Praise for *Christianity for the Rest of Us*

"This book is so full of good news that I keep it next to my Bible. With her clear vision of congregational transformation and her ability to read the signs of the times, Diana Butler Bass is the soft-spoken prophet many of us have been waiting for. What is more, she assures us that what we hope for is already underway. Anyone looking for a flourishing church will find one in these pages, along with concrete practices for renewing the congregations we know best."

—Barbara Brown Taylor, author of *Leaving Church: A Memoir of Faith*

"In the spirit of the much exaggerated death of Mark Twain, Diana Butler Bass demonstrates that the so-called mainline neighborhood church is alive and well, which is for so many of us, very good news indeed, given the alienation of fundamentalism or secularism: thank God for this good news."

—Peter J. Gomes, Harvard University

"Diana Butler Bass shows, with eloquence and clarity, why the church for modern seekers is just around the corner. What a hopeful book, confirming something many of us have long suspected—our little corners of the Kingdom are changing the world, one heart at a time."

—Philip Gulley, co-author of *If Grace Is True*

"This is Diana Butler Bass at her very best—a warm, candid, totally engaging scholar taking a look at main-line Christianity in this country and telling us with gusto why she likes what she sees. Bravo!"

—Phyllis Tickle, Religion Editor, *Publishers Weekly* (retired)

"Not only does this book confirm the dictum to 'think globally and act locally,' but teaches us that to think traditionally today we must act very creatively! Diana Butler Bass is teaching us how to "discern" the living Body of Christ, which is clearly both within and beyond any single Christian group or denomination today. This book is ecumenical hope!"

—Fr. Richard Rohr, O.F.M., Center for Action and Contemplation, Albuquerque, New Mexico

"Full of careful insights and analysis, *Christianity for the Rest of Us* is a book of great encouragement and hope for mainline Protestant churches who will hear the message."

—Frederick H. Borsch, author of *The Spirit Searches Everything,* retired Episcopal Bishop of Los Angeles, Professor of Anglican Studies and the New Testament, Lutheran Theological Seminary at Philadelphia

Christianity for the Rest of Us

Christianity
for the
Rest of Us

HOW THE
NEIGHBORHOOD CHURCH IS
TRANSFORMING THE FAITH

Diana Butler Bass

HarperSanFrancisco
A Division of HarperCollins*Publishers*

All biblical quotations are taken from the New Revised Standard Version unless otherwise noted.

CHRISTIANITY FOR THE REST OF US: *How the Neighborhood Church Is Transforming the Faith*. Copyright © 2006 by Diana Butler Bass. All rights reserved. Printed in the United States of America. No part of this book may be used or reproduced in any manner whatsoever without written permission except in the case of brief quotations embodied in critical articles and reviews. For information address HarperCollins Publishers, 10 East 53rd Street, New York, NY 10022.

HarperCollins books may be purchased for educational, business, or sales promotional use. For information please write: Special Markets Department, HarperCollins Publishers, 10 East 53rd Street, New York, NY 10022.

HarperCollins Web site: http://www.harpercollins.com

HarperCollins®, ♨®, and HarperSanFrancisco™ are trademarks of HarperCollins Publishers.

FIRST EDITION

Library of Congress Cataloging-in-Publication Data
Bass, Diana Butler
Christianity for the rest of us : how the neighborhood church is revitalizing the faith / Diana Butler Bass. — 1st ed.
p. cm.
Includes bibliographical references.
ISBN 978-0-06-083694-8
ISBN-10: 0-06-083694-6
1. Community—Religious aspects—Christianity. 2. Church work.
3. Church membership. 4. Church growth. 5. Church renewal. I. Title.
BV625.B38   2006
280'.40973090511—dc22   2006041144

07 08 09 10 11   RRD(H)   10 9 8 7 6

To my in-laws, Bill and Courtenay Bass,
who embody the best practices and passions
of mainline Protestantism.

CONTENTS

Part III

From Tourists to Pilgrims
215

INTRODUCTION

Christianity for the Rest of Us

In the fall of 2005, I was the keynote speaker at a conference on vital churches. About 175 people had come to spend the day discussing how mainline Protestant congregations might find new ways of being faithful in a changing world. The day opened with the event chaplain, an Episcopal priest, taking those attending through a spiritual exercise of centering prayer. She directed us to look around the room one last time as she turned down the lights; then she asked us to close our eyes. In the semi-darkness, she drew our attention to where our feet touched the floor and had us listen to our own breath. From the breath, she said, God would give us a sacred word on which to meditate. Her words, she related, were "holy and blessed." "Breathe," she told us, "breathe your sacred words." About every ten seconds, she demonstrated centered breathing by intoning her own words, "holy and blessed," and inviting us to breathe ours.

As I listened for a sacred word to arise from my breath, I confess that I struggled. Even in the quieting environment of the church parish hall, the only word that came to my mind was "anxiety." I tried to banish it, reaching out for holy blessedness, but only anxiety remained.

What caused my anxiety? The whole thing struck me as painfully ironic. Many people probably think this scenario aptly describes mainline Protestantism: liberal churchgoers sitting around in the dark with their eyes shut.

Although the priest's spiritual exercise was a terrible metaphor for church, it saddens me that churchgoers themselves play into this stereotype—acting as if church is about closed eyes in the semidarkness, seeking the comfort of God's holy blessedness. As I let myself breathe anxiety, however, my eyes popped open, refusing to shut. I glanced around the room realizing that people need to open their eyes to see what is going on around them. And I confess: I have little patience for spirituality that seems self-absorbed and isolating. Most of my life has been a search for authentic spiritual community, a church with its eyes wide to the world, nothing phony or contrived. As the priest tried to center us in prayer, I wondered if we instead needed to be decentered, to be more realistic about the current state of affairs and imagine what possibilities God might have for us.

Unlike those who persist in believing that mainline Protestantism is a religion with eyes shut, I know different. For the last three years, my job has been going to church. As the project director of a research study on vital congregations, I have spent hundreds of hours in worship, attending programs and events, talking with clergy, and interviewing church members. I did not visit just any churches, however. No suburban megachurches or revivalist congregations with famous television preachers for me. Rather, I journeyed with a surprising group of contemporary pilgrims—those folks who gather in mainline Protestant congregations, communities that describe themselves as theologically centrist to liberal-progressive and are part of denominations that trace their lineage back to colonial America.

I hung out with brand-name Christians—Methodists, Presbyterians, Lutherans, Congregationalists, and Episcopalians—observing, listening, and paying attention to what is happening in their often-ignored churches. When I told people of my quest, they sometimes chuckled: "Vital mainline churches? Must have been a short journey!" Or editorialized, "Aren't those the 'frozen chosen'? What's so interesting about them?" After all, many said, repeating the conventional wisdom, "Only conservative churches can grow."[1] Critics consider the old mainline denominations culturally irrelevant and hopelessly confused. According to most reports, politically conservative evangelicalism is the only vital form of the Christian faith. Other Christians do not even seem to exist.

I knew, though, that "other" Christians existed. I am one—an Episcopalian who has found a meaningful way of life through ancient traditions, social justice, spiritual practices, and emotive worship. The religious right seems to have hijacked American Christianity, and I can barely stand reading the news about religion and politics. Although most of my friends are "other" Christians, too, we feel pretty isolated. So, like the biblical character Joshua, I set off to spy out the land and find some like-minded pilgrims, hoping to discover a different kind of Christianity—a Christianity for the rest of us—by listening to real people in the pews, finding out what makes their churches work, and giving voice to their understanding of the gospel.

Sometimes, I felt singularly alone in my quest to explore the undiscovered country of vital mainline churches. During the time that I have been tracking mainline vitality, evangelical voices have grown louder and more insistent that they—and they alone—are the true Christians, the ones with true doctrine, true morals, and true politics. The power of their claim was backed by their electoral pull in the 2004 presidential elections. But that victory did not mollify religious conservatives. Instead, their leaders seem ever more aggressive in their attempts to create a kind of "one-party" Christianity in this country. Indeed, in the week I wrote this, yet another book was released attacking the mainline and proffering its explanation for "why Americans are fleeing liberal churches for conservative Christianity."[2] During much of the last decade, I have felt like the voice crying in the wilderness. When people asked me what I was writing about, I typically responded: "The other Christians. The ones you don't hear about in the media. The quiet ones."

A few years ago, not many people knew what I meant, but now, more often than not, they respond, "Thank goodness. That's me! I am tired of feeling so alone!" There are more of the "other" Christians than I expected. As this journey progressed, I discovered more and more traveling companions. The other Christians practice this different kind of Christianity for the rest of us—a faith that is open and generous, intellectual and emotive, beautiful and just.

In all the congregations, I discovered Christians who are reaching toward new language to express these ideals, recreating structures that embody spirituality, and relocating themselves in larger, public practices of faith and politics. In recent years, there has been talk of "emerging" Christianity, of a "new paradigm" faith that is adapting to changes in a pluralist, post-Christian world. Some of my friends refer to it as transformational Christianity. Indeed, the mainline churches in my research represent an "emerging" shape of Protestant Christianity.[3] Or, perhaps, as one friend of mine says, "Your churches are the *reemergent* ones! They are moving into the future by reengaging their best past." Emerging or reemerging, there is something happening in the pews—something that could transform American Christianity.

Although I have long been interested in what makes a good church, this particular journey took shape as a three-year research project of spiritually vital mainline Protestant churches.[4] The study was not a quantitative project; I did not attempt to count how many mainline churches were vibrant, healthy congregations or how many people might consider themselves the other Christians. Rather, I was looking for a renewal in the practice of Christianity in mainline churches to discover whether a common pattern, language, and spiritual logic were taking shape in a variety of congregations in different parts of the country. If enough congregations were experiencing a similar enough transformation, it would be possible to discern and describe a possible emerging trend in religious practice. To do this, I identified fifty mainline congregations in which new things appeared to be happening, and where people were growing deeper and experiencing a new sense of identity by intentionally engaging Christian practices.

The churches came from six denominations, were located across the country (with the majority in the Midwest and South), defined themselves as theological moderates or liberals, and represented a variety of demographic characteristics common in mainline churches. They ranged in size from 35 to 2,500 members, with the average congregation numbering just below 300. Before the study, only a few of the fifty pastors had met and none of the congregations was fully aware of the work the others were doing. The fifty churches participated in various kinds of qualitative research as I attempted to glean stories from their life together through interviews, open-ended surveys, and, when possible, Sunday visits. More than 300 people from the fifty congregations contributed to the research that resulted in thousands of pages of data.

Of the fifty participating churches, ten became key in-depth sites where researchers spent from two to three weeks over several months. These were: Redeemer United Church of Christ, New Haven, Connecticut; Goleta Presbyterian Church, Goleta, California; Calvin Presbyterian Church, Zelienople, Pennsylvania; Cornerstone United Methodist Church, Naples, Florida; Saint Mark Lutheran Church, Yorktown, Virginia; Phinney Ridge Lutheran Church, Seattle, Washington; Church of the Holy Communion (Episcopal), Memphis, Tennessee; Church of the Redeemer (Episcopal), Cincinnati, Ohio; Epiphany (Episcopal), Washington, D.C.; and Iglesia Santa María (Episcopal), Falls Church, Virginia. We befriended the pastors and staff and got to know the congregation through what sociologists call participant-observer research. We tried to experience the churches as if we were members—attending everything from worship to Sunday school, board meetings to prayer groups, retreats, and concerts. In return, they opened themselves to us, treating us almost as family. I vividly remember one Sunday: as my family and I walked into Saint Mark in Yorktown, Virginia, after five or six visits, the pastor jokingly asked when I was sending in my pledge card.

Most of the stories in this book are drawn from the ten congregations studied in-depth, with the other forty providing general data, grounding the larger context of the study, and serving as a validation group for the research findings. As people in the study told me, the stories repeated here resonated with their experiences, and many said they "saw themselves" in these narratives. Unlike academic studies that disguise research sites, I chose to use the real names of the churches, pastors, and paid staff members—as a reminder that these are actual places where real people care for one another, worship God, struggle with pain, and attempt to be faithful. But, to protect the privacy of the many people who shared their stories with the research team, I have assigned pseudonyms to individual congregants. Christianity for the rest of us is not my invention, a vague hope of what I wish Christianity could be. Rather, it is what real people in real churches taught me by sharing their stories.

Many people think mainline Protestantism is dying, that it is going the way of the dodo in favor of a more lively form of conservative Christianity found in suburban evangelical megachurches. I do not deny that mainline Protestantism is in trouble. Some of its institutions, unresponsive to change, are probably beyond hope of recovery or repair. I also believe, however, that lively faith is not located in buildings, programs, organizations, and structures. Rather, spiritual vitality lives in human beings; it is located in the heart of God's people and the communities they form. At the edges of mainline institutional decay, some remarkable congregations are finding new ways of being faithful—ways that offer hope to those Americans who want to be Christian but are wary of the religion found in those suburban megachurches.

Although I have the appropriate academic credentials to conduct such a study, this is not a cool, detached research report—the sort that might be published by a scholarly press. Instead, it is the narrative of a pilgrimage. At the beginning, I did not intend to go on a journey with these churches. I was interested in how old Protestant churches, congregations that are theologically moderate to liberal, were renewing themselves and finding new spiritual vibrancy. My job was to investigate religious change and to find out where, why, and how it was happening.

I embarked on this quest to find faithfully innovative Protestants, but what I found on the journey surprised even me. From Seattle to Naples, Florida, from Boston to Santa Barbara, California, I discovered mainline churches that were deepening spiritually and, often, growing numerically. The fifty congregations involved in my study were not usually the largest in their towns. Rather, they were solid, healthy churches that exhibited Christian authenticity, expressed a coherent faith, and offered members ways of living with passion and purpose. They exuded a renewed sense of mission and identity, often having emerged from dire circumstances of decline, crisis, threatened closure, or spiritual ennui. The congregations embraced no evangelistic strategy, no programmatic style of church growth. Rather, they were their own best selves—creative and traditional, risktaking and grounded, confident and humble, open and orthodox. They were often in tension with local fundamentalist Christians or, surprisingly, their own denominations. And sometimes both.

Their paths of renewal varied, but I discerned a similar pattern across these very different communities. Mainline renewal is, as one Lutheran pastor told me, "not rocket science." As he said, "You preach the gospel, offer hospitality, and pay attention to worship and people's spiritual lives. Frankly, you take Christianity seriously as a way of life."

All the congregations have found new vitality through an intentional and transformative engagement with Christian tradition as embodied in faith practices. Typically, they have rediscovered the riches of the Christian past and practice simple, but profound, things like discernment, hospitality, testimony, contemplation, and justice. They reach back to ancient wisdom and reach out through a life sustained by Christian devotional and moral practices. They know the biblical story and their own story. They focus more on God's grace in the world than on the eternal state of their own souls.

For me, something odd happened along the way. As the congregations shared their stories of faith, hope, and love, I realized how deeply discontented I was with business-as-usual church. They began to teach me more than I ever expected about what it means to be a Christian today. As the months of visiting and observing unfolded, I noticed changes in my perspectives about contemporary spirituality, my understanding of Christian faith and community, my own spiritual practices, my sense of congregational vitality, and, most surprising, my political views. In the process, I realized that I was no longer just studying them. Rather, we were on a pilgrimage together.

This book is, therefore, a kind of report from the field, a story of insights I gained from going on a pilgrimage with the people in some remarkable Christian communities. By taking you on this journey, I hope you might change your perspectives, understandings, practices, and passions about Christianity, too.

The idea for this project started around 1994. I was living in Santa Barbara, California, where, through a series of unexpected events, I began attending a progressive Episcopal congregation. In my graduate studies I had read every recent book on both mainline and evangelical Protestantism—all of which said, in varying degrees of nuance, the same thing: mainline Protestantism was dying because it was theologically liberal; evangelical Protestantism was growing because it was theologically conservative. Liberal religions cannot sustain vitality. Only conservative, demanding religions can.

What, then, was the problem? For many years I had been associated with conservative evangelical Protestants. Despite many good things they taught me, and the many faithful individual evangelicals I knew, I increasingly experienced their communities as narrow and inhospitable. Moreover, I worried about the increasing political partisanship in evangelical congregations. The liberal church that I joined was just the opposite—full of lived grace, an open invitation of God's love, and refreshingly unpartisan. Much to my surprise, it was growing—in fact, growing rapidly. How could it be that conservative communities failed to practice Christian virtue while the more liberal one succeeded? According to every theory I had read, the Episcopal congregation should be dying. But it was not.

I suppose that some people might have dismissed this as a fluke. I could not. The question nagged at me. When most scholars look at mainline Protestantism, they explore issues of decline. Why are churches failing? I am interested in other questions: Why do some succeed? How are those churches finding new life in a time of religious change? What can those of us seeking a meaningful Christianity learn from them? What does their vitality mean for the rest of us, for Americans interested in spiritual and religious issues? I have written about these questions in several forms: spiritual autobiography, political theology, and congregational studies.

Despite my interest in church, however, I am not very interested in institutional, or "organized," religion. Having grown up in the 1960s and 1970s, I share my generation's skepticism for institutions of all sorts, and especially political and religious ones. For some reason, *religious* institutions have always struck me as terribly oxymoronic. Religious institutions often lack any sense of spirituality and are the least dynamic of all institutions. Rather, I am interested in spiritual community, and the local expression of such community in congregations. Of course, congregations are institutions, but unlike denominations, they are more fluid, often receptive to change, and potentially the most innovative. Beyond the congregation, however, mainline Protestant institutions are in a state of deep crisis and desperately in need of renewal. After this journey, I am more convinced than ever that if American religious institutions are to regain their spiritual grounding, they will need to listen to and learn from the spiritual practices of local congregations.[5]

Along the way, the congregations taught me something important about the Christian faith. Institutions do not hold Christians together.

Tradition holds them together, to one another, to the past, and to the future. In one particularly lively exchange with a group of Episcopal bishops who were deeply concerned with the crisis and collapse of the worldwide Anglican Communion (the global organization of which the American Episcopal church is a part), I posed the question "Would there still be Anglicanism if the Anglican Communion suddenly disappeared?" They answered, "Of course." Then, we began to talk about how Anglicanism existed before the Anglican Communion (1874), before the Episcopal church (1786), before the Church of England (1534), and even before Catholic Christianity came to England (606). As the bishops delved into their own history, they insisted that a form of Christianity recognizably Anglican had existed since the 400s, mostly in Celtic tribes in Great Britain. Anglicanism was not an organization, it was a lived tradition and a commitment to particular spiritual practices, nimbly adjusting to innumerable cultures while remaining connected to its original spiritual impulses through history. The same is true for other forms of Protestantism. My journey of going to church taught me that we are, again, in a time when faith would live through rebirthing its tradition, not through maintaining or improving its inherited structures.

I welcome you to this pilgrimage. This is not a pilgrimage of geography. We will not be journeying to a sacred site, like Canterbury or Lourdes. Rather, we will be traveling through a broad spiritual landscape—contemporary American Protestantism—as we move through places, reflections, activities, and time. We will do what pilgrims do: tell stories all along the way. Like campfire tales, really. Surprising, sad, and funny stories with spiritual and theological morals.

The journey begins with a question, "What happened to the neighborhood church?" The answer is deceptively simple: Many old neighborhood churches are failing. The old way of organizing American religion has vanished. In the wake of the loss, however, some Christians are rebuilding spiritual community, and a new kind of Protestant church is being born. The people I met are building upon tradition, faithfulness, and wisdom to offer a distinct alternative to a Christianity based on personal salvation and moral certainty. They are creating a new kind of neighborhood church.

Next, we may ask, "How do we get there?" As with any worthwhile spiritual journey, there are many possible paths. Although no single way exists, there are, however, signposts to let us know that we are heading toward beauty, goodness, and truthfulness. Christians call these signposts "practices," the things they do together in community that form them in God's love for the world. We will follow the signposts and see where they lead.

Finally, we wonder, "Are we there yet?" Every pilgrimage has a destination, and this one is no exception. Emerging Christianity is about change—about changing from spiritual tourists to pilgrims—about transforming our selves, our congregations, and our communities. We are going there, to a change of heart that revolutionizes one's whole life.

The churches along my way had not closed their eyes to change. Indeed, they were wide-eyed congregations in which new things were happening, lives were being transformed, and grassroots communal actions offered new possibilities for the body politic. None of the congregations I visited practiced business-as-usual church. All were reaching toward a future they could not fully see—a future of faith, hope, and love.

If you are satisfied with your local congregation, if you like the kind of Christianity that offers certainty and order in an age of change, if you think church is about closing your eyes, this book is not for you. It is not for the comfortable, the certain, and the religiously content. If you feel anxious, however, consider this an invitation. I invite you on my pilgrimage to some very different kinds of churches, old Protestant churches that have found new life in the face of change. They reminded me that Christianity is a sacred pathway to someplace better, a journey of transforming our selves, our faith communities, and our world.

At one time, I thought I was alone. But the rest of us are here. There are many pilgrims on this road. Welcome to our pilgrimage. We are glad for your company.

PART I

What Happened to the Neighborhood Church?

ONE

The Vanished Village

I grew up in a village that has vanished. The village was not destroyed by a war in someplace like Iraq or by a natural disaster such as the tsunami in Indonesia. For that matter, its buildings still stand—a scant fifty miles from where I currently live in Virginia. Each morning, when driving my daughter to school, I pass a freeway exit that would take me there: "North 95—Baltimore." That is where I was born and grew up. Baltimore, Maryland, in the 1960s. Or, more specifically, the neighborhood of Hamilton in Baltimore along a street called Harford Road. Although Hamilton exists on the map, my childhood universe—an urban village of the 1960s—is gone. It is almost as if it never existed at all. The names may be the same, but there are no maps, and no freeway exits, back to the place that once was.

When I was a little girl, Hamilton was populated by hard-working families, many of German ancestry, almost all of whom were Catholics, Lutherans, or Methodists. We belonged to the last-named group and attended Saint John's United Methodist Church of Hamilton. My Hochstedt ancestors were among the founding members of that congregation. Grandpop Hochstedt owned a flower shop in the center of Hamilton, on Harford Road itself, a family business begun by his grandfather in 1884. The entire extended Hochstedt clan, including my parents, worked there. Every day at noon, we would close the shop for an hour, cross the back driveway to my grandparents' house, and gather for family dinner. My great-grandfather, a local celebrity of sorts, owned the first motorcar and first telephone in the neighborhood, laid the cornerstone for the public elementary school, and was the captain of the volunteer fire department.

From my house, it was one mile to Saint John's. In that mile, a tiny urban village existed—a complete world of school, work, play, relations, and worship. When I was seven or eight, I used to walk the entire mile—from home to school to the public library to the florist shop and, finally, to the church—by myself. I now marvel that my parents let their young daughter traverse city streets. If I am honest, however, I realize that I was never really alone. All along the route, their friends, neighbors, and other small business owners looked out for me. Everybody knew them; everybody knew me. We all looked out for one another.

Not only did we look out for one another, but everyone in the village seemed to believe the same things about God and morality. Parents, pastors, teachers, librarians, politicians, businessmen, and police officers—specific religious preferences aside—shared a common view of what it meant to have a good life. From an early age, I knew the answers to every ethical question: "Be nice," "Follow the rules," or "Do unto others as you would have them do unto you." Everyone in Hamilton was a Christian (although it was hard for the Lutherans and Methodists to admit that the Roman Catholics were really Christians). We knew about Jews—mostly from the Bible—but we never actually met any. Some Pentecostals lived on the margins of Hamilton (my grandmother embraced that faith to the consternation of the Hochstedt patriarchs), and we knew that—somewhere—black people had their own churches. But that was the limit of religious diversity. Hindus, Muslims, and Buddhists lived in exotic, faraway countries.

For my family, Saint John's served as the village church. There, in the chilly church basement, the walls painted in a World War II surplus green, I first learned about the Bible and Jesus. My Sunday school class sat in tiny chairs, placed in rows facing the teacher who told us Bible stories, helped us memorize the books of the Bible, and explained the mysterious geography of the Holy Land on a set of worn maps. On the wall behind us were pictures of Abraham and Abraham Lincoln—reminding us of the close link between our biblical faith and our faith in democracy, and that church and state believed the same things about God and doing good. My Girl Scout troop met down the hall, in a space lined with pictures of the Men's Bible Class stretching back to the church's founding.

We all knew our place in this world. It was a world of boundaries, rules, and roles. Social class, race, ethnicity, birth order, and gender determined everything. We believed that God made it that way. All his life, my father, the second son, struggled with his role, condemned to the financial whims of the rightful heir, his profligate older brother. And me, my father's daughter? In the early 1960s, I knew what would lie ahead: marriage to a high school sweetheart, children, and working for my cousin Eddie (the first son of the first son) in that same flower shop. Some of the adults talked of the younger generation attending college, but I was never sure how that would happen. Although I was born into this boundaried world, I always chafed under its rules and roles. Part of me always wanted to leave.

Things did change on Harford Road—unanticipated and, for some of its inhabitants, unwelcome change. And people did leave. Not long ago, film director John Waters depicted Harford Road in his sexual comedy *Dirty Shame*. In it, the residents of Harford Road awake one morning in the 1970s and find their entire world transformed from a working-class Christian village to a sexualized urban playground. I remember Harford Road changing, too, but not from the perspective of the sexual revolution. I remember the changes brought on by family pressures and cultural change—from women resisting their assigned roles and black people protesting in the streets. In 1972 my parents moved to Arizona.

Most of the cousins went to college—none became florists; none still live in Baltimore. After my grandfather died in 1985, my uncle sold the flower shop. And that period of my family's history, a history that had unfolded on one mile of a Baltimore street since their arrival in the New World a century earlier, came to a close. I was born into a world—an all-encompassing, ordered village, and a way of life—that was dying even as I was being formed by its last breaths.

The village vanished. And even though I am only in my midforties, I feel ancient when I return to Hamilton's haunted streets. Everyone I knew is gone; we have all become wanderers in a different world. On the streets of Hamilton, only the buildings remain. I can look through the windows of my grandfather's shop—the windows that I looked out of as a young child and first began to see the world—and gaze into the sterile office supply store that has taken its place. Someone ripped out the bountiful azaleas that graced my mother's yard and paved over the entire lawn. The bakery, the movie theater, the drug store soda fountain, the Kresge's department store—all gone.

However differently we see it, John Waters and I agree on one thing: old Harford Road is gone, completely gone.

Maybe our childhood worlds exist only through the romantic haze of memory. Certainly things always change. But my story about old Harford Road is neither a sentimental journey nor a lament about isolated change in a single urban neighborhood. Rather, Harford Road is a sort of spiritual parable that helps us better understand what Jesus once called the signs of the times. This small story of sadness and loss, of people struggling with identity and change, reveals a much larger reality. Hamilton is an outpost of a vast social revolution—the lived experience of one group of related families and friends as the entire world entered into one of the most significant periods of transformation in three centuries.

When I was born in 1959, things had not changed on Harford Road for a long time. Yes, there had been new inventions like motorcars and telephones and airplanes overhead. This kind of visible change came slowly—mostly through the addition of machines that made everyday life easier for the inhabitants. Although the village looked different in 1959 than it did in 1900, its internal structures, the way Hamiltonians viewed the world, the village's language, values, and ideals, along with its roles and expectations, remained essentially unchanged.

Hamilton was a microcosm of working-class and middle-class America. Similar patterns of family, faith, business, education, and politics were repeated across the country, in different ethnic communities and through time. Life for my parents, grandparents, and great-grandparents differed very little from generation to generation. The vast majority of people shared a worldview based on order, reason, and objective truth—all based on the idea of a benevolent Creator. They acted out their roles on these assumptions, and they trained the children in the village to be good citizens and good Christians in this interconnected and self-contained world. The only thing that worried us was that the Communists in Russia did not follow the same rules. But we equally assumed that good always triumphed over evil. Everything would be all right in the end.

Interestingly enough, we did not have to worry about the Communists. Their village fell. What we did not expect, however, was that our village would fall, too. Everything was not all right in the end. Many of the same pressures—politics, economics, philosophy, globalization, technology, multiculturalism and science—would change Baltimore as much as they did Moscow. A new world was being birthed in massive cultural fragmentation and emerging global chaos.

Hamilton reflects the changes. The once all-white Hamilton Elementary School is now racially diverse. The neighborhood's number of families with children stands at less than 20 percent—well below the national average—and in stark contrast to the family-oriented streets of my childhood. The neighborhood comprises a near equal split of married and single people, leading me to guess that there is a growing gay and lesbian population in Hamilton's reconfigured universe. Overall economic health has declined. Crime and unemployment rates are fairly high. The available data point to a neighborhood in transition, if not decay. Hamilton exists as a fractured space, a collapsed world; it is a place struggling for new meaning, identity, and vitality.

Hamilton is not alone. All over the planet, villages are vanishing. We know that everything is changing, that some sort of new world is emerging. Everywhere. And we have no idea what it is becoming.

What about religion in this emerging world? Amid the change, everyone talks about religious diversity, Christian and Islamic fundamentalisms, new spiritualities, rising agnosticism, Eastern meditation and prayer practices, religion in the global south, and suburban evangelical megachurches. All sorts of faiths are being rediscovered and new ones are being born. From my own experience, however, I kept wondering: What about Saint John's United Methodist of Hamilton, the spiritual center of the lost world? What about the old Protestant traditions?

I first encountered God through the rainbow prisms cast by Saint John's stained glass windows. I was baptized at the church in the spring of 1959. To me Saint John's will always be a glistening Easter Sunday sort of world, graced by the fragrance of lilac and lilies, its days turning like hymnal pages. Despite all the change in the neighborhood, Saint John's United Methodist still stands. The church recently celebrated its hundredth anniversary.

But Saint John's does not stand as a bulwark of the glorious Protestant past. A quick perusal of the church's website tells a much sadder story. Few people appear in the pictures of the church; most of the shots are of an empty sanctuary and parish hall. No longer able to afford its own pastor, the congregation shares a minister with another Methodist church. There is talk of closing or combining the church with another. Clearly, the remaining congregation is trying hard to find its way in this new world—it recently joined an organization called the Center for Progressive Christianity and is reaching out to gay and lesbian persons. The church newsletter boldly proclaims "Faith for a New Age and Time."

Saint John's United Methodist Church of Hamilton embodies the struggle of the old Protestant religion, that which is called *mainline* or *liberal* Protestantism. Sometimes, critics blame theological and political liberalism for the problems of these churches, but Saint John's story points in another direction. It bespeaks the power of ties, the ties that once held together old Hamilton. What gave life to Saint John's was an established pattern of relationships—friends, family, neighborhood, community, and history—ties that bound its people into a single, comprehensive universe, that urban village. Once those ties were broken, the church could not sustain itself. The world into which Saint John's was born died. When Hamilton died, the church struggled—and is still struggling—to figure out where it fits amid the fragmented worlds that now surround it. I have no idea whether Saint John's will survive.

As I learned in Sunday school at Saint John's, however, churches are more than buildings. People are the church. As the neighborhood fractured, the people of Saint John's scattered, becoming spiritually unmoored in a changing world. What happens to people, people who are part of an ancient tradition, when everything around them shifts? How do they move on in faith?

I sometimes wonder what my life would be like if my family had continued to attend Saint John's, if we had stayed in the neighborhood as it collapsed around us. Would I still be a member, one of the remaining few? Would my faith have struggled to live, just as Saint John's faith appears to be struggling? Would I have given up on my family's traditional Protestantism? Become a skeptic or a New Age seeker? Maybe a Roman Catholic, a Jew, a Buddhist? I do not know.

Of course, staying at Saint John's did not happen. We left the village. We were among those families who aided the collapse, who broke the ties of the old neighborhood. Although lines of my family's history in Baltimore stretched back to 1800, my parents abandoned tradition and moved our family to Scottsdale, Arizona, in 1972. No one could believe that we would willingly move to a desert. There, in the western wilderness, we would have to make a new home. We became spiritual nomads.

It is not easy being a spiritual nomad, but it is a widespread phenomenon, part of the cultural condition loosely referred to as "postmodern."[6]

Many people, like me, were born in traditional religions and still carry vague memories of how the world was before everything changed. Many more, however, especially those born after 1965, were born nomads, people birthed into an unhinged world. To them, the world of Hamilton is as distant as that of the American Revolution. Wherever we are on this timeline of change, however, we all know the relentless anxiety of living with massive cultural transformation. Of this, sociologist Zygmunt Bauman says, "One can think of postmodern life as one lived in a city in which traffic is daily re-routed and street names are liable to be changed without notice."[7] I once heard author Phyllis Tickle remark, "Postmodern, post-Christian, post-Protestant, and postdenominational. What do all these posts mean? That we know where we have been but that we have no idea where we are going!"

Throughout my journey, I heard people reflect on these changes. Steve Jacobsen, minister of Goleta Presbyterian Church, just north of Santa Barbara, California, told me that a guiding principle of his ministry is to "map out a clear path for faith in the postmodern world." He believes that the church needs to be a place where Christians can intellectually "unwind where our culture is" and, in the midst of any anxiety that causes, create time for silence, "believing in the power of imagery, music, story, feeling, and spontaneity." One of his goals is to help his congregants understand "the importance of community, because we are a mobile culture, and the importance of roots and commitment." Across town, at Trinity Episcopal in Santa Barbara, a woman insisted, "I have been glad that my church is now marginalized in the secular culture, so that it might explore what it means to not be twinned with power."

In Seattle, Pastor Don Maier, the former minister of Phinney Ridge Lutheran, remembers when "we were in a different time in this country and a different time in the church." That time, he says, is gone. When he began his ministry at Phinney Ridge, theologians were "just beginning to talk about the post-Christian era or the end of Christendom." They may have theorized postmodernism, but he experienced it on the ground. Many people he called on in his pastoral duties were "barely baptized, never taught" about Christian faith. Every evangelism program the church tried failed. He confesses, "We didn't have an adequate way to embrace those people and give them the path that they needed to take." On Seattle's postmodern frontier, where 80 percent of people claim no religious affiliation, nothing seemed to work for "adults who had no experience with the life of the church or the life of Christ." Eventually, Phinney Ridge developed a process, called The WAY, to help adults understand the spirituality, moral vision, and practices of a Christian way of life. He laughs, "It doesn't happen by osmosis! It had to be intentional for us."

It is not just people in places like California or Seattle who have experienced these changes. The Reverend Jesús Reyes, the Episcopal priest of Iglesia Santa María in Falls Church, Virginia, serves a congregation made up mostly of recent immigrants to the United States. "They are truly aliens, almost in the biblical sense, strangers wandering through a foreign culture." He ably speaks of both their needs as newcomers to the United States and larger cultural shifts—here and in their home countries. As he speaks, I realize his comments apply to all serious Christians, not just his Spanish-speaking parishioners. "What they need is community. What they need is the family. A different type of family. That's where I see my mission."

Nomadic spirituality, that sense of being alien, strangers in a strange land, is almost a given of contemporary life. Having moved from Baltimore to Arizona when I was thirteen, leaving the village behind, I learned what it means to wander in the desert. Although my parents settled at a Methodist church in Scottsdale, I joined a conservative evangelical congregation and my journey—that of staying Christian in a post-everything world—began in earnest. That journey would wind me through fundamentalism, the charismatic movement, and classical evangelicalism, before eventually returning me to mainline Protestantism as a changed person of faith. After I came back to mainline religion, I found myself in numerous churches, all vital, all lively, none in decline—and all willing to become communities where spiritual nomads could practice the Christian faith as pilgrims.[8]

I have often heard people remark that churches do not like change, that they provide refuge from change, or that they resist change. Some Christians today fear cultural change, opting instead to make pronouncements about a God who is "the same yesterday, today, and forever" and insisting that they alone know the way to and the mind of God. Christianity, they say, is not about change. Christianity is old-time religion. They build churches to protect people from change, often in anonymous, suburban, gated spiritual communities, where they recreate a vision of some cherished Christian past. They venture out into the world to try and force the rest of us back to the perfect world of their fathers.[9]

I cannot figure this out. In the New Testament, Jesus asks everyone to change. With the exception of children, Jesus insists that every person he meets do something and change. The whole message of the Christian scripture is based in the idea of *metanoia,* the change of heart that happens when we meet God face-to-face. Even a cursory knowledge of history reveals that Christianity is a religion about change. *The Christian faith always changes*—even when some of its adherents claim that it does not. As I learned on my own journey, the other Christians more comfortably navigate change and are doing so these days with surprising grace.

There are, however, many ways to cope with change. In M. Night Shyamalan's film *The Village,* a group of people escape the contemporary world's chaos by constructing an alternative community, a haven completely separated from the rest of society, protected by strict and unvarying rules, customs, and beliefs, all based on the model of a nineteenth-century pioneer town. They marry and have children, all the while sheltering the community's young from the outside world. Ultimately, town elders—the only ones who know the secret—discover that even a carefully guarded world cannot withstand forces of transformation. In a moment of crisis, they must send someone out of the village in order to save what they most value about life in the village. They choose a blind girl, so that she might not see and be contaminated by the world. Her journey beyond the village is terrifying—but she finds that love, salvation, and redemption lay only outside the walls and in risking the unknown. Although she is blind, her eyes are metaphorically opened—and she is the only one who can truly see.

There seem to be different sorts of Christians today, those who prefer to build walled villages and do not want to see, and those who take risks in the wilderness and are willing to open their eyes. For nearly two decades, scholars have identified risk-taking spiritual types as "seekers," those individuals on a journey of faith that moves beyond the faith traditions they inherited into new religious territory. In religion, the seeker story is old news.

What if the story is not just the journey of a single blind girl? An individual seeker? What if those wanderers in the wilderness joined together? What if the whole village went on a journey to see?

On my journey, I traveled with those who are more comfortable in the wilderness, people who were willing to explore the new terrain around them. Yet they did not travel alone. I found that in the breakdown of old villages, Christians are forming a different sort of village in congregations across the country. Not spiritual gated communities or protected rural villages. Rather, their new kind of village is a pilgrim community embarked on a journey of rediscovering Christianity, where people can forge new faith ties in a frightening and fragmented world. For those I met, change was not always easy, and their churches were not perfect. But they embodied courage, creativity, and imagination. And risk. In reaching toward a new kind of Christianity (which is, as I hope will become obvious, actually an old kind of Christianity), they serve as a living guidebook for spiritual nomads who are seeking to find wisdom's way.

TWO

Remembering Christianity

In the early 1990s I taught church history at an evangelical Christian college in California. One of my classes, American Christianity, focused on the role religion has played in our nation's history, politics, and culture. Most of my students came from conservative homes and churches. They were pleased when I argued that secular historians had largely ignored religion in American life. However, they were not happy when I pointed out that the Founding Fathers had less-than-orthodox theological ideas and less-than-pious personal lives. Every year an exasperated student would protest, "But Professor, fifty-two of the fifty-four signers of the Declaration of Independence were Christians! They founded America as a Christian nation!"

At first, it seemed odd that students regularly challenged me with the same statistic. Then, I discovered that the vast majority of them had seen the same video, *America's Godly Heritage*, by an amateur historian named David Barton. The film argues that the United States was founded explicitly as an evangelical Christian nation. Large numbers of evangelical

churches and schools use his material to "correct" the secular interpretation of American history.

In recent years, conservative evangelicals have created a kind of cot-
tage industry out of America's Christian heritage. From his television
pulpit, Florida pastor D. James Kennedy weekly assails contemporary
secular society's historical blindness and extols the nation's Christian
past. Paul Marshall and David Manuel produced an influential textbook
called *The Light and the Glory* that opens with God directing Christopher Columbus to found the New World. Across America, conservative
Christians are claiming history as theirs—remaking the past in their own
theological image of a Christian nation, even a specifically evangelical
Protestant one.

In many ways, it is tempting to ignore this as the uneducated carping
of people who believe the world was created in six twenty-four-hour
days. And it was not difficult to award low grades to students echoing
such claims. Over the years, however, I think I may have been a little
tough on those students. After all, most of them lived in southern California, in a society marked by historical amnesia. Unmoored in time,
those young Californians were searching for a place in the human story,
a place that connected them to history, where they might belong. They
sought to find meaning in the present—and where a hopeful future might
head—through returning to the past. They were attempting to find the
way forward by linking with what they believed to be some ancient
American memory. In doing so, they rather naturally reached to religion
as a way of weaving a past: *As the ancients believed, so we believe.*[10]

I can understand their quest. After all, I too am unmoored. My family history and its religious traditions were all severed when Hamilton vanished. When we moved west, I lost touch with the history that
formed me. That was hard on me. I have always loved history as a sort
of spiritual exercise, with its imaginative way of entering the past and of
connecting with others' stories. Religion and history always intertwine;
religion carries the traditions of the past, and history shapes faith. Perhaps I loved history because, even as a child, I could feel the decay of

the world around me. I sensed the sadness of something sinking and an urgent need to find a life raft of the past to navigate the present. I needed to remember times that were slipping rapidly away. Maybe I needed to believe there could be resurrection.

At the center of Old Town Alexandria, Virginia, near where I now reside, stands Christ Church, an Episcopal congregation founded in 1767. They still meet in their original—and largely unchanged—building. George Washington owned a pew at Christ Church. A few generations later, Robert E. Lee was confirmed there. The church's graceful brick exterior and the refined white interior with its brass fixtures and box pews bespeak the measured Protestant faith of the Founders. A few blocks from Christ Church stands the Old Presbyterian Meeting House, nearly identical in rational graciousness, where Washington's memorial services were held. Daily I drive down a road called Quaker Lane, no doubt named after the brothers and sisters in the Quaker society that once met at the edge of town. Christ Church, Old Presbyterian Meeting House, and Quaker Lane embody Protestant memory.

But Protestantism is not Alexandria's only story. Saint Mary's Roman Catholic Church was founded in 1795. Catholicism came late to Virginia, but across the river, Roman Catholics had established the colony of Maryland one hundred years earlier. Because I was born and raised in Maryland, I understand the cords of American Catholicism, with its democratic impulses, its emphases on religious community and education, and its struggle to find a place in the New World. In elementary school I learned of my colonial ancestors' "sacred trust" to create a safe haven for Catholics and to open the way for later religious freedom in America. Seeing Saint Mary's in Alexandria, established so quickly after the Constitution was written, reminds me of the precious—and sometimes fragile—American memory of religious toleration and the separation of church and state.

Nor is Alexandria's spiritual memory exclusively Christian. Across the street from Christ Church, a small sign marks the site of the first

Jewish synagogue in Virginia. Their current building is right across from my office at Virginia Seminary. When I drive to Target, I travel along Powhatan Street, a way named for the Native American chief who once ruled twenty-five tribes in northern Virginia—and whose daughter, Pocahontas, married an Englishman and converted to Christianity. I always wonder how much of the old ways remained in her soul. And I wonder what the forests and the Potomac River looked like then, her tribe's places of worship and awe.

These are the links of America's religious past: Protestant, Catholic, Jewish, and Native American. The link of memory may be tenuous—obscured, perhaps, except to those with eyes to see. Through architecture and name, however, I find myself daily in their stories.

Unlike my evangelical students in California, I cannot claim that America is a singularly Christian nation. Alexandria always reminds me differently, and I remember that ancient faiths entwined from the outset of American history. If I listen carefully, the links of their memory still jangle, forming a chain that connects me to a religious past—a past of spiritual nomads, a past in which people were dislocated in time, a past in which they had to relocate in God. Alexandria's stories are not of stability and changeless tradition. Rather, they are stories of exile and return, of people searching memory, of seeking home. And, for the Protestants who came here almost three hundred years ago, theirs was a quest to remember Christianity in a strange new world.

What kind of Christianity marked the early American landscape? Was it only, as some people think, some sort of evangelical Protestantism? Millions of Americans are searching for a usable past as they seek to remember faith in a changing world. Evangelical Christians, like David Barton, are forging a chain of memory that enables conservative Protestants to make sense of their place in history. They are creating a past by remixing history—as if they were updating an old Elvis song for a new generation.

Although like-minded Protestants might appreciate this effort, the evangelical version of a Christian American is unsettling to many people. It portrays the Founders as saints, a pantheon of larger-than-human characters whom God personally inspired and directed. Because of their faith-filled heroism, and because God scripted the action, every event of American history is good, godly, and pure—a sort of postbiblical revelation enacted on American soil. That includes, of course, trying to explain away doctrinal irregularities and moral failings—and ignoring the fact that American Christians committed wholesale evils like slavery, the genocide of native peoples, persecution of non-Protestants, racism, and violence against women and children. And it ignores religious diversity, with sad, tragic, and challenging memories of Christianity. Remixing the past by taking out the unpleasant bits is a dangerous thing.

The evangelical version of American history is not just a divine drama, however; it is also a morality play. Spectators are asked to do more than watch. Believers become heirs and actors, people required to follow the script as revealed to the Founding Fathers by God in Jesus Christ. In other words, conservative Protestants are not comfortable with the idea that their view of history is just that—*their* view. Rather, they want to enshrine their view as *the* story of our national past. Indeed, most of these Christian histories seek to dominate all other stories and reshape American history according to their reading of the past.

In recent decades, mainstream scholars of American religion have rejected dominating stories and become more interested in stories about Catholics, Jews, and Native Americans. We live in an age of stories—not a single story. There is nothing sinister about this; it is not a subversive plot to undermine America's Protestant heritage. Rather, scholars acknowledged that America's Protestant story was well known. What twentieth-century American schoolchild did not know about George Washington and established churches like Christ Church? Instead, historians turned to those "other stories," seeking to construct narratives of minority faith traditions. They created a new web of stories in which Americans live, rather than allowing a single story to dominate.

In this process, however, Christian stories got a little lost. At first, mainline Protestants did not notice that their story had been displaced (indeed, many welcomed the new variety of stories), but evangelical Protestants worried about the change. Popular historians like David Barton began to tell their version of the Protestant story. Academically rigorous and respectable conservative evangelical historians, like Mark Noll, told a much more sophisticated version of the Christian America story. However nuanced, all these stories emphasize Protestant belief, doctrinal clarity, moral purity, and evangelical certainty. Whether evangelical Protestants read popularizers like Barton or intellectuals like Noll, they have a usable past. They know the stories that link them to the ancestors. They remember a past.

But what of the *other* Protestants? The Protestants who go quietly about their business without media fanfare or public policy statements? The ones whose churches are struggling? What stories link them? Is there a usable Protestant past for the rest of us?

European Christians politically established the United States, but this fact does not make us a Christian *nation*. In fact, our ancient spiritual stories draw from four major taproots, only two of which were Christian: Native American, Jewish, Roman Catholic, and Protestant. Of all these stories, Protestant memory is surprisingly conflicted and obscured. Secular Americans fail to appreciate the ways in which Protestantism shaped—and still shapes—our culture. And evangelical Protestants have seized the whole Protestant narrative, effectively silencing Protestant stories that do not fit with their agenda.

Yet once—not so very long ago—not all Protestants were understood to be evangelicals or fundamentalists or political extremists. Instead, Protestantism served as a cultural center point, a way of being in the world, a set of traditions and practices that framed American life. To understand who we are as a people, to understand our location in sacred time, it is important to tell some new stories about an old, old faith, the Protestant taproot. Indeed, Protestant congregations have often been a kind of moderating force in American culture, providing communal ballast in times of change and trial. We need stories that speak of the middle ground, the ancient American center between secular skepticism and Christian fundamentalism.

Sitting on an elegant street downhill from Yale Divinity School, Church of the Redeemer, a congregation of the once-dominant United Church of Christ, looks every bit the part of a New England establishment church. Its elegant white spire, brick exterior, and clear glass windows echo the theology of my grandparents' world—orderly, pristine, and understated. Redeemer's current building dates to the 1920s, when Anglo-Protestantism formed the religious foundation of the nation, but the congregation is actually much older with a more complex and surprising history. It was founded in 1838 by a brilliant and intellectually rebellious Yale theologian, the Reverend Nathaniel William Taylor.

Taylor was rebelling against New England Calvinist orthodoxy, the fundamentalists of his own day, the tradition he had inherited from his Puritan ancestors. He did not, however, reject Calvinism wholesale. Instead, he reworked it, constructing a theology nicknamed the New Divinity. Concerned with the Calvinist question of sin, Taylor argued that sin was not passed on biologically from Adam and Eve to the whole of the human race. Rather, he believed that "sin is in the sinning," a free-will human choice.

In the process of reworking New England Calvinism, Taylor argued against both the extreme skepticism of the Enlightenment and the extreme enthusiasm of evangelical religion, both of which rejected traditional Protestant theology. His New Divinity constituted a "creative third way" in theology and rendered the once formidable New England Calvinist God a more benevolent divinity in harmony with the spiritual longings of the day.[11] From the clay of American Calvinism, Taylor fashioned an open faith that encouraged personal religious commitment and social responsibility.

Thus, he positioned Redeemer as an innovative heir of Puritanism, bearing an ancient tradition, between the two religious poles of his day.

It was a new kind of Puritan congregation for a new time. Throughout its history, Redeemer has embodied Taylor's moderation and continued his interest in reforming tradition. Some seventy years after its founding, Dr. Watson Phillips, a later pastor, remarked, "When my life work is ended here, I want to leave this church compact, harmonious, consecrated.... I am not anxious about its doctrinal position. I am deeply concerned about its spirit, its point of view, the way it related itself to the practical problems of the modern community."[12]

As Redeemer learned, however, creative middles are often problematic. They depend on moderating extremes, and often have a hard time holding together; middles need to be periodically reinvented. By the 1970s and 1980s, Redeemer's creative third way had not been reinvented in a long time. Rather, it had chosen sides and become part of New Haven's mainline liberal establishment. When the liberal establishment started to decline (yes, even in New Haven), Redeemer's congregation declined right along with it—to the point of nearly closing the once great church.

Then, in 1996, the Reverend Lillian Daniel, a young minister arrived knowing the congregation would either die or be renewed under her watch. Her own spirituality defies characterization—she grew up an Episcopalian, had an evangelical conversion experience, graduated from Yale Divinity School, and is passionately committed to both Christian tradition and social justice. Lillian embodies a creative third way in American religion, a blended sort of Christian theology and spirituality that draws from deep wells of tradition and yet is generously open to change and the remaking of those very traditions. Her own creative middle meshed with Redeemer's ancient pattern of faith and sparked a renewal in the old congregation.

Today, Redeemer pulses with spiritual energy—deepened by the practices of prayer, testimony, and doing justice. A new generation of churchgoers has arrived, many of whom had never been part of a Christian congregation before. Redeemer is not the biggest church in New Haven, but it is fully alive and welcoming students, townsfolk, married families, gay and lesbian members, and the homeless into its community of faith. "We have a revival going on in our church," says one congregational leader, "just not an evangelical one. A revival. And that's an interesting way to look at our mainline liberal church!"

A creative third way. And a "new divinity" to boot.

In his book *Hellfire Nation*, James Monroe argues that "The United States is so susceptible to moral combustions—to witch-hunts, moral panics, crime wars, and prohibitions—precisely because it is such an open and fluid society."[13] Protestant ministers often fuel these moral fires, and their congregations often serve as gatherings of God's righteous warriors. Such churches are exclusive churches—places from which the saints can exclude sinners and launch godly crusades. Exclusive congregations insist that you join their spiritual side (usually by being "born again" and living by a certain set of rules) before you are considered a full member. Hellfire nation, based in excluding congregations, is the essence of David Barton's Christian America.

While hellfire is certainly part of the Protestant story, there is another part as well. When American Protestant ministers were not busy preaching hell, some—like Nathaniel Taylor—envisioned different paths and constructed creative third ways. Creative third ways provide open spaces amid cultural questions and tensions. Typically, such open spaces are found in congregations that value comprehensiveness over exclusion. For these Protestants, church is the sacred space where saints *and* sinners gather to hear God's word, engage practices of prayer and service, and be transformed through participation. There is no spiritual test to come in, no intellectual position to which one must agree. This is the vision of the comprehensive church, a congregation not torn asunder by the riptides of cultural extremism, but a place where Christian practices frame all of life and, in the words of the old hymn, "heal the sin-sick soul."

Christians have long struggled between these visions of Christian community. Classical theology framed the tension by posing a question: is the church "the gathering of the saints" or "a hospital for sinners"?

When Christian congregations are gatherings of saints, then hellfire is the sure result. Such communities must maintain clear boundaries of who is "in" (the saved) and who is "out" (the unsaved). Saints believe specific things about God and morality, allowing for no ambiguity or questions, and demonstrate their faith by resisting everything they deem idolatrous or evil. By its very nature, this version of Christianity must extend its reach in a quest to eradicate all forms of sin that threaten the purity of the church. In American history, the church as the gathering of saints has been a persistent form of Christian community.

The other form, the church as a hospital for sinners, has been sometimes less obvious in our national life. This vision does not emphasize personal salvation in terms of heaven and hell. Rather, this kind of church recognizes that all human beings are sickened by sin and need healing. Faith is a matter of trust in God; morality is enacting God's justice; salvation is God's wholeness or *shalom*. This kind of church comprises a variety of folks—some with a variety of ills and some at different levels of spiritual wholeness—all pilgrims together on a Christian way. The comprehensive church is a fundamentally modest body, and it makes few grand claims about eternity and salvation. Rather, these communities emphasize life in this world. They offer ways of being Christian, also called practices, that enable people to live better and more faithfully in God.

But the saints-and-sinners church typology should not be considered a simple theological dualism. Another powerful image of Protestant churchgoing emerged in the middle of the twentieth century, when mainliners forgot both the gathering of saints and the hospital for sinners. Many mainstream congregations became a kind of Christian version of the Rotary Club, understanding the church as a religious place for social acceptability and business connections. In a very real way, mainline Protestants retained the ideal of comprehensiveness while jettisoning the idea that people are spiritually sick and need healing. Everyone was welcome—with no spiritual demands other than to conform to some sort of generalized Protestant morality. As a result, many mainline congregations forgot the practices that originally formed their traditions, making participation in their churches optional at best and irrelevant at worst. By the time I was born in 1959, church was an extension of post-war middle-class aspirations, run by bureaucracies in the faith business.

Thus, the ideal of church as a hospital for sinners occupies a comprehensive middle space, the mediating territory between Christian exclusivism and secularized inclusivism. Although the comprehensive congregation has appeared to vanish from the American landscape, it was a widely held understanding of congregational life for much of our history. Indeed, the comprehensive church—the ideal of the village church that included saints and sinners alike—is the oldest pattern of American congregational life.[14] However many settlers came to America intent upon creating the pure church, many thousands more Europeans came to the New World and simply recreated the village parishes of their former homes. Remembering Christianity means remembering this forgotten way of being church.

Before the mid-twentieth century Christ Church in Alexandria exemplified the older pattern. As a religious version of American domestic architecture, its original structure was similar to a squire's house. Instead of housing local nobility, however, the parish church was God's house. Unlike at the squire's house where one had to be invited in, God welcomed all Alexandrians home. There, every Sunday morning, the rich and noble worshiped alongside the middling classes and the poor. Slaves sat with their owners in family pews (not in separate balconies). The ceiling was painted crystal blue to represent the sky, the high vault of heaven under which humanity lived. The windows, clear and bright, bathed the entire congregation in the light of God's reason, a spiritual brightness accessible to all. It was not a perfect world; like all eighteenth-century Anglo-communities, it was riddled with inequities and injustice. But it was symbolically and theologically structured as a comprehensive universe under God in whom all people could find a home. It was a kind of Protestantism that tied people together through a shared way of life in community—not through fear of eternal punishment.

Traditional American Protestantism was not all hellfire and damnation religion. Beyond the thunder there whispers a more ancient wisdom that welcomes all, saints and sinners, to God's house. Once upon a time in America, Protestant congregations were village churches that offered weary immigrants a new home in a new world. Can we remember a kind of Christianity that offered hospitality for pilgrims in a strange land?

We are all pilgrims in a strange land now, exiles and immigrants wandering in the new world of this post-everything age. Most of us have forgotten the village churches of our ancestors, forgotten that they, with their comprehensive way of life, once defined the Christian faith. We have forgotten the enchanted universe of places like Christ Church—with the blue sky and bright sunlight of coming home to God. Indeed, through much of the twentieth century, the old village churches became secularized and lost their sense of wonder, transcendence, and passion. This loss of holy beauty hastened their decline. The church as the gathering of saints—with all its crusading zeal and supernatural power—overcame the fading vision of the village church. Despite the noise of the saints' assemblies, however, that more ancient wisdom still calls. We need to remember another way.

In 2004 I was at another Church of the Redeemer. This Redeemer is a big, diverse Episcopal church in Cincinnati, Ohio. There, a twenty-something woman testified to finding the congregation as her church home. She had visited all manner of churches and spiritual gatherings. Then she came to Redeemer. Its liturgy, the beautiful old words of worship, drew her in. "It was overwhelming," she said, "it just feels ancient, and that's very comforting; it connects us with our ancestors." She stayed and joined the community.

Many people today, religious nomads isolated in time by modern amnesia, are trying to relocate themselves in the past. To get connected with the ancestors. To find their way back to an enchanted world. If you look, you can see people remixing history everywhere. The past has become contested territory as a map to our future. Because of this, the Christian America, that hellfire nation, of David Barton and other conservative evangelicals has tremendous cultural appeal. It is a reading of the past that makes sense to those seeking certainty in an uncertain landscape. But it is also a political agenda to convince Christians that God has a particular future in mind for us—a future that, not surprisingly, looks exactly like a policy statement from the religious right.

Theirs, however, is not the only version of history available to spiritual nomads. Other Christians are remembering the past differently, reaching back to the ancient wisdom of the village church, a tradition that, at its best, both grounds a community and opens its doors to wayfarers. Two colleagues of mine once referred to this as "porous monasticism," a kind of Christian community of practice that is both spiritual and open at the same time. Its doors are not barred by threats of eternal damnation. Rather, signposts of Christian practice—the things people do together in community for the sake of God and the world—mark its sacred space.

In my journey, I have come to think of such congregations as the new village church, a place where pilgrims can remember Christianity. There, the beauty of saintliness is, as theologian Edith Wyschograd suggests, "the flash of sanctity" amid the mundane—the holiness of a reenchanted world. Even as old villages are vanishing, some Christians are remaking the tradition of the village church as they reconstruct spiritual community around this ancient American ideal. And, perhaps not unexpectedly in this transient age, their new village church is spiritually mobile: a pilgrim community on a journey together.

THREE

The New Village Church

During the time I taught at the evangelical Christian college, I was also a member of Trinity Episcopal Church in Santa Barbara, a vital, faithful, and deeply passionate Christian community. Yet it had not always been that way. For more than two decades, the church suffered from a fairly typical set of mainline Protestant woes: numerical decline, financial crisis, poor leadership, deferred repair of its historic building, and loss of hope. In the mid-1990s, however, things changed. Through a process of prayerful discernment, offering radical hospitality, developing new patterns of leadership, and experimenting with innovative worship, the church turned around. Trinity not only stopped the decline, but in just a few years the congregation tripled in size. They created a congregation on the shards of the old one, a new village church that is responsive to the longings of a changing world.

Trinity is a politically and theologically progressive church, an heir of classical Protestant liberalism. Since 1970, churches like Trinity have not fared well.[15] According to the conventional view that only conservative churches grow, Trinity should have died. But it did not. It came back

to life by *heightening* the liberal aspects of its identity. The congregation
called an openly gay minister, created inclusive-language worship services, and actively engaged a variety of controversial political causes.

So, if liberal churches die, what about Trinity? I did not like the overly politicized faith of my childhood church, yet I loved being part of
Trinity. What was different? Eventually, I came to realize that the mainline churches of my childhood had essentially capitulated to American
culture—their political practices of charity and social concern were ba-
sically secular. Saint John's United Methodist in Baltimore did not differ
fundamentally from the United Way, the Rotary Club, or Hamilton Elementary School. From all accounts, Trinity in Santa Barbara had been
the same. These mainline congregations, while they did many worthy
things, paid little or no attention to people's spiritual lives. They simply
assumed that people were Christians, that they knew how to be, think,
and pray like Christians.

Trinity's leaders realized that they could no longer assume that people
were Christians—and that church could not serve as a social-service in-
stitution, a political party, or a business. The primary job of church is
to be a spiritual community that forms people in faith. They did not
abandon the classic traditions of Protestant liberalism; rather, Trinity
linked its progressive vision to a new sense of spirituality and a renewed
appreciation for Christian tradition. Walks for the homeless and walking
the Labyrinth. Living wage and a way of living the Benedictine rule. Attention to inclusive language and deep attentiveness to the Bible. Social
justice and spirituality joined in an open community of practice. People
said they came because they were hungry for exactly what Trinity offered. They wanted a different kind of Christianity than that of their
childhoods, but they still wanted to connect with the Christian tradition. They wanted the Bible, prayer, and worship. They wanted open,
nonjudgmental, and intellectually generous community. They wanted
to serve and change the world. And they wanted it all to make sense in a
way that transformed their lives. Their new village church is a congregation that is both spiritual and religious.[16]

*   *   *

My pilgrimage to find the emerging mainline really began at Trinity. Participating in that congregation, and writing about it, made me wonder if there were other mainline congregations creating new church. Now, having spent three years journeying across the mainline, I have worshiped in many such congregations. Not all of them share Trinity's specific political commitments, but some do. They are unique places, with their own personalities and histories. Yet, they are distinctly mainline Protestant in their history, outlook, and theology. They, too, are finding vitality by linking their sense of identity to a new emphasis on spiritual practice and Christian tradition.

Interest in spirituality is not new in American religion. Our history is marked by periods of intense spirituality, usually followed by a return to more authoritative sorts of religion. Since colonial days, American faith has often bounced between the poles of ecstasy, usually termed "spirituality," and order, typically tagged as "religion." I was born in 1959, a period of religious order. Beginning about 1970, however, we have moved increasingly toward the other pole, toward "spirituality." For the last twenty years, scholars have reported on this development.[17] Some observers refer to this as "the spiritual revolution."[18] Despite a marked attempt by some groups like the Southern Baptists to reassert authoritarian religion, in the summer of 2005 *Newsweek* magazine could claim in a cover story that "Americans are looking for personal, ecstatic experiences of God, and they don't much care what the neighbors are doing."[19]

The *Newsweek* story emphasized individualistic styles of spiritual practice and concluded that Americans are far more interested in generic "spirituality" than in "religion." As I read the story, though, I noticed something strange about the report. The story seemed to vary from the magazine's poll on religious practice. According to its own poll, only 9 percent of Americans defined themselves as "religious," while 24 percent said "spiritual but not religious." However, a surprising 55 percent of Americans defined themselves as both "religious *and* spiritual." While

84 percent said that spirituality was "very" or "somewhat" important in their daily life, 68 percent confessed that their "practice" was "the same" or "mostly the same" as their childhood religion. And almost three-quarters claimed that their religious practices were "very traditional" or "somewhat traditional."[20]

Although *Newsweek* emphasized individual—and even exotic—forms of spirituality, its polling pointed toward a different possibility: Americans want to combine their concern with personal spirituality with more traditional forms of religion. If true, we may be witnessing a surprisingly unique moment in American religious history, a time in which the old poles of personal ecstasy and institutional order are collapsing in on themselves and creating a new kind of religious pattern. The magazine may have missed an emerging story of a much larger cultural shift.

In a book published two years before the *Newsweek* article, Princeton sociologist Robert Wuthnow criticized this sort of religion reporting as missing the point:

> But suppose that this view of spirituality were wrong. Suppose that the more colorful, esoteric expressions of spirituality captured media attention simply because they were colorful and esoteric, while most of the public's interest in spirituality was being absorbed by organized religion. Or, suppose, at least, that most people who developed a serious interest in spirituality wound up pursuing that interest through religious organizations.

He goes on to suggest, "To be sure, the quest to know God may arise from existential yearnings, from illness and loneliness, or from moments of wonder about the ultimate mysteries of life. But these vague yearnings and experiences have to take shape. They have to find *carriers,* vehicles of expression to help people to make sense of their feelings."[21]

In my journey with vital mainline congregations, I found faith communities that were reenvisioning and re-forming both their traditions and their practices in a new spiritual communalism. In some places,

Americans are reknitting old religions with a lively sense of God's presence as experienced in spiritual practices *in community.*[22] My mainline congregations embody this change. They are "religious and spiritual" churches, *carriers* of a vital, lively faith.

By weaving personal spiritual quests with more traditional forms of religious life in community, mainline churches can be renewed. Such churches, like Trinity in Santa Barbara, do grow when this pattern is evident. Vital Christianity is not about being conservative, about being foot soldiers for the religious right. It is about being responsive to people's spiritual longings and experiences, and drawing from tradition and history to help make sense of it all. A congregation grows when it draws its worldview and practices from scripture, engaging the Bible, as Marcus Borg so memorably says, "seriously but not literally."[23] Mainline churches decline when they neglect scripture and prayer, discernment and hospitality, contemplation and justice. I have witnessed the old mainline recovering faith through an emerging set of practices of passionate Christianity, in communities that are both spiritual *and* religious.

What do spiritual and religious communities look like? On my journey, three interrelated characteristics, forming a trinity of vitality, came into focus—giving shape to the new village church: tradition, practice, and wisdom.

Tradition, Not Traditionalism

Cornerstone United Methodist in Naples, Florida, is a new congregation, founded in 1996. They worship in a modern building in a recently constructed suburb, surrounded by sun-washed white houses and clear blue lakes. Inside the church, there is a rock band, overhead projectors, and a thirty-something pastor with a ponytail down his back. "I think we could probably count on the fingers of only three or four hands the members of this congregation who have been in church all their lives, or are cradle Methodists," Scott, a member of the church, told me. "That's okay, you know. We are Methodists and we want to continue the Methodist tradition, but this is a new way of looking at it. A new way of practicing Methodism." He said that "all this leads to the openness that allows the Holy Spirit to move." Their worship, he said, is an "amalgamation of old and new," with weekly Eucharist, icons, praise music, candles, high-church liturgy, and the ponytailed preacher wearing a chasuble (an elaborate robe modeled on medieval clerical clothing and worn today mostly by Roman Catholic and Episcopal priests). "You know," Scott laughed as he talked about communion, "that's the one ritual in the church that was actually given to us by Jesus. It doesn't get much older than that in our tradition!" But they have a professional-quality praise band, too. He stresses that the combination "is a great way to draw people in."

Scott knows the pitfalls of boring faith—he used to be an Episcopalian and struggled with chilly religion for a long time. He also spent time with fundamentalist-type Episcopalians and grew weary of their emphasis on uniformity and authority. Scott was seeking an expressive, hospitable, open form of faith when he found Cornerstone, a church that has given him real enthusiasm for being a Christian again. But he is also critical of too much emotion. "You can have all emotion and nothing else. You end up falling flat." He sees his congregation's intentional mix of spirituality and tradition, of ecstasy and order, as "the yin and the yang" of the Christian life.

Located in a part of Florida where everything, including their church, is new, the people at Cornerstone United Methodist share a common enthusiasm for tradition. A member of the praise band referred to the church as "cutting-edge traditional." One woman, a former Southern Baptist, claims that until she came to Cornerstone, tradition typically meant "ritual," or "we always say this, we always do that." But, now, after studying church history and learning about ancient Christianity, she says, "It is very symbolic, but it's not ritual. It's very meaningful every time I go through it." The church, she insists, "makes tradition part of our lives."

Some people worry about a revival of tradition. After all, Christians traditionally excluded women from the ministry, supported racial seg-regation, confused church and state, and held slaves. Perhaps tradition is best left in the past. Indeed, during my Methodist childhood we es-chewed tradition in favor of being "modern." In the 1960s and 1970s, *tradition* was a negative word. Yet, in the *Newsweek* poll, 71 percent re-sponded that their religious practices were "very traditional" or "some-what traditional." Tradition has become a positive term.

Like the people at Cornerstone, all the mainline Protestants I met were busily reclaiming tradition. However, they understood tradition as a fluid, dynamic, and critical process, making a distinction between the life-giving "Great Tradition" that religion scholar Huston Smith refers to as "the voice of peace, justice, and beauty that emanates from the Christian soul," and authoritarian, exclusive tradition*ism* as practiced by some contemporary American Protestants.[24]

As one Pittsburgh Presbyterian said, "We are really trying to be a church that knows tradition and at the same time moves into the future." A mainline pastor in Washington, D.C., described the new emphasis as "recovering the practices of the early church and offering them in a way that the contemporary or emerging church can use and find meaning in." None of the churches treated tradition as a museum piece to be guarded; rather, they understood it as the clay of Christian experience—material that successive generations of believers must craft with faithful care.[25]

Practice, Not Purity

Calvin Presbyterian Church is located in Zelienople, Pennsylvania, a half-hour north of Pittsburgh, in the Beaver-Butler Presbytery (regional association of Presbyterian churches). It is arguably, as a Presbyterian friend tells me, "one of the most conservative presbyteries in the coun-try." Of the eighty-seven Presbyterian churches in their region, only seventeen are growing. Of those seventeen, Calvin is the only one to have posted growth every year for a decade.

Why is Calvin growing? "In most mainstream churches, you'll find two different things happening," explained Shawn, a member. "On one side, the growing churches are the more conservative churches, and the dying ones are termed—for lack of a better word—liberal churches." But, he confessed, "We would probably fit into that mold of the liberal church." Shawn credited growth to the congregation's emphasis on spirituality and prayer, an emphasis "that makes us completely different" from other liberal churches. He stressed, however, that "We are not an evangelical church." Tim, a fellow church member, agreed: "We have deep faith and spirituality in our church." Melissa said, "Our church gives people the ability to grow deeper. If you want to take your spirituality deeper, the opportunity is there."

Calvin models the spirit of liberality, emphasizing acceptance instead of doctrinal purity and diversity rather than uniformity. Yet, faith at Calvin is not some sort of bland secular toleration; it is a robust, transformative expression of being in relationship with God. The people of Calvin *act* like Christians. The minister concedes that the church is not attractive to some conservative evangelicals, "We try to be grounded in scripture. I think our message is grounded in the Bible. People who are looking for fundamentalism or literalism won't get that."

While they resist labels, members readily confess that people seeking "black and white on issues," what one woman called "that narrow thing," would not be comfortable at Calvin. Members hold a variety of views on social issues, and single-agenda Christians would, they admit, find Calvin's cultivated diversity—a diversity that includes both political and theological conservatives and liberals—unsettling. Congregants are careful to discuss this, trying to maintain their cherished virtue of spiritual acceptance, but gently criticizing what one member called "a certain judgmental conservative ethic" that bedevils other congregations in their region. "Their agenda," said another, "is ensuring their own salvation." Shawn says, "On one hand, we're not heavy on doctrine, what you believe, or whether or not you 'fit.' We're liberal and open. On the other hand, we want to meet your needs from the very personal basis of your relationship with God." They do the things that Christian people should do, but they do them in an open, inclusive, and nonjudgmental way. The people of Calvin form community around Christian practice, not around moral or theological purity.

In all the congregations I visited, there was a steady critique of exclusivist Christianity. Although not particularly bitter, the pilgrims I met regularly distanced themselves from narrow forms of religion. "Oftentimes, I hear someone say 'I hate organized religion,'" Kate at Calvin told me. "So I say we're a very disorganized religion. We are not dogmatic in any particular way." Shawn tried to explain Calvin as "a God-centered, prayer-centered church as opposed to a program- and belief-centered church." Each was reaching for language to describe their congregation—committed but not exclusive, personal but not individualistic.

Emphasizing open practice instead of purity is not easy given the current political context. Many told me how hard it was to share their faith because the media had conflated "Christian" with "fundamentalist," leaving them bereft of a public vocabulary to talk about their beliefs. A Seattle Lutheran tried to explain it, "We're really walking the walk that the people of the Bible, that Jesus and the disciples, talked about. We're supposed to do it. This church really makes you think about the idea that Jesus was a liberal. The stuff he preached and the way you are supposed to live is radical." Or, as one churchgoer in her sixties told me bluntly, "I have a deep personal faith. I am outraged by the 'righteousness' of the conservative Christian right." Another minister confessed that while she had "evangelical leanings," she had a "marked distaste for the politics of exclusivity that often gets thrown in with that theology." In an ironic twist, these mainliners saw themselves as more faithful to the gospel, and therefore more at odds with the culture, than conservative Christians, whom they believed had been co-opted by worldly values of success, consumerism, and political power. Through the course of my research, the people I met engaged a Christian way of life in congregations that challenged the prevailing stereotype of faith.

Wisdom, Not Certainty

The Church of the Holy Communion is an Episcopal congregation in a genteel part of Memphis. The church's elegant buildings, well-tended lawns, and old shade trees bespeak the gracious Christianity treasured throughout the American South. There is more, however, to Holy Communion than this esteemed tradition. Outside the church, a large banner advertises the upcoming visit of Elaine Pagels, the scholar and best-selling author of works on the Gnostic gospels. On Tuesday evenings, a book group discusses her *Beyond Belief: The Secret Gospel of Thomas.* Pagels's visit has caused quite a ruckus in the neighborhood. Many Christians in Memphis think she is a heretic and that no church should invite her to speak. William, a lay leader in the church, laughs when he talks about her visit, "I tell people about the wonderful speakers we have here, like Elaine Pagels or Karen Armstrong, and they say things like, 'Oh my God, they're coming to Memphis?!'"

William was brought up Southern Baptist but, as an adult, went to church only sporadically for twenty years. After a long search, he found a home at Holy Communion. He confesses that he never knew that Christianity could be an adventure: "There's so much here for people to learn and grow." He repeats himself with a kind of wonder, "There's *so much* you can learn. It's like you're entering a space where things happen and you learn from them." Like others I spoke with at Holy Communion, William loves asking questions, thinking about faith from a variety of perspectives, and learning in spiritual community. But at Holy Communion, knowledge is tempered by prayer. William sighs, "No matter how much we read or study, we'll never fully know God."

It is difficult for William to explain completely what it means to be part of a church that welcomes controversial thinkers like Pagels. "I don't think it's a black and white type church," he says of Holy Communion. "Maybe wisdom is a good way of putting it. It's a search for meaning and growth without saying it has to be one way or the other.

I've heard a number of parishioners say that is the thing they like about it, it's not just black and white."

The people I met along the way were on a quest for wisdom rather than certainty. If practice meant acting like Christians, engaging a Christian way of life, wisdom referred to knowing God. Practice meant *doing* Christian things; wisdom meant *thinking* like Christians. Counter to the prevailing view that people want certain answers, mainline pilgrims rest comfortably with ambiguity. They resist dogmatism in favor of being part of a community where they can ask life's questions—a circumstance that they identify as necessary for the spiritual life. As one Cincinnati Episcopalian put it, "The questions are very important. Sometimes more important than the answers. Because we can't know what the real answers are exactly anyway." A churchgoer in Washington, D.C., told me, "The whole thing is not being about definite answers but about community."

All of this reflects an opened-ended quality of questing, upholding the idea that the Christian life will always be incomplete in this world. Dora, a member of Holy Communion, commented, "The moment that we think we know, we've lost our perspective on wisdom. The search and the journey is, maybe, to get to the point where I'm at peace with what I do understand, and understand that there is more." A member of Calvin Presbyterian Church explained, "There are people in the world who want to be told this is what's right and this is what's wrong. It's black and white. But we tend to attract people who are more interested in the questions and the mysteries of these things than they are in the answers to them."

Like many mainline Protestants, the people who shared with me were well educated and articulate, but they embarked on the Christian intellectual life with surprising spiritual modesty. To them, wisdom was not esoteric, a secret for only mature believers; rather, wisdom was a spiritual gift whereby thinking (the head) and knowing (the heart) joined and opened the way to God. They insisted that certain things remain in the realm of mystery, and that Christian character calls for humility in understanding the ways of God. While outsiders wrongly interpret this characteristic in mainline religion as wishy-washy, the people I met cautiously portrayed it as wisdom, a quality of prudent discernment and human limitation.

The pilgrims I met taught me that tradition, practice, and wisdom compose the Christian way of life, the shape of a vital spiritual community, giving form to their longings for home. Tradition connects Christians to the past, practice is the calling in the present, and wisdom pushes toward a future of eternal love. The church engages tradition through remembering in preaching, teaching, and sacraments; it engages practice by doing a Christian way of life; and it engages wisdom through a life of knowing God. Together, tradition, practice, and wisdom are the architecture of the new village church, the one embarked on the Christian pilgrimage: a trajectory of the soul's direction in God.

| Individual or Congregation | Past TRADITION Remembering | > | Present PRACTICE Doing | > | Future WISDOM Knowing | GOD Shalom |

But the trajectory is not just linear. Tradition, practice, and wisdom also form three interconnected and timeless circles of faith, wherein each quality and disposition shapes, informs, and leads to the others as individuals and congregations move around the circles:

By combining the linear dimension of tradition, faithfulness, and wisdom with the circular relationships of the three, this triune spirituality moves forward in time, in effect mapping out the pathway of Christian pilgrimage as individuals and congregations move both around the circle and through time:

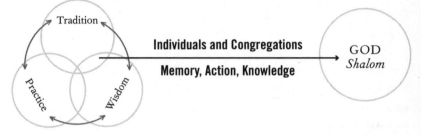

Christianity teaches that the forward movement is not an endless, repetitive cycle. Someday the journey will culminate in peace, what the scriptures call *shalom,* when God restores the entire universe in love. This motion through time is the Christian pilgrimage—a trinity that moves toward consummation in our individual lives, our congregations, and, eventually, in human community and history.

New village churches are not built through niche marketing, sophisticated programming, capital campaigns, and architectural plans. Indeed, all of the study churches rejected standard church-growth strategies. As the Reverend Holly McKissick of Saint Andrew Christian Church of Olathe, Kansas, reported, "We are not offering a 'product' that everyone wants. When we started this congregation fifteen years ago, we were intentionally open, inclusive, and justice-oriented. The prevailing wisdom on how to start a new church was: mirror your neighborhood. Ask what people want and give it to them. We have tried to mirror the gospel." Like Saint Andrew, all the research churches are built on practicing faith in community, places where people travel a way of faith together toward *shalom.* Although they have buildings, new village churches are primarily the communal journeys of a people finding a home in tradition, practice, and wisdom.

FOUR

Finding Home

I met Judith, a thirty-something mother of two young children, over dinner at a friend's house in Seattle. Extroverted and warm, she wanted to share her spiritual journey. She now attends Plymouth Congregational Church, an active, politically progressive mainline congregation in downtown Seattle. But she grew up in a small Episcopal church in California where her parents were "core members." She remembers that, as a child, religion was "very important" to her. At age thirteen, however, Judith's world crumbled. Her parents divorced and her mother left the church; her father stayed, but things were never the same. "My church life," she says, "completely blew up at that point. I floated through my teen years." At college, she stopped attending church regularly. She would go to an occasional service, "but it really didn't resonate too much." While a college student, Judith met her husband, "a kind of non-practicing Catholic." They married and moved to the Northwest.

Her husband, she says, did "not have much interest in going to church on Sunday. I always felt like something was missing, but I didn't want to be the kind of person who went to church without their spouse." She admits that they "struggled" a bit with the issue when their first child was born. "How do you instill values in children without going to church?" she asks rhetorically. After the birth of their second, they decided to return to church but did not know where to go. One of her husband's business associates told them about Plymouth. It sounded interesting to him, and he asked if she wanted to try it. She told him, "I am going to jump at any chance to go to church."

They went to Plymouth together as a family. On that first Sunday, Judith says, "it felt like home from the beginning. I found a place where I can be myself." She recalls the time when the feeling of being home overcame her—during a family camp they attended in their first year at the church. "I ended up crying a lot that week," she confesses. She needed time alone to figure out her feelings.

> *I went to a beautiful meadow at the camp. My group leader suggested that I walk a labyrinth. And so I walked. I saw a rock on the ground that said "Trust." I kept walking and I saw a rock on the ground that said "Be Brave." I started sobbing as I walked. I started saying to myself, "It is going to be all right now. It is going to be all right now." I realized as I walked that this was related to my loss of my church life when I was a girl.*

Now, as a wife and mother herself, she "had it back," faith, family, home, church. That which had been broken was made whole. "As I left the labyrinth, there was a rock that said 'Thanks.' I am very grateful to God"—she pauses for a moment, wondering what the reaction will be—"for speaking to me through the rocks!"

Her words bring to mind Jesus' words that "even the rocks and stones" will call out God's glory. She laughs softly. "I felt very loved by the earth and God at that moment." After years of floating, she felt grounded again. Home. Finally.

*   *   *

Born in a mainline Protestant home, Judith eventually came back to that tradition, albeit in a related denomination. Sociologists refer to people like Judith as "returnees." Since the late 1980s, mainline congregations have seen an influx of people returning home.

On my journey, the vast majority of people I met did not grow up in the churches they currently attend. For almost everyone, their spiritual and personal quests had taken them away from their childhood faiths— if they had any—through periods of longing, questioning, and a sustained search to "find home." Their stories often described a kind of religious displacement; many of the people depicted themselves almost as spiritual refugees. Because of their sense of dislocation, themes of homecoming and return dominated their faith stories. For these people, however, finding home does not necessarily mean returning to the villages of their youth. Indeed, as in Judith's case, they have discovered that you cannot go home again—that home is by way of another route, the unexpected journey, a quest or pilgrimage.

Several years ago, I belonged to a church that had a community within it called Rivendell, after the house in *The Lord of the Rings*. Different sorts of people belonged to the community; they came from diverse backgrounds and had different reasons for belonging. But, like Frodo and his unlikely collection of friends, all were on a spiritual quest to do that which God called them to do—a mission that could only be accomplished in a community of diverse sorts. I thought about the Rivendell community often while on my journey, for the people I met were much the same. Not everyone was a returnee like Judith. There were exiles, immigrants, converts, and villagers—all of whom made up a band of contemporary pilgrims on a quest to find home.

Exiles

In New Haven, Connecticut, the Church of the Redeemer is part of the United Church of Christ, a Congregationalist denomination whose roots stretch back to New England Puritanism, one of the oldest forms of American Protestantism. The church had fallen on hard times, and in the mid-1990s it looked as if it might close. But, with the arrival of a new young minister, the Reverend Lillian Daniel, the church began to turn around and began attracting many new people, most of whom came from other religious traditions.[26]

"I first walked through those doors about seventeen years ago," says Jim, a Roman Catholic. His wife, a Protestant, had then joined Redeemer. He did not like it much. He says that Protestant services are "all too long" compared to the thirty-minute mass at his parish. He confesses that after one particularly painful ninety-minute service, "The Church of the Redeemer and I were not off to a good start."

But he kept coming back, mostly with his wife for special occasions, and admits that "there was something about this church." However, deep emotions tied him to his Catholic parish, although it was in a steep decline. "I still loved Saint Peter's, even as it was falling apart around me; it was still a beautiful church. It was the first church I ever went to, the church that my mother and I used to walk to every Sunday when I was a little boy, right next to the school of the same name in which I spent some of the most wonderful years of my life." As an adult, however, Jim began to question some of the church's teachings and he admits to a "disagreement" between himself and a "couple of priests" as to "what constitutes a good Catholic." The argument, he says, "was potentially devastating to me." He shared his pain with Rev. Daniel, who "assured me that God was with me." Although he is still technically a Catholic, Church of the Redeemer is now his home.

Jim speaks of his journey with the pain of a displaced person, a reluctant spiritual refugee from Roman Catholicism. Adding to his sense of loss, he says, "They tore down Saint Peter's not long ago. The church and the school. To this day, as I drive on I-95, I can't look over at where that beautiful campus and those two wonderful buildings used to stand." At odds with church teaching and suffering from the closure of his old congregation, Jim has learned that church is more than a building.

Speaking of what makes Redeemer special, Jim addressed the congregation directly, "It's you. You people sitting out there in those pews. You make this church unique."

Jim was not alone at Redeemer. Other Roman Catholics shared that Redeemer welcomed "even struggling Roman Catholics!" One young woman said, "To my surprise, I began to feel more at home here than at my own church." She continued, "For the first time in my life, I had the wonderful experience of worshiping God without laying aside any of my convictions about the equality and dignity of all people, whether man or woman, gay or straight, young or old." Although she, like Jim, remains Catholic, she and her fiancé plan to wed at Redeemer, "We felt that New Haven is our home right now, and that this is our church."

Besides offering a spiritual home to displaced Roman Catholics, Redeemer has also welcomed a large number of people from Dixwell Congregational Church, the historically African-American UCC congregation across town. Like Redeemer, Dixwell had had a glorious history, especially under its powerful spiritual leader Doc Edmonds during the civil rights era. After Doc retired, however, the church struggled with new leadership that steered the congregation in a very different direction. In the mid-1990s, Doc left his old church and began worshiping at Redeemer. A number of his former parishioners and his own family members followed.

Among those who came to Redeemer from Dixwell are Aaron and Madeline, an active, well-educated, successful couple in the early years of retirement. As lifelong churchgoers, they have served in many leadership roles at both Dixwell and Redeemer. One Sunday, they drove me around New Haven and took me to Dixwell. They proudly told me of their former congregation's history, describing marches, sermons, and sit-ins, and even explaining small details of the church's unusual architecture. They shared the sad story of its conflict and decline, and their eventual self-imposed exile to Redeemer. They are still emotional about having to leave Dixwell, but they love Redeemer. Madeline praises her new congregation as "open and accepting" and appreciates the "wide diversity of backgrounds" of the congregation.

Being deeply formed in the gospel of civil rights, both Madeline and Aaron believe that church should "be about building bridges." Aaron says that one of Redeemer's primary strengths is "its practice of hospitality—this is a church that has open doors." He extols the "level of trust in the congregation," where people can "air disagreements and feel safe." Perhaps as a counterpoint to his experience at Dixwell, Aaron says that "Redeemer is a church that could disagree and still hold each other in Christian fellowship." He tells me about fighting well at Redeemer, and about his Friends in Faith group: "It is really about love, about relationships. Love like in a family. That's what we have at Redeemer."

New England Congregationalism was originally a religion of exiles—those people who fled England for the sake of religious conscience and attempted to make a spiritual home in the New World. Standing in this ancient line, Church of the Redeemer is a church of exiles. Along with the disenfranchised Roman Catholics and displaced African-Americans, former fundamentalists, coming-out gays and lesbians, homeless people, and students have all found Redeemer a good place for exiles to call home.

Immigrants

On Sunday, July 18, 2004, the people of Iglesia Santa María (Episcopal) in Falls Church, Virginia, worshiped in their new church building for the first time. The Reverend Jesús Reyes did not preach his sermon from the pulpit that day. Rather, he stood in the center of the congregation, welcoming the gathering of several hundred Spanish-speaking immigrants to their new home. "La Iglesia Santa María is a new house in a time of *fiesta:* Holy Communion. The body of Christ brings us into this new house where Christians can share a meal." Everyone listened intently as Jesús opened his arms wide, saying:

Our tradition of communion is one in which each of us, with our hearts and our individual personalities can come together in a new community. No one is excluded from the table of the Lord. This is the central message of the Eucharist. We are the people of God—and we are immigrants. Think of the joy of going home to the house you grew up in, with the smell of mother's cooking in the kitchen, the tastes of food, the sounds of family. Here, like your mother's table, the Lord's table welcomes you home. Here we are an extended family in the Spirit through communion. You are all members of God's house.

At the words "mother's cooking," one woman sitting near me wiped her eyes. The man next to her blinked stoically so as not to show emotion. Jesús's words, so poignant for these new Americans, underscored their obvious spiritual longing for home. Many of these people would not return to the country of their birth, nor would their children live in their parents' homeland. These were double-immigrants, for everyone here was born Roman Catholic. In addition to leaving their home countries, they also left Mother Church. They must make a new home in God, seeking a better life for themselves and their families in a foreign world.

Iglesia Santa María is the first freestanding Episcopal Latino congregation in northern Virginia. Founding members Marguerite and Eduardo Rodríguez are a hardworking young couple who have managed to buy a modest ranch house in the suburbs. "This is the first house we've owned in this country. It is not big, but it is comfortable." They anxiously looked forward to the people of Santa María having their own church. "Churches are created to put all people together," Eduardo says, "to create a community where you can feel as a family." Marguerite smiles and adds, "We feel very happy to have our own house, own space. It will be the same for the church. When you have your own church, your own space, you can go to the kitchen and make coffee. It is your space. You own it." Eduardo talks about why they want to move to their own building from the space they share with an Anglo congregation. "You are going to the church to find something you need"—he struggles a little with the English—"the emptiness you feel when you come from your country. That's why it is important for us to have a church."

Images of home, family, children, and community are rife at Santa María. One woman shared her dream for Santa María with me, "that we become a giant family that believes in Christ; we share obligations; share sorrows; share happiness; one grand family!" On the first day at the new building, sixty children led the processional—all carrying food and flowers to the altar. In the basement, there is a Latino-American martyrs chapel, with a shrine to the Blessed Mother, designed to remind the young people in the church why their parents fled their homelands. "Honoring our martyrs," Jesus tells me, "is a way of honoring our families, their sacrifices and our roots." During Sunday worship, large families sit together, often three generations. Children run and laugh during the service. And Padre Jesús stands in the center, praying, preaching, and passing out bread and wine. I imagine him as a village priest in Mexico, surrounded by God's family, blessing them. After the service, María, another founding member, smiles and tells me, "It is our own house now. We see this church as our second home."

Being with the people of Santa María, I realize that I, too, am an immigrant. Although I hardly speak their language, I feel deep kinship with them and wish I could tell them in Spanish how welcome they have made me. Having moved away from Baltimore as a teen, I experience a certain sense of homelessness, of being a perpetual immigrant. You do not have to cross national borders to be an immigrant. City to city, state to state, many Americans make a life away from the homeland.

For me church has also become my dwelling. As I walked forward to take communion at Santa María, surrounded by so many other immigrants, I felt like I was home. Jesús smiled as he pressed a wafer in my hand, and I swear that I caught a whiff of my mother's kitchen.

Converts

"I definitely need constant and continuing conversion as I am such a superb sinner!" laughs Deanna, a member of Phinney Ridge Lutheran Church in Seattle, Washington. "You don't want to know, and I don't want to think about, how many of the Ten Commandments I've broken in my wild past."

Deanna did not grow up as a Christian, or in any religion. A few years ago, when she decided to join Phinney Ridge, she called her parents—one in Washington, the other in North Carolina—to find out if she had been baptized. Neither could remember. "They can't recall much of my child-hood," she says cryptically. "All my life, I've felt like an orphan."

She found her way to the church in a time of personal crisis, when she felt overtaken by depression and could not figure out the source of her negative emotions. "I felt bad for no known reason." Then, she realized that "something in me felt unforgiven."

I began to review the world religions in my mind, looking for a balm for my crabbiness. Of all the world religions, I found Christianity the least understandable and appealing. I mean, couldn't they find a more appealing symbol than a dead guy on a cross? How inviting is that? However, upon reviewing and searching for an inspirational figure to help me out of my funk, I thought of Jesus. Wasn't his big gig forgiveness?

This did not make Deanna feel better. "So I began to mutter to myself, 'Okay, Jesus, if you are the big guru of forgiveness, give me forgiveness, how about sending some my way?!'" Angry and upset, she screamed at God, "I've tried to be good, what am I not forgiven? If you're the great forgiver, then give me some ——ing forgiveness NOW!"

Much to her surprise, she "felt Jesus' presence in the room." She says that, "wordlessly, he communicated that he'd been waiting a long time to be asked and that forgiveness was mine." Immediately, she felt "peaceful and calm," feelings that "stayed with me the rest of the day."

She struggled to figure out what had happened, but she had the strangest sense that she had really experienced "a visit from Jesus." Knowing that she had to "look into this fellow named Jesus a little more," she walked into Phinney Ridge, the church right down the street from her house, the next Sunday.

Deanna considers herself "skeptical bordering on cynical, an unlikely candidate for organized religion." But the congregation welcomed her warmly and invited her into their adult inquirers' process called The WAY. The idea intrigued her: she realized that "this is not a do-it-yourself deal. I need fellow travelers to teach me, to hold my hand, and to remind me of Jesus' promises." She embarked on a pilgrimage of getting to know Jesus. "Through The WAY," she says, "I found a way to a heavenly father and divine family. I learned new ways to pray; how to read the Bible; to enjoy fellowship and be part of community."

Although her parents could not remember, Deanna persisted in her quest to find out if she had ever been baptized. She tracked down distant relatives, made dozens of calls, and finally located the congregation that her grandmother had belonged to when Deanna was a baby. The church secretary told her that the baptismal records had been destroyed in a fire. Deanna was disappointed. But three weeks later, the secretary called back to say that she had tracked down other records. On January 6, 1956, Deanna had, indeed, been baptized. "I was overjoyed," she recalls, "I was a child of God all along and I didn't know it."

In an urban neighborhood in secular Seattle, Phinney Ridge attracts people like Deanna—converts to Christianity. I heard a number of stories like hers, from people who grew up with no religious tradition but found, almost always by divine accident, new life in the church. "Spiritual questers do find a home here," says Pastor Paul Hoffman. "The challenge is to create Christians, and not just spiritual people." They work hard to introduce people to the Christian tradition and, in the process of doing so, have created familial community. "You develop some meaningful friendships," says Bob, a sponsor in The WAY, "really meaningful relationships within the congregation."

In much of American Protestantism, conversion is viewed as an individual event: a convicted sinner gets born again by praying a prayer of salvation, asking Jesus into the heart. This simple act, done at revivals, prayer meetings, or with a television evangelist, ensures entrance to heaven. At Phinney Ridge, however, conversion is not an individual event. Rather, as it was in the earliest days of Christianity, conversion means joining God's people, being incorporated into the body of Christ. Finding oneself a child of God means finding family.

In the context of family, people like Deanna learn that they must be "continually converted," learning and relearning the way of faith in community. Conversion is not a single prayer. Conversion is pilgrimage. "My need to get to know this Jesus fellow and find out about forgiveness kept me coming back," Deanna says, "and keeps me coming back." She confesses, "I still sin with great regularity." But her family at Phinney Ridge neither forgets nor abandons her. They are there with "that eternal welcome mat and acceptance" helping her with her "continuing conversion."

Villagers

Barbara and John Hickman are not returnees, exiles, immigrants, or converts. They are lifelong Lutherans and have been members of Saint Mark Lutheran Church in Yorktown, Virginia, for twenty-two years. Barbara and John have stayed; they hung around the village. Born Protestant, raised in Protestant congregations, they are faithful members who have done nearly every job in their local church. But for all their geographical stability, Barbara and John are pilgrims, too. Over the years, their faith has grown deeper and their congregation has increasingly become their family. They have been on a journey while staying put.

One afternoon, a group of us gather for lunch to talk about Saint Mark. Most of the people in the group are long-term members of twenty years or more. Everyone talks about how much the church has changed in recent years, how "Pastor is growing the church spiritually," as June puts it. "We Lutherans may have spirituality," she says, "but we don't talk about it very well! We are learning to talk about it." They begin to tell me stories of deepened faith, of how much more meaningful being Christians has become to them. When it comes to Barbara and John, the conversation stops, the others waiting in respectful silence, as if not sure what their friends will say. But Barbara and John want to share. They vividly remember when their spiritual lives changed and their church became their family in a new way.

One April day in 2002, the Hickmans received a phone call. Linda, their daughter-in-law, a young mother of a toddler, had died. The police said it appeared to be suicide. In complete shock, Barbara and John phoned their pastor, Rev. Gary Erdos. Gary told them to wait at home; he would accompany them to their son's house. Barbara and John agreed.

Gary later told me that when he arrived at the Hickmans' house, Barbara and John were in the driveway. "Barbara was physically shaking, mumbling that she didn't know how she was going to make it through this." John was talking to a neighbor, and Gary overheard him saying, "God has brought us to our knees before, now our faces are in the dirt." Gary hugged them (Barbara and John warmly remember this kindness) and drove them to their son's house.

When they arrived, Barbara and John worried about how their daughter-in-law's body would be handled. Unable to view the tragedy themselves, they asked Gary to make sure "she was all right." Would he go with the coroner and deputies to tend her body? Although he had never seen a violent death before, Gary agreed. Barbara sighs, "He treated her like a person instead of a crime scene." After Linda's body was removed, John asked, "Do you think she's in heaven?" When Gary answered yes, John said, "Good. Because I don't want to go there if she isn't."

Barbara and John confess that in the midst of their deep sorrow and confusion, they also felt mortified. After all, a member of their family had committed suicide, an act that some think is the unforgivable sin. How would their congregation react? Would anyone care? Could they hold her funeral in the church? Would people understand? Where would she be buried?

Barbara shakes as she tells the story. John puts an arm around the back of her chair, gently supporting his wife. Gary, she tells me, "was amazing," insisting that the family hold the funeral at Saint Mark. To Barbara and John's astonishment, hundreds of people gathered to celebrate Linda's life. There was no gossip, no hints of judgment, and no intimations of blame or shame. Rather, the congregation did everything possible to support and care for the family, especially their son and granddaughter. John said, "I'm ashamed for speaking of how our face was in the dirt, because Saint Mark has picked us up and carried us through all of it in Jesus' name. I believe we have seen Jesus."

At the time, the congregation at Saint Mark had just renovated its building, turning a dilapidated nursery into a chapel. The chapel is airy, marked by a sense of spiritual openness, with glass, white walls, and light-hued wood. Directly opposite the entry is a small pulpit. The wall behind the pulpit is a honeycomb of nooks, a few with elegant pottery, the only decoration in the room.

The first time I saw that chapel, I thought it a creative way to display art—until I looked closer and realized that it is a columbarium. The pottery jars are urns artfully designed to reflect the person whose ashes they hold.

The most beautiful urn is a vibrant sea-blue, encircled by a gold metal sculpture of three swimming dolphins, two adults and a baby. It holds Linda's ashes. "She loved the ocean," John explains. "The dolphins represent their family." Barbara says, "The church president insisted that she be the first person placed in the new columbarium." She continues, "He wouldn't let us pay. He said, 'We know you can afford to pay for it, but if you would like to bury Linda at the church, giving this to you is something we all believe to be a way we can live out Jesus' command to love God and love our neighbor.'" The congregation, she says, "took a tragedy and created redemption."

Across the table, Sarah looks at them with tears in her eyes. "It meant a lot to all of us," she assures them. "If you ever get a notion that you aren't loved around here, someone will correct it." As another woman told me, "Saint Mark has truly become our extended family."

I heard many quiet stories of faithful churchgoers who never left; they never really doubted or felt a need for exotic spiritual experiences. They taught Sunday school, served on committees, baked casseroles, and invited their friends to church. But staying did not mean remaining the same. Sometimes pilgrimages knock on your front door. Their journeys took them deeper and farther than they had ever anticipated. Like Barbara and John, they testified to the amazing grace of finding home in their own backyard.

Saint George's Episcopal Church in Arlington, Virginia, was founded a century ago, in what was once a middle-class neighborhood of single-family homes. Now, the old housing stock has been torn down and replaced by urban malls, office buildings, high-rise condominiums, and metro stations. These days the charming, English village–style church sits right in the middle of a highly mobile and always changing urban landscape. Yet, here, surrounded by the churning city, people find home. Says one member, "I walked into this church in November 1998 after a two-decade absence from church. My partner and I were embraced and intentionally invited to become part of this community. We were and are seekers from different religious traditions. He is from a fundamentalist Christian tradition and my background is Roman Catholic." A woman from the congregation testified, "I knew from the start that I'd found my church home." Another person added, "Saint George's and Saint Georgians have become part of my family."

I heard such comments everywhere. The images of home and family were striking, even surprising. Before 1960, American Christians understood spirituality primarily in terms of dwelling—of church buildings, familial faith, and generations of participation in a single congregation. After 1960, however, the spiritual style of the country shifted toward seeking as the population moved south and west and as anti-institutional, antiauthoritarian baby boomers opted out of traditional religion.[27] The seeker ethos was so powerful that one sociologist depicted the baby boomers as a "generation of seekers," people on a near-perpetual quest for religious experience.[28]

At first, much of the search was directed toward personal experience, increasingly exotic, eclectic, and rebellious ways of experiencing God. Along the way, though, some seekers expressed a desire to settle. The quest changed. Some no longer sought episodic spiritual ecstasy but longed for a spiritual community, a home, where they could forge new, non-biological family ties and connect with a religious tradition.

Sociologist Wade Clark Roof has described this pattern as "a shared experience," in which the "journey extends not only forward but into the past, toward rediscovery and reclaiming Christian spirituality." He quotes Sara Caughman, one such seeker, who is now an active Episcopalian, as saying, "Many people start out walking as if they are alone but discover fellow travelers along the way."[29]

But people like Sara could not just go back to the old village. It did not exist anymore. She joined an Episcopal congregation that had been in decline for two decades. Along with a small group of like-minded pilgrims, she chose to resettle a dying church and help revive it by reconstructing the Christian tradition in community. They focused on spiritual practices, "learning that spirituality—if it is to have depth—requires cultivation by means of habit and shared activity."[30] In turn, the emphasis on practice opened them to understanding and connecting with the past, finding roots in tradition. Going home to tradition, however, did not mean recreating their parents' church. Rather, her congregation is marked by "its celebration of openness and diversity." They have managed to create a new village church, to find a new home, and root in tradition in ways that are open, fluid, flexible, and dynamic. In the last ten years, Sara's congregation has experienced dramatic growth by combining spiritual impulses of seeking and dwelling in a new emphasis on tradition and Christian practice.

Sara would find fellow travelers on my journey. In fact, I heard many stories like hers. The pilgrims I met understood home, family, and tradition in dynamic ways, weaving together a spiritual-quest orientation with their desire to construct new kinds of church. They are trying to remember the Christian tradition (if they ever knew in the first place), what practice means in daily life, and what the wisdom tradition offers. They are pilgrims traveling together to God, creating new homes and families along the way.

PART II

Ten Signposts
of Renewal

Off the Map

Like most people these days, I use computer directions when I travel. I love the convenience and sense of authoritative assurance they provide in strange cities: "Go .5 mile ahead and turn right; proceed for 1.7 miles and turn left." After many trips, however, I noticed that online maps direct travelers to the single—and most obvious—route on interstates and major highways with no mention of road construction or rush-hour traffic patterns. Unlike the old paper maps of my childhood, computer-generated directions give the impression that there is only one way from point A to point B. Armed solely with electronic directions, I stick to their route, afraid that if I fail to follow the little arrows and mile markers, I would be lost.

Not long ago, returning home to Virginia from Pennsylvania via MapQuest, my husband and I got caught in a locally notorious construction mess on the Baltimore beltway. My frustrated husband asked, "Is there another way?" I grabbed the worn paper atlas from the backseat as we exited the freeway. Using old-fashioned street signs and intuition, we navigated through neighborhoods to an unused secondary highway—where there was little traffic and an open road. My husband remarked, "That's a good route. It's a reasonable way even if there isn't any traffic!" We found a better way that eventually brought us safely home, an alternative route that we created by following the signposts on the ground.

Some Christians think that faith is like a set of MapQuest directions—that there is only a single highway to God. After all, Jesus said, "I am the Way, the Truth, and the Life. No one comes to the Father except by me." He is the map. And Christianity is a kind of vacation destination, a place you wind up in to escape hell. Such Christians claim that God has a plan for your life, a route you must follow or you will be lost in this life—and damned in the next. They even have things like "four spiritual laws" and "forty days of purpose" that tell you how to get there. Like computer-generated directions, this road is predetermined, distant, and authoritative. You cannot exit this freeway or deviate from the route without peril. Taking a creative risk, as I did in my recent journey through Baltimore's old neighborhoods, will not lead you home. Instead, it leads directly to hell and destruction. Who cares about a few spiritual traffic jams or construction zones? Better stick to the map. Follow the plan.

But what if Jesus is not a MapQuest sort of map, a superhighway to salvation? What if Jesus is more like old-fashioned street signs in a Baltimore neighborhood, navigated by imagination and intuition? Rather than a set of directions to get saved, Jesus is, as his earliest followers claimed, "the Way." Jesus is not the way we get somewhere. *Jesus is the Christian journey itself,* a pilgrimage that culminates in the wayfarer's arrival in God. When Jesus said "Follow me," he did not say "Follow the map." Rather, he invited people to follow him, to walk with him on a pilgrimage toward God.

How, then, do we get there? How do we follow the Jesus way?

You have to exit the highway, risk getting lost, and follow the signposts on the ground.

In Seattle, at Phinney Ridge Lutheran Church, they understand that Jesus is not a destination on a divine map. Rather, Jesus is the way. In 1993 the church initiated "The WAY," a process of welcoming people into a life of Christian pilgrimage. Many churches offer newcomers a four- to six-week program of membership; after a few classes people simply sign up and typically sign a pledge card, too. Not at Phinney Ridge. Instead of a quick membership class, they offer a full year of mentoring and teaching to form people of faith: "the goal is to help them at their own pace to come into a living relationship with Jesus Christ that takes over the center of their life."[31] They are not trying to make members; rather, they are trying to make pilgrims.

Since its inception, more than three hundred people have embarked on The WAY. One of those pilgrims, Joan Henderson, recalls first entering the church:

When I walked in the front door at Phinney Ridge on Easter a decade ago, I had no idea that I had been invited, but I had been. I was invited by the Holy Spirit. But the invitation was so subtle I didn't know anything was at work other than me trying to get my way. I wasn't interested in following anything or anyone. I didn't want to be changed, I wasn't looking for community. I just wanted to get our girls baptized so they could get admitted to a Catholic school. Quick and clean. In and out. I've come to refer to it as looking for a drive-through baptism.

Joan has come to believe that the Christian life is one of "continuing invitation," where through the "stirrings of the Holy Spirit, Christ calls us to follow." Around her neck hangs a necklace, a gift from a friend. It reads simply SHOW UP. The pilgrimage begins with that invitation— and God keeps asking us to show up through grief, confusion, joy, hopelessness, and fear. "In every situation," she says, "Christ is in the middle offering an invitation...."

"I showed up and Phinney Ridge welcomed me, welcomed our whole family. I did all I could. I showed up. That was it. And that was a lot." And they "showed up" for her. "I've never been the same," she says gratefully.

How do you go on the pilgrimage? Show up. Begin the way.

MapQuest will not take us to this place. Maps are about seeing from above, about perspective from a god's-eye view, about getting to a destination by avoiding the pain. Christianity is not a map religion. Christianity is a religion of the streets, of signposts on the ground, of people walking along the way. To borrow from French philosopher Michel de Certeau, the Christian story "begins on ground level, with footsteps," where the pilgrims' "intertwined paths give their space to spaces" as "they weave places together."[32] There can be found traces of holiness, traces of faith in the city. Christianity is a kind of vast spiritual and historical migration, a mobile city of pilgrims, all on their way to a country where there are no maps.

Although no map can fix the way, there are signposts to point Christians in the right direction, toward the wisdom of God, toward love, toward home. Things like hospitality, contemplation, healing, testimony, and justice. Christians call these signposts "practices," the activities drawn from our tradition that we do together in community. Practices form Christians in faith as they deepen their trust in God's love and strengthen their love for the world.

From the earliest days of the Christian faith, Jesus' followers, known as people of the Way, were recognized by what they did—practicing hospitality and forgiveness. Too often, contemporary Christianity seems to be a religion about belief, a kind of spiritual club that can be joined by agreeing to a statement of faith.

But emerging Christianity is not about pure doctrine or agreeing with a set of philosophical presuppositions. The kind of Christianity enacted in the congregations where I traveled is more like a recovery group: "Act as if . . ." If you act like a Christian by joining in its practices, by following its tracings, you may well become one. Being a Christian is not a one-moment miracle of salvation. It takes practice. It is a process of faith and a continuing conversion. And it can be a long walk.

Practices invite weary nomads to join the journey, to find home, to create a different kind of village, to enter the memory of Jesus. And practices serve as signposts along the way, pointing toward the tracings of others who have marked the Christian path. Without them, we would be lost.

FIVE

Hospitality

WELCOMING STRANGERS

On a Sunday morning in January 2005, my family and I drove south from Saint Petersburg to Naples, Florida, to attend church. Crossing the Sunshine Bridge as ocean fog danced in the dawn, I relished the tropical ease of travel along the coast. Indeed, this is a tourist mecca. And Naples, our destination, is famous for the hospitality of its beautiful hotels. If only for a week, its lush resorts, chic spas, and upscale restaurants offer tourists healing respites from foul weather and demanding jobs. These oases create an alternate reality of peace and tranquillity, a momentary lull in the chaos of contemporary life. At those hotels, however, you pay a premium for such care. In Florida, hospitality is an industry that offers weary consumers the product of welcoming care. For those fortunate enough, such extravagant hospitality is, indeed, restorative—even while it is temporary and illusory.

If vacations are easy in Naples, being a Christian—at least a mainline one—is hard. For those who want to attend church, southwest Florida offers the usual array of conservative evangelical megachurches. For those who want to pursue the good life without God, the beach and golf courses beckon. But for those seeking another way, between fundamentalism and secularism, a way of pilgrim faith, finding community is not easy.

On the edge of Naples, away from the beach, along a commercial boulevard, sits Cornerstone United Methodist Church. As is true for much of the Sunbelt, brand-name Protestantism is not flourishing in Naples. But Cornerstone, a new mission congregation, is prospering, especially spiritually. In stark contrast to the hospitality industry that surrounds it, the congregation welcomes Naples's many wayfarers into restorative community. Hospitality at Cornerstone is as extravagant as that offered by the resorts, but it is not illusory or ephemeral. It is genuine.

On this surprisingly hot Sunday morning, we arrived a little early. A number of people smiled at us and said hello. Nearly everyone followed the greeting with a question: "Where are you from?" "We live outside Washington, D.C.," my husband replied. "Oh, there are lots of people here who used to live in Washington." At Cornerstone, they seem accustomed to asking strangers whence they have come.

We are not the only ones to arrive early. An early morning praise service, offered as a kind of spiritual warm-up before the more traditional liturgy, has attracted several dozen people. They are dressed casually in shorts, jeans, and golf shirts. Some wear T-shirts bearing the logo CORNERSTONE UNITED METHODIST CHURCH. Although most people here this morning are white, they clearly come from various social backgrounds. Everywhere, people welcome each other. Warm greetings and hugs abound. A preppy-looking retired man is talking to a man covered with tattoos. Senior citizens, young families, and single people mingle in the entryway. There are several people from other ethnic backgrounds, too. A man who appears to be Haitian chats with some teens. An African-American musician is warming up with a Latino friend in the band. The minister, Roy Terry, is standing with them. A long ponytail falls down his back. Three black-clad teenage girls with pierced noses and Goth makeup approach an elderly woman in a wheelchair. One by one, they lean down, kiss the woman on the cheek, and ask her how she is doing.

The sign out front says Methodist, but I was raised Methodist and this does not look like any Methodist church I remember. It appears to be a congregation in which wayfarers and strangers have become friends.

When I was a girl at Saint John's United Methodist Church in Hamilton, no one mentioned the Christian practice of hospitality, of welcoming strangers into community. Perhaps hospitality was an unspoken norm, something Christians just did. More likely, however, it was because we had accepted a cultural practice of hospitality. In the 1960s rounds of cocktail parties, dinners, and picnics at the homes of family or friends constituted hospitality. Mostly, my childhood church failed at hospitality for a simple reason: there were no wayfarers to welcome! We entertained those we knew. And, in my neighborhood, everybody knew everyone else. New people entered Saint John's only through birth—and there were lots of births.

With the old patterns of the village broken down, however, the Christian practice of hospitality has reemerged as foundational to the spiritual life. Contemporary Americans are nomads, what Catholic writer Henri Nouwen once called "a world of strangers, estranged from their own past, culture, and country, from their neighbors, friends and family, from their deepest self and their God."[33] In such a "world of strangers," where fear, anger, and hostility build walls between people and chip away at communal soulfulness, Nouwen proposed that "if there is any concept worth restoring to its original depth and evocative potential, it is the concept of hospitality."[34] For Nouwen, hospitality is the "creation of a free space" where strangers become friends. "Hospitality is not to change people, but to offer them space where change can take place."[35]

Although Nouwen wrote those words in the 1970s, they have become even more truthful in the intervening decades. Sociologist Zygmunt Bauman makes the point that in our contemporary, fragmented world, the only "rational choice" left to people in the West is to adopt the pose of "tourist" or "nomad" in relation to religion and spirituality. In every possible way, the changes of the late twentieth century cast us all out—a kind of contemporary exile from the Garden—forcing citizens of Western nations to become travelers in an unfamiliar world. Nouwen's "world of strangers" may not be an evocative enough term for what has happened in our society. Now, even "seeker" is passé, for seekers hope to find something. Bauman argues that there may well be nothing to find—that we are perpetual wanderers through unmarked country, randomly collecting experiences and souvenirs along the way.

On that Sunday morning at Cornerstone, my family and I arrived as tourists—indeed, following the worship service we were scheduled to drive to Disney World for a short vacation. Roy and his family, along with several members of the church's leadership team, insisted on taking us out for lunch. We lingered on the church porch for a time and then piled into cars and headed for a local restaurant.

Crowded around a large table, the adults shared stories about their spiritual journeys and their excitement about Cornerstone. I hoped that my seven-year-old, Emma, was not too bored. Being a little person in a strange state at a table of adults can be a trying experience for even the most patient child. In the midst of their marvelous hospitality, with its energetic conversation and laughter, I noticed that Roy's teenage daughter, Emily, was talking to Emma. She was listening intently to the older girl, and the two even went off together for a short walk outside. After lunch, she showed Emma her car—a red 1966 Mustang convertible that she had earned for herself by raising and selling a pony. Emma was completely enthralled, later telling me that she wanted a car just like that when she turned sixteen. Although Disney World beckoned, Emma clearly enjoyed making a new friend. And I marveled at the easy way that a teenage girl offered hospitality to the smallest stranger at the table.

A year (and about a dozen congregations) later, I asked Emma which was her favorite church among all that we visited. Without hesitation, she said: "Roy's church." When I asked why, she responded, "I loved the rock music and Emily was really cool. She was nice to me." Emily had, quite literally, transformed a tourist into a friend through the practice of hospitality.

In the twentieth century, most of us came to believe that travel is easy. Language barriers lessened, air travel was quick, and global hotel and restaurant chains provided familiar comforts to those away from home. Through most of history, however, travel has been hard. Being a traveler meant putting oneself at risk, exposing oneself to the perils of unknown lands. The early Christians knew this, and developed their language of pilgrimage and journey against this dangerous landscape. Those same early Christians—eventually followed by medieval monastic communities—also developed their practices of hospitality as a way of caring for God's wayfarers.

If emerging Christianity is, like its ancient ancestor, a faith of travelers, of pilgrims on a way, it should be no surprise that hospitality would, once again, find itself at the heart of Christian life. In our context, hospitality opens the possibility of Nouwen's "free space" where strangers become friends—and equally offers travelers safe passage through dangerous country.

Occasionally, I have attended churches with "hospitality programs" or "welcome committees" where friendliness seems little more than a phony act to get newcomers to join the church. At such places, hospitality typically follows a secular model—such as the neighborhood Welcome Wagon of the 1960s, which, for all its friendliness, was essentially a way to promote certain stores and products. In some churches "hospitality" appears to be a code word for promotion, with the church as the primary product. Hospitality is an instrument used for another end: to sign people up as pledging members.

True Christian hospitality is not a recruitment strategy designed to manipulate strangers into church membership. Rather, it is a central practice of the Christian faith—something Christians are called to do for the sake of that thing itself. Hospitality draws from the ancient taproots of

Christian faith, from the soil of the Middle East, where it is considered a primary virtue of community. Although it is a practice shared by Jews and Muslims, for Christians hospitality holds special significance: Christians welcome strangers as we ourselves have been welcomed into God through the love of Jesus Christ. Through hospitality, Christians imitate God's welcome. Therefore, hospitality is not a program, not a single hour or ministry in the life of a congregation. It stands at the heart of a Christian way of life, a living icon of wholeness in God. "We don't care who you are," explained one Cornerstone member, "where you came from, what color you are, what your background is, with whom you share your life. You are here, now, at Cornerstone and you are a brother or sister in Christ."

Some of Cornerstone's people have never been part of a church before; others had previously been members of strict and conservative denominations such as the Southern Baptists; a few have joined from other mainline Protestant congregations or from Roman Catholicism. Very few grew up in Florida. Marsha, a congregational leader who was reared in an Anabaptist tradition, confessed that after moving to Naples, she did not go to church. "For eight years," she says, "we wandered around." Arriving at Cornerstone, she and her husband found the sense of freedom welcoming. "There's a lot of freedom here to be who we are. I think that's really neat."

That sense of freedom exemplifies Christian hospitality. "Somehow, the way we do church equalizes. We are all the same," said one woman trying to explain the congregation. Sameness, however, does not mean conformity. "You walk in and you don't feel pressure to conform. There are a lot of churches you go in and everybody looks like they came from a cookie cutter. They're always the same and if you don't fit in, then you don't feel comfortable." But hospitality, a radically biblical and democratic practice, opens the way for all people to be the same under God, part of the same family, welcomed for who they are in all their uniqueness. "We're who we are," said Scott, a former Episcopalian. "Real, honest to God, real." Another member recalled his experience in a different congregation where he was treated as an "outsider" for not being "*conservative* enough and, therefore, not *Christian* enough." Evidently, that congregation offered hospitality based on one's voting record.

Sadly, many Americans experience congregations as judgmental places with strict rules of appearance and behavior. But God's hospitality demands otherwise—that all are welcome. At Cornerstone, an easy sense of authentic hospitality extends across the congregation. Praise band members look like working-class biker guys that churches usually ignore. At one point in the service, a guitarist said, "I was frightened because I hadn't been in a church before. [But this congregation] didn't feel like being herded as cattle. Music got me in the door."

Although hospitality at Cornerstone is free, it is not without cost. Indeed, Christians who enter into the practice of welcoming the stranger know that it is risky—and sometimes dangerous. Hospitality is not a tame practice, an option to offer only to those who are likeable. As the ancient Christian theologian Gregory of Nyssa reminded his flock, "The stranger, those who are naked, without food, infirm and imprisoned are the ones the Gospel intends for you."[36] Hospitality can be frightening at times.

The people at Cornerstone know this. One man shared a story about Rick, a man who challenged the congregation's hospitality. "He comes with tattoos, addiction problems, and even long braids of different colors all over his head." But, he insisted, the congregation accepted Rick as a human being in need of God's love: "People still saw HIM." Still, it is risky welcoming Rick because "he continues to struggle with life issues and is in and out of jail because of his addictions and inappropriate behavior." Yet the people at Cornerstone know and accept him, holding him accountable for his faith journey and actions. "This is not the kind of miracle story people like to hear," the Cornerstone member admitted, "but it is a part of the real world."

At Cornerstone, they speak of living out the "apostolic core" of Christianity, a reference to a brief sentence in the Book of Acts: "They

devoted themselves to the apostles' teaching and fellowship, to the breaking of bread and the prayers." An essential part of that early Christian
teaching and fellowship was hospitality, a practice that awed even the
Roman opponents of Jesus' first followers.

A few centuries later, as the Roman Empire broke down amid social chaos and violence, Saint Benedict charged monastic communities
to "receive guests as Christ" and to embrace the poor, outcast, strangers,
and pilgrims. The heart of Benedictine spirituality is hospitality: a Christian community is not a closed community but extends welcome and
shelter to all, regardless of class, status, or respectability. Joan Chittister,
a contemporary Catholic writer says, "Hospitality means we take people
into the space that is our lives and our minds and our hearts and our work
and our efforts. Hospitality is the way we come out of ourselves."[37] Or,
as two Roman Catholic writers put it, "Guests are crucial to the making
of any heart."[38]

In the eighteenth century, early Methodists claimed that their faith
was a religion of the heart, an allusion to founder John Wesley's famous
description of his own conversion, "My heart was strangely warmed."
But anything involving the heart involves risk. Whether they are welcoming newcomers, retirees, immigrants, Goth teenagers, biker-guy
guitarists, liberals, little girls on their way to Disney World, or recovering convicts, the people at Cornerstone open their hearts.

At Phinney Ridge Lutheran Church in Seattle, a world away from
Cornerstone in Naples, people have discovered the same power of hospitality. As at Cornerstone, congregants witness to the power of welcoming love. "There's a lack of judgment here," one woman related.
"You know, at some churches you go and you feel like people are looking at you and sizing you up. That doesn't happen here. Everybody is
just glad to see you. They gave me a little loaf of bread the first time I
was here. I was so touched." Another remembered being welcomed by
a woman in a wheelchair: "When I tell her that I am visiting, she asked
me to sit and chat with her. She tells me that she is now living in a group

home (she has cerebral palsy, I think) but was recently homeless because of mounting medical bills." At Phinney Ridge, the practice of hospitality opens hearts so wide that the congregation *hosted*—a word drawn from the lexicon of hospitality—a Tent City for the homeless on the church's front lawn. "There's a lot of talk among churches about reaching out to the community and it never happens," said Sandra, a member of the church, "but our church hosted Tent City. It really makes you think about what churches are supposed to be doing. I mean, what would Jesus have done? He would have hosted Tent City!"

Hospitality changes both the host and the guest. Indeed, in many cases, the roles of host and guest appear reversed. At Church of the Epiphany, an Episcopal congregation in Washington, D.C., they host "The Welcome Table," an 8:00 A.M. worship service, breakfast, and small group Bible study for about two hundred homeless people every Sunday morning. There, guests are called by name (instead of number as is the case at most social service agencies in the city) and dine on china with real silverware as waiters (other members of the church) pour their coffee. When guests leave after the meal, a congregational host says, "Thank you for coming." "But we should thank you," a homeless man said to one of the hosts in my hearing. The host quickly responded, "No, we thank you. You have given to us."

At first, those who attended Epiphany's traditional 11:00 A.M. service simply referred to the 8:00 A.M. people as "the homeless." Gradually, however, "the homeless" have become "guests" and, now, in many cases, "homeless members," or "members who live on the streets." Or simply Joe, Wanda, or Ted. When the service was initiated, the liturgy included no collection because the regular churchgoers thought it inappropriate to ask guests to contribute. However, homeless members insisted that their service should include a traditional offering. They wanted to give back to the church. As the priest reported to me, "They felt like they were not real members and asked to contribute." Daniel, a member of the traditional congregation, recalled how moved he was the first time he acted as an usher at the homeless service: "As the plate passed down the rows, I watched poor people turn their pockets inside out and throw loose change and crumpled dollars in the offering. I almost cried. I learned more about giving that morning than in a thousand sermons."

Offering hospitality to strangers has become a powerful aspect of Epiphany's identity, a practice that has revolutionized both the parish and the members' self-understanding. They now donate office space to *Street Sense,* the newspaper written, published, and sold by Washington's homeless community. *Street Sense* vendors are quickly becoming an important part of the congregation. And, in the spring of 2006, Epiphany began taking hospitality to the streets—the church now offers noontime worship in a local park and serving bag lunches to all who attend.

One of the oldest themes in Christian literature about hospitality is the deliberate confusion of the roles of host and guest.[39] This role-switching emphasizes an important point: as a pilgrim of Christ, you will sometimes be the host and sometimes the guest. The second-century writer Diognetus, reminding his readers about Christian identity, said that "Every foreign land is to them as their native country, and every land of their birth as a land of strangers."[40] Or, as the great early Christian preacher John Chrysostom put it, "Don't you know that we live in a foreign land, as though strangers and sojourners?"[41]

Christians have always been hosts and guests, natives and strangers, citizens and sojourners. In our contemporary world of strangers, tourists, and nomads, Henri Nouwen proclaims, "When hostility is converted into hospitality then fearful strangers can become guests.... Then, in fact, the distinction between host and guest proves to be artificial and evaporates in the recognition of newfound unity."[42] In a time of hate-filled extremism, some Christians still long for a world of nonviolent love, of reconciling peace. Of human wholeness, of true brother and sisterhood, in God's compassion. For them, hospitality opens the way to practicing peace, doing a tangible thing that can change the world.

As Martin Marty, a noted Lutheran theologian, says, "In a world where strangers meet strangers with gunfire, barrier walls, spiritually landmined paths, the spirit of revenge, and the record of intransigence, it sounds almost dainty to come on the scene and urge that hospitality has a strong and promising place."[43] In every congregation I observed, hospitality ranked as one of the strongest practices. But it was not just tea and cakes. Like Cornerstone, Phinney Ridge, and Epiphany, the other churches I visited all demonstrated that hospitality is not dainty by practicing it as a way of overcoming fear and isolation. Although hospitality takes many forms, from the kiss of peace bestowed by a Goth teenager on an elderly woman, to offering bread to a stranger and thanking a homeless person for coming to breakfast, the core practice remains the same: Christian people, themselves wayfarers, welcome strangers into the heart of God's transformative love.

SIX

Discernment

LISTENING FOR TRUTH

"We need to hear with our hearts," proclaimed the Reverend Randolph Charles in his Easter sermon at Epiphany, "and hear with our souls." On that first Easter morning, he continued, Jesus comforted the grieving Mary Magdalene by calling her name and then by giving her something to do: "Go to my brothers and say to them, 'I am ascending to my Father.'" Mary, her tears dried and her heart full of hope, listened to Jesus and obeyed. She went and announced to the fearful disciples, "I have seen the Lord!"

"This is what God continues to do," said Randolph. "The resurrected Christ calls us by name, and God wants us to do something. Easter calls us into knowing the risen Christ and making Christ known." The Easter life, he insisted, consists in finding our true identity in God and in knowing that God has given us a vocation, "something to do." In the resurrection, we are opened to the fundamental truthfulness of Christianity: that God loves us and calls us by name; that God asks us to participate in the unfolding of divine beauty. In Christ, we find both our truest selves and the reasons for our existence. Randolph ended the sermon by leading the congregation in prayer, "Risen Christ, I want to hear you call my name. What do you want me to do?"

That Lent, in the weeks leading up to Easter, two dozen members of Epiphany met on Wednesday night for something called Group Spiritual Direction. The evening started with a contemplative candlelight service—silence, scripture readings, and a story or poem in the place of a traditional sermon. There are mostly women here, but a few men are present. A surprising number of people in the small congregation are young adults. Like every gathering at Epiphany, this is a diverse group, white and black, straight and gay. One homeless man made this his spiritual practice for Lent. After the quiet worship, the congregation disperses into five smaller groups designed to help participants sense the work of God's spirit in their lives.

The Church of the Epiphany is located in Washington, D.C. From political speeches to television punditry, Washington is a talking town. Words are the coinage of the realm. Everybody has something to say; few people listen. And fewer of those words are true. In Washington, words are not about truth, they are about power. Although it may seem cynical to say so, words are about getting other people to submit to the speaker's view of reality. Yet, here, only three blocks from the White House, these tiny groups of Christians are learning to listen, to hear the truthfulness of God, by sitting in a quiet candlelit room. There are no speeches, no panel discussions, and no debates here, only the deeply countercultural act of silence. After ten minutes, the facilitator, Elaine, a gentle woman in a wheelchair, asks, "Would someone like to present? What is going on in your life?"

When ready, someone shares. Someone always shares. There are stories of love, work, doubts, fears, health, and relationships. The speaker, who is never interrupted by the group, tries to focus the presentation on God's presence in the midst of these concerns. After she finishes, the group remains silent for a few more minutes. Their job is not to fix the problem or offer advice to the presenter. When they begin to speak, they reflect the story back to the presenter through images and questions that occurred to them during the silence. The presenter is not defensive or protective. Rather, she holds the response—almost as a gift—allowing the insights of others to more deeply craft her original story. As the response lessens, the group slips into silence once again. This rhythm—silence, sharing, silence, response, and silence—carries the congregation through these Lenten evenings to that glorious Easter morning, where the congregation imagined itself as Mary Magdalene: "Risen Christ, I want to hear you call my name. What do you want me to do?"

Christians believe that human beings have the capacity to hear, see, touch, and feel God—a genuine sensing of truth and beauty through which we know God and know God's will. Christians call this discernment. Some Christians depict this capacity as a supernatural gift, a miraculous directive, or an extraordinary mystical experience. Others view finding God's will as a mechanical process; if you follow "four spiritual laws" or go through "forty days of purpose," you will know your life direction. But Christian tradition points toward something more mundane: discernment as a practice that can be developed through participation in reflection, questions, prayer, and community.

Discernment is a gift to the whole of the Christian community, one that can be strengthened and nurtured by engaging the practice. Discernment serves as a kind of spiritual compass, helping us negotiate the unfamiliar territory of our truest selves as we seek to find meaning in God's call. Indeed, discernment often takes the form of questions: Who am I? What does God want me to do with my life? How can I be true to both myself and God? It is easy to understand discernment as an individual process, but in the study congregations, discernment was also a corporate practice. The churches learned to ask questions of God, then listen carefully for God's inner wisdom for the community. Who are we? What does God want us to do? How can we be faithful to God's call? Next to hospitality, discernment was one of the most widely spread spiritual practices among the research churches. Given the larger cultural context, this makes a good deal of sense. Since we live in a "country with no maps," discernment must guide contemporary pilgrims. Vital Christianity necessarily involves the practice of discernment.

Robert, a member of Epiphany, relates that "I'd long been interested in mindfulness." Having grown up in East Coast liberal Presbyterianism, he traces this back to his early fascination with the New England Transcendentalists, especially Emerson and Thoreau. "It was only after I came back to church at forty," he admits, "that I began to try to ground that mind in God and to try to determine—through study, reflection, and conversation with others—how to base my decisions on what God would have me do rather than on my own preferences."

Robert started attending an Episcopal church in California where he was a member of a "base community," a reflection-oriented Bible study. Each week, ten people gathered to ask questions of the scripture text for the upcoming Sunday sermon. Where has God been in our lives this week? What is this reading saying to us in our lives? What would it have us do? Through this small group, Robert learned that discernment is not "a vague, ineffable process" but is "actually the most practical of practices, for it helps us determine what it is we should do." He is quick to add, however, that discernment is not some sort of secular "weighing the pluses and minuses, or evaluation of desired outcomes." Rather, discernment is "serious reflection on scripture, grounded in prayer and informed by experience. It is both deeply personal and entirely communal."

Over the last decade, Robert's practice of discernment has deepened. For a couple of years, he took a break from full-time office employment, opting instead for freelance work. In 1999 he was part of a small group that read Parker Palmer's *Let Your Life Speak*. Palmer's reflection on vocation, along with his description of a Quaker "clearness committee," led Robert to return to full-time work as a manager of a nonprofit organization, which involved moving his family to Washington, D.C. There he joined Epiphany and, with Elaine Edwards, helped design a congregational process of discernment—of which the Lenten evening series was a part. "Discernment," he says, "is the way that Christians talk about deciding on a course of action that they believe is grounded in God's will and that will help realize the reign of God. It is closely related to theological reflection but goes beyond reflection to decision making."

Episcopal priest Richard Valantasis argues that discernment is the "most critical issue in postmodern religious formation." He asks, "How does a person know that what one does, or thinks, or feels is right, or holy, or of God?" All the old standards for guidance have ceased to function. In a pluralist society, no one group—and no one kind of Christianity—holds enough authority to legitimize its own forms of truth (although some are making the attempt!). "So," Valantasis continues, "how do seekers discern what is best or right to do? How does one distinguish what is godly and good from what is ungodly and detrimental?"[44] Some mainline Christians have given in to the dangers posed by these questions. The danger is often termed *relativism*, a kind of do-what-you-will, everything-is-equally-true philosophy—a charge often hurled at more liberal Protestants by their fundamentalist rivals. The questions are hard ones: if the old village and all the old answers have vanished, then how do seekers determine goodness, truthfulness, and beauty?

From my observation of American religion, many Protestants tend toward the easy path when it comes to questions of goodness, truth, and beauty. One extreme seeks clarity and a return to Absolute Truth (capital *A*, capital *T*) as found in the Bible and 1950s America. In Ohio, for example, an influential evangelical minister runs a Christian think tank called the Center for Moral Clarity. On its website, you can click on issues like "abortion" and "homosexuality" and read God's opinion on the subject. The other extreme was recently demonstrated in the case of an Episcopal priest in Pennsylvania who started druid services in his congregation with the hope of reaching some local neo-pagans. Without thinking, he simply adapted to the pluralistic culture surrounding the congregation. (And, after some public embarrassment, his bishop defrocked him.) Most mainline Protestants would never go as far as this minister in his relativism, but it remains a fair critique that many are de facto relativists. Such people accept the consequences of moral relativism—they do not want to be disturbed by difficult questions of moral goodness—and privatize their faith and personalize morality.

But there is a third way between the Center for Moral Clarity and Episco-druid worship, between the old way of doing things and postmodern relativism. Frederick Schmidt, another Episcopal priest, argues that discernment is fundamentally a practice of asking "God-questions" instead of "I-questions." According to Schmidt, I-questions are "driven by the need for self-actualization and a sense of entitlement."[45] I-questions are the basis for both the Center for Moral Clarity and the druid worship: What am I going to do to defeat evil? What am I going to do to reach out for God? In both cases, knotty ethical problems are solved by what "I" believe or what "I" think is best.

Although I-questions are a necessary part of life, they do not constitute a Christian practice of discernment. Schmidt suggests that God-questions are the basis of discernment, "the task or process of distinguishing the spirit or presence of God at work in the world from other, competing spirits in an effort to determine where the spirit of God may be moving." God-questions shift our focus from what we do to what God is doing, by helping us understand where we fit in the larger economy of God's hope for the world. As a result, "discernment is theological, ethical, and critical" and is a process "guided by the light that our spiritual traditions provide."[46]

In recent years, Epiphany has been changing from a congregation that asked I-questions to one that asks God-questions. The focus has shifted away from what individuals want of and from the church to what God wants of Epiphany and its people. But God-questions are not God-proclamations. Although discernment was a foundational practice in all the vital congregations in my study, in no case was finding God's will equated with some infallible doctrinal Truth, an answer handed down from on high for all eternity. Rather, in every congregation, discernment involved asking God-questions and listening for the movement of the spirit in the world today. Mainline Christians had found new pathways by paying attention to God in the context of reflective questioning and making faithful connections between the past, present, and future.

At first, this surprised me—because discernment is neither easy nor obvious spiritual work. But perhaps it should not have. Roman Catholic theologian Frank Rogers notes that "new applications of the practice of discernment are emerging all over the world today." Discernment, he claims, "helps us to find better paths toward the future.... In a world of relational rupture, gang violence, cultural intolerance, and rampant self-deception, this practice helps us to discover ways to live that heal and bring life rather than contribute to the pain around us."[47] At Epiphany, an urban congregation in the middle of Washington, D.C., a city that surely matches this description of the world, people are listening for God's way toward a life-filled future.

Discernment does not simply confirm our hunches or intuitions. Instead, it is a perilous practice that involves self-criticism, questions, and risk—and it often redirects our lives. Renee Grayson, still in her twenties and a lay leader at Epiphany, testifies to the guiding power of discernment in her own spiritual life. Initially, she resisted becoming involved at Epiphany: "I wanted to take things slowly, ease into the community." Yet, she felt an inward "tug-of-war" that God was calling her out of her church "comfort zone." One Ash Wednesday, she learned that the church was offering a special evening program. "Nah," she thought, "I'll go another time." She left the building and headed for the Metro. As she rode down the escalator, she felt she had to go back to join the Wednesday evening group. "I rode the escalator back up and returned to the church, getting a book and signing up for the class."

As a result of participating more deeply in the church's ministry, she says,

I have seen, heard, and felt God's presence in the "day to day." And my relationship with God has deepened exponentially in the last six years. I've learned it is a relationship that requires paying attention, taking action, and making difficult decisions. It requires me to get out of my comfort zone and to take risks.... I've learned if I say yes, God will help me with the rest.

Renee's practice of "paying attention" initially turned her around in the Metro station. Eventually, it caused her to leave her position with a nonprofit organization and seek ordination in the Episcopal church. To discover this calling, she had to go through structured discernment processes both in the church and through the bishop's office. "A few years ago," she laughs, "I struggled with whether or not to participate in a six-week Lenten program. Soon, I will be off to seminary. The irony is holy."

"Discernment requires that we pay attention," writes Catholic theologian Wendy Wright; it "is about feeling texture, assessing weight, watching the plumb line, listening for overtones, searching for shards, feeling the quickening, surrendering to love."[48] You have to pay attention when you are not entirely sure where you are going.

Discernment is an odd guide, however, for it not only points the way on the journey but is a sort of destination in itself. Theologian Mark McIntosh, who has studied the history and practice of Christian discernment, suggests that it entails more than listening for the spirit. He identifies five phases of discernment: faith, distinguishing between good and evil, practical wisdom, sensitivity to pursue God's will, and finally, contemplation of wisdom. Together, these five movements of discernment form a "pattern of the discerning life" that takes us beyond technique-driven and self-interested popular spirituality. When discernment moves an individual or community toward contemplative wisdom, transformation—the risky turnaround of our lives—results. McIntosh insists that through the discerning life we meet truth, as "the beauty of holiness," and we enact truth as the way of God in the world. Truth is not some absolute and unchanging philosophical, moral, or political position. Rather, truth is a "living reality" that everything exists in communion with God.[49] Ultimately, this insight is linked back with transformative compassion for the world—that which Christian tradition calls wisdom.

The New Testament refers to such a transformation as *metanoia,* meaning a radical change of mind and heart that redirects our whole being—just like Renee Grayson's ride back up the Metro escalator. Evangelical Protestants have long defined *metanoia* as an act of individual choice in which we are born again. Even as I write, Larry King was interviewing evangelist Billy Graham on CNN. A video of an old crusade played with a younger Graham asking, "Have you been changed? Have you experienced a time of dramatic turnaround? If not, you must choose. You must accept Jesus, follow the narrow way, and be born again."

In emerging Christianity, discernment is the spiritual process through which *metanoia,* being "born again" in God's truth, beauty, and love, occurs. Thus, discernment points the way, guides the way, and becomes the way—the way that begins with God-questions, that winds through wisdom, and ends in the healing of the world. This is what Jesus meant when he said, "I am the Way."

The way of discernment can take many forms—among them, reflecting on scripture in base communities, instituting Quaker-style clearness committees, participating in congregationwide call and vocation processes, committing to individual and group spiritual direction, and following a monastic prayer practice modeled on those of the early desert fathers and mothers, Benedict, or Ignatius of Loyola. Indeed, discernment is an ancient Christian practice, one that stretches back to the New Testament itself: "Beloved, do not believe every spirit, but test the spirits to see whether they are from God" (1 John 4:1). For centuries, discernment has been understood as the way of spiritual maturity. The early Christian monk Antony the Great of Egypt identified the practice as that which separated pseudoreligion from faith: "Some have afflicted their bodies by asceticism, but they lack discernment, and so they are far from God."[50]

Much of what I witnessed on the road involved congregations engaging ancient practice in contemporary settings. But their discernment processes were hardly arcane or elitist. Rather, they tended toward simplicity—telling stories, asking straightforward questions, listening to answers. Indeed, in many cases the power of discernment lay in its simplicity and its accessibility to the whole community.

In Cincinnati, Ohio, the practice of discernment transformed the Episcopal congregation at Church of the Redeemer. COR, as parishioners fondly call it, was founded in 1908 in the upscale Hyde Park neighborhood. Although COR struggled during the Depression, by the end of World War II, it was flourishing. In 1957 the congregation built its present sanctuary to accommodate the crowds of young families. The following year, NBC broadcast the Palm Sunday service from Redeemer. Former minister Jim Hanisian describes the congregants then as "captains of industry" and recalls that "They worried about how to be good board members, because most of the people sat on a number of civic boards. If you talked about outreach in those years, you'd be talking about on which boards people served." Redeemer was rich, socially powerful, politically moderate, the old-fashioned "Republican party at prayer," and the very model of postwar Protestantism.

And, in the 1960s and 1970s, it collapsed. When Hanisian arrived in 1979, the church budget totaled $87,000 and eighty-nine people attended worship. "Then we went down some more the next week," jokes Hanisian, "because they'd seen me!"

That began ten hard years of turning around the congregation. Hanisian remembers his early priorities: "The vision was competent ministry ... raise the money, the resources, get new people. Developing programming that made sense to the needs of the people. Minister pastorally to the parties that needed reconciling."

In the mid-1980s, however, Hanisian embraced a personal practice of centering prayer. "I was the president of my Episcopal youth group.

I went to an Episcopal college. I went through Episcopal seminary. I'd been a priest for twelve years, and no one ever told me about this prayer." He introduced the practice to COR, and by 1986 hundreds of people had participated in a congregational course on centering prayer. Hanisian realized that he had "a praying church, something they'd never been before." The prayer foundation opened the way for deeper Christian formation, for new ministries to develop, and for the restructuring of the leadership boards.

To Hanisian and the new leadership team, however, something still seemed to be missing, despite the success. People still seemed to think that church was something you did, that ministry was a kind of spiritual work. Lynne Thornton, a member of the vestry (the governing board of a local Episcopal church), recalls, "From 1991 to 1995, a different spirit flew in. The Spirit. It literally blew in.... It was very much about discerning if God was present. And discerning where God was calling you. It was about call. Those were the words we used deliberately: call, discernment, ministry."

Using his doctor of ministry research as an opportunity, Hanisian created a congregationwide process of discernment based on the question "Where is God in your ministry?" Each member of the vestry interviewed ministry chairpersons, asking them that God-question and gathering the responses from the church leadership. A few people wondered if Hanisian had "lost it," but they went along to "humor the rector." Others felt uncomfortable with the whole idea. Marsha, a vestry member at the time, recalls, "You know, in the beginning it was difficult, to start to do this God-talk. We hadn't been used to doing that. To go with somebody, sit down one-on-one, pray with them, and to talk with, you know, God-talk." Still, she and the others did it.

Susanna, the chairperson of the pastoral board, remembers getting the call for the vestry interview. She admits that she tried to avoid the exercise: "I was totally intimidated!" Eventually, though, she scheduled the appointment.

We began with prayer, which was calming, and we started to talk, trying to answer the question "Where do you see God in your ministry?" It was eye-opening. I hadn't really stopped to think about it that way, and it allowed me to say, "I do see God in this," or "Maybe I don't, and maybe I should look around at something else," or whatever. But it was a new awareness [of God] that evolved into a relationship.

Tom, another member of the vestry, recalls conducting those interviews and the responses of his fellow parishioners. "The reactions in those early days were interesting. I did three [interviews] the first time." He describes the process as a "window opening" in his understanding of the congregation's spiritual life. He remembers a contrast between two interviews: "[One man] shared all of his perspectives on faith he gained from ministry. Another looked at me like I had two heads, 'This isn't about God. This is just something I do.'" Oddly enough, when the research for the minister's dissertation was completed, the congregation did not want to stop asking the question. But the question changed as the process affected the whole church. As Tom said, "All of a sudden, it became 'Do you see God in everything you do?'"

Tom's story illustrates what happens when discernment becomes internalized: "It is in our minds, in my mind, myself. I'm more open to encountering God. I'm more aware when it happens. If you aren't looking for it, you will never see it. Well, I'm looking for it because it has become part of what we do. I might not have noticed God's presence before, but I'm more attuned to it now."

Listening, paying attention to the Spirit, new awareness. When pursued in community, discernment became a shaping practice that, quite literally, transformed Church of the Redeemer. As Richard Valantasis remarks about the importance of discernment, "The old ways, good as they were, may not apply to new situations, while new circumstances demand a creative engagement with God to point an individual, a community, or even the world in the right direction."[51] After a midcentury slump, Church of the Redeemer began moving into God's dynamic future—something they have continued to do for the last twenty years with ever-greater maturity—because Redeemer's people have learned to listen to the Spirit.

Back at Epiphany in Washington, D.C., the idea for Group Spiritual Direction arose from a smaller group in the congregation. In the summer of 2004 Randolph Charles, the rector, asked a few parishioners if they would be interested in forming a group for the eventual purpose of introducing the larger congregation to the practice of discernment. No clergy would be involved; this would be a lay-led process. For several months they met, practicing the practice that they hoped to share with the church. Introducing discernment would be a change for the congregation. Epiphany is a very hands-on church, with a congregation that delights in good works, not unlike the busy Church of the Redeemer in the days right before the "Where is God in your ministry?" question. Discernment would ask them to step back, to listen before acting, lift awareness, and learn to sense God's presence in all that they did.

Elaine Edwards, whose life was transformed when she was diagnosed with multiple sclerosis, is a trained spiritual director and was part of the group. She was excited by the prospect of helping Epiphany grow deeper. "People are searching for meaning," she says; "they want to connect with spirit. I'm not sure mainline churches can satisfy that need. But we're trying to create space for that at Epiphany." She continues, "We are opening the congregation to a greater experience of the Holy Spirit. We are asking more of people than just coming to church on Sunday. I think Epiphany is ready for that."

Elaine is right. The hunger is palatable. And, as theologian Mark McIntosh points out, Easter may be just the right time to begin:

From their first encounter with the crucified and risen Jesus, believers have been drawn into a worshipping community where truth has given itself to be known in the creation of a new life together. Spiritual discernment has arisen naturally and most necessarily for such a common life, because it

reflects the pressure of a living truth—refusing partiality and bias, push-
ing beyond individual understanding, opening the discerning community
to the creative, self-sharing life from which all truth springs. Discerning
truth could never be a lonely form of life. The truth humanity hungers
for seems far too large a feast for solitary diners. It requires a sharing far
too joyful for any but the truly wise. For they alone discern the depth of
thanks most justly due so great a giver. Knowing the giver in each gift,
they are themselves set free from small desires and awake to God's desire
in every thing; they discern its truth in praise.[52]

As Randolph Charles recently told me, "It is just time. It is time to pay
attention to the promptings of the Spirit and move on with them to God's
future." Discernment welcomes pilgrims to the feast.

SEVEN

Healing

ENTERING *SHALOM*

On a hill at the edge of the Pennsylvania town of Zelienople, Calvin Presbyterian Church stands overlooking the neighboring valley. In 1805, in that valley, a group of German settlers led by George Rapp founded a spiritual community called Harmony. Unlike some of the more exotic religious experiments of the early Republic, the Harmonists were a quiet group, patiently awaiting the arrival of their Lord through simplicity, prayer, industry, healthful living, and community. There, on the edge of the American wilderness, these earnest utopians constructed a way of life designed to nurture divine harmony between God and humanity that would welcome Jesus—and his long-awaited kingdom—into their midst. The Harmonists longed for the wholeness of the universe to be restored, for the vision of unity between God and humanity, of health, happiness, and peace, to be made real. To make their point, they constructed one of the earliest gardens in the country—modeled after their imagined Garden of Eden. For these colonists, harmony meant reordering their communities according to God's original intention.

Harmony is a lovely, old-fashioned, sort of word. And, in a culture racked by division and invective, it is seldom heard in our public discourse. Although we typically think of harmony in relation to architecture or music, it is a word with deep political implications: agreement, accord, or concord. Harmony is the overcoming of division, hatred, and discord; the mending of what is displaced or broken. In short, harmony is a kind of healing or making whole, the creation of what is disordered into what is ordered. To find harmony is to find balance, to touch the center point of wholeness.

The Pennsylvania Harmonists died out by the late nineteenth century (no doubt due to their practice of celibacy!). But, in some ways, the spirit of their dream—for Christian harmony—has migrated up the hill to Calvin Church. At first it might seem odd to link the Presbyterians on the hill with the old hope of the German settlers of Harmony. But harmony is not just the utopian dream of some isolated religious group. On one Sunday morning worshiping at Calvin, I heard echoes of that ancient American dream in a hymn written by the current pastor and the music director, "I'm Gonna Change All That."

> *The Lord's gonna come, but my heart isn't ready.*
> *Oh, the Lord's gonna come, but my soul isn't right.*
> *Not enough faith, not enough love, not enough Thee.*
> *But I'm gonna change all that, I'll be transformed by love.*
> *I'm gonna change all that, make room for the dove.*
> *For my soul's gonna be a place for God to live and laugh, to*
>   *heal and love.*

Unknown to these contemporary Presbyterians, they had stumbled back to the founding hope of their valley, embodying harmony in community as a way to prepare for God's coming. In the biblical tradition, harmony manifests salvation, from the root word *salvus,* meaning "to heal." Throughout the scriptures, harmony is way of life practiced by a community with healing at its center. And Calvin Church takes healing seriously.

Calvin's pastor, Graham Standish, preaches harmony—"Christ's vision was one of spiritual, mental, physical, and relational balance, integration, and wholeness."[53] Although he rejects some sort of perfectionism or utopian idea of harmony, he nevertheless believes that this sort of integration leads to healthier living and healing. As a trained therapist and spiritual director, Pastor Standish argues that "imbalance" is one of the central problems of our time. "The Christian faith," he says, "calls on us to live a radically different kind of life: a life of balance with Christ as the balancing fulcrum. It calls on us to question and reject the Western kind of life that is rooted in stimulation and activity, and instead to live a life that is rooted in God."[54]

Calvin Church has come to believe that healing is the work of God, based in the power of Christ and the Holy Spirit, and that we open ourselves to it through prayer. Early in his ministry at the congregation, Graham felt compelled to "recover the ministry of healing that was part of the ancient church" and to restore the practice of healing prayer. Although the church moved into the practice slowly, today it is central to their life together. Prayer ministers visit and anoint the sick with oil; prayer groups meet weekly for intercessory prayer; healing prayer is offered after every Sunday service. A small anteroom off the sanctuary serves as a prayer chapel where candles can be lit for the sick. Outside, a rough-hewn labyrinth creates sacred space for those seeking balance through walking meditation. Many of the prayer ministers knit prayer shawls, praying for those who will receive the shawls as a tangible sign of God's embrace.

Although Graham originally sensed that God was calling the congregation into healing prayer, leadership has passed to a layperson, Diane McClusky, who now serves as the congregation's prayer minister. Diane is also a third-level Reiki master and massage therapist. Following the call for balance, she sees healing as coming not only through spoken prayer but also through integrating body work: knitting, massage, reflexology, Reiki, and walking the labyrinth. In its space, worship, and practices, Calvin models the vision of the church as a hospital for sinners, a kind of congregational hospice that welcomes all to God's healing grace.

People at Calvin are quick to point out, however, that healing is not just personal or inward. As one member, Scott, says, "Incorporating spirituality of prayer and trying to find God in [all] places has given life to the whole mission of loving each other. Through that love, you spread the gospel." Another pointed out that healing prayer "is an attempt to reach needs away from the church, not necessarily here in the building." They understand the link between healing and salvation: God's healing is offered for the sake of the world. The people of Calvin Church do not focus on the idea of "personal salvation" in the way their evangelical neighbors do. Instead, for them God's salvation is a process of healing whereby they are transformed—and, in turn, they open themselves to transforming the world.

Quaker writer Parker Palmer suggests that "The gift we receive on the inner journey is the insight that the universe is working together for good." He continues, "The structure of reality is not the structure of a battle.... Harmony is more fundamental than warfare in the nature of reality," or what he would later call a "hidden wholeness."[55] The writer Phyllis Tickle believes that a new kind of Christianity is emerging, one that will be marked by its emphasis on "right harmony." If Calvin Church is any indication, she may well be right. In a tiny patch of sacred geography in western Pennsylvania, some Christians have been living harmony for a long time.

Not long ago, a reporter called and asked me about the practices of vital mainline churches. "What do they do that is different? What's new?"

"Well," I began to answer, "they practice things like hospitality and healing ..."

He interrupted. "Healing? All churches do healing! There's nothing new about that."

"Healing *is* ancient," I replied. "What is new is that these mainline churches are practicing it. When I was a girl, growing up in the Methodist church, nobody talked about healing." He protested again. I changed the subject back to hospitality.

But his comments got me thinking. Why the renewed interest in healing—especially from a faith tradition that had largely lost the practice?

In my childhood Methodist church, healing was not often discussed. We learned about Jesus healing people in the Bible, in that remote world that seemed to exist only on the yellowed Bible-land maps in our Sunday school classrooms. Healing was an ancient miracle or—as we became more theologically sophisticated—an ancient metaphor, largely inaccessible to modern people. Healing, it appeared to me, was part of premodern history. In an enlightened society like ours, healing had become the business of doctors and hospitals; we awaited miracles of new medicines and cures. Except for faith in science, faith had nothing to do with it. This was the work of researchers and surgeons. Although occasionally we would celebrate Jesus as "the Great Physician" or hear in a sermon that Saint Luke was a doctor, healing—with the exception of giving money to medical missions—was certainly not the work of the church!

Even in our Methodist world, however, we heard rumors that some Christians still believed in healing. They were mostly Pentecostal faith healers and revivalists who held tent meetings and met in storefront churches. My parents—and my pastors—referred to them as Holy Rollers and looked down on them and others who did not share our scientific sensibilities. They recognized that good people sought supernatural healing, but they equally thought them victims of religious crooks and spiritual snake-oil salesmen. Indeed, by the twentieth century, mainline Protestants had, in effect, accepted the modern dualism of science and faith and overreacted to the excesses of supernaturalism. Although Christian in name, they functioned as secularists in regard to healing. As a result, they downplayed Jesus' healing ministry and relegated healing practices to the world of science.

Eventually, the antisupernaturalism of mainline Protestantism left many people cold and sent them searching for a more transcendent God. Healing has become a key theme in contemporary spirituality, growing more dominant as the population ages. Scholarly research projects explore the links between faith and wellness, entire magazines focus on spirituality and health. Pentecostals are no longer alone in their belief in supernatural healing; many people pray for health, hoping that God will reach into the soul and touch their deepest needs. There exists a strong cultural current of desire to feel and experience God's power personally and to participate in God's purposes for humanity—people want to be part of healing the universe.

Salvation, being changed or transformed by God's grace, is a key concept in Protestant Christianity. For some Christians, salvation primarily means being rescued—getting "saved" from one's own wretched and sinful life and, after death, from the torments of hellfire and damnation. For a long time, for mainline Protestants, salvation seemed to mean being a good person, a good citizen, helping others and "being nice." In recent years, however, in some quarters of the old mainline, salvation has become much more spiritually robust. There, healing has become a defining metaphor for salvation. For mainline pilgrims, salvation entails several levels of healing: emotions and the psyche, physical wellness, human reconciliation, and cosmic restoration. The language I heard about healing revealed that many mainline Protestants have rejected the antisupernaturalism of their forebears. Instead, they are tracing their way back to a supernatural God.

Calvin Presbyterian embodies this change. One member attributed the "malaise of the church to lack of focus on spirituality beginning with the fights between conservative and liberal Protestants in the 1960s. The liberals focused on social justice—a very good thing—but they did it without spirituality, which they left to the evangelicals.... Calvin is a mainline church trying to recover this aspect of faith." At Calvin, however, recovering spirituality is no mere imitation of evangelical religion. Instead, it is a profoundly biblical retelling of salvation as experienced in God's healing power.

At a conference on spiritual practices, Diane McClusky is teaching a workshop on "Christian Reiki," the practice she has developed at Calvin Church. She is an elegant, middle-aged woman with blond hair, wise eyes, and a beautiful deep blue shawl draped over her shoulders. She stands in front of a class of eighteen women, some ministers, a few Sunday school teachers, and a couple of nurses. With the exception of one Roman Catholic, all are mainline Protestants. No one except Diane is from Calvin. Reiki is a healing art, she explains, a light touch "energy massage" that originated with a Buddhist teacher in Japan. Today, Reiki is gaining a following in the United States. "Many Christians think it is weird," says Diane, "like black magic or witchcraft, spooky, you know." But she insists otherwise. "It has brought me closer to God, to Jesus, and to the Holy Spirit. After all, as Christians we try to follow the example of Christ. Christ touched people and healed them. Christ sent his followers out to teach and heal." She looks around the room at her students, some of whom appear just a little skeptical. "At this time in the world, when so many people are lost and hurting, we need every skill we can get to help us to heal one another."

Diane wants people to experience God's salvation. "Reiki means 'Spirit breathing' or 'Spirit breath,'" she tells us. I immediately think of the first chapter of Genesis, where the Spirit hovers over the waters as creation begins. "I take this to mean that the Holy Spirit uses our bodies to breathe healing into those who need it." She laughs. "Some people have called me a Pentecostal! I don't really know what they mean by that. But I love Jesus and believe that the Holy Spirit heals. He uses us as the conduit, a channel for God's healing."

She quotes a few verses from the New Testament and then reads a passage written by the medieval Catholic mystic Teresa of Avila:

> *Christ has no body now on earth but yours,*
> *no hands but yours, no feet but yours.*
> *Yours are the eyes through which to look out*
> *Christ's compassion to the world;*
> *Yours are the feet with which He is to go about doing good;*
> *yours are the hands with which He is to bless men now.*

Satisfied that the group grasps the theological dimensions of her Christian Reiki practice, she demonstrates the actual technique. One woman is ready to become a first-level Reiki healer; with her permission Diane takes her through a Reiki treatment that serves as the initiation.

For many minutes, the room is bathed in soft light, with gentle music playing. Diane walks around the woman, holding her hands just above the woman's body, surrounding her with spiritual energy, occasionally touching her gently. While she works, the room seems surprisingly alive as the women watch intently. Several look more relaxed, as if their own bodies are releasing pain. A couple of women quietly cry. Even the skeptics seem to sense God's presence. After the session, one woman reports that, while watching, she experienced a complete healing from pain. The women share their insights, chatting excitedly with one another, hugging, praying, and weeping just a little. A few, who clearly had not connected before the conference, now treat one another as warm friends. Through Diane's afternoon workshop, the women have formed a new community. She concludes, "I just know that Jesus is with me; he is my Friend and my Guide." She then tells the women to "open themselves" to see Jesus in all things, and let Jesus direct all that they do.

At Calvin, healing is an expression of God's harmony—what the Hebrew scriptures refer to as *shalom*, God's "dynamic wholeness."[56] Writing about *shalom*, Protestant minister Bruce Epperly and Jewish rabbi Lewis Solomon claim that it entails both personal and communal healing: "Though it was seldom fully realized, the Divine order of the universe was reflected in the ordering of the dinner table, ethics toward citizens and strangers, and justice toward the poor."[57] Biblical scholar Walter Brueggemann, who is widely influential among mainline Protestants, describes *shalom* as "the central vision" of the Bible in which "all of creation is one, every creature in community with every other, living in harmony and security toward the joy and well-being of every other creature."[58] In short, *shalom* is closely related to salvation, the healing of the disordered and broken into the harmony of its created wholeness. As another writer says, "the kernel of *shalom* is communal harmony."[59]

At Calvin, *shalom* emerges out of a deep sense of oneness with God. As the church has learned to pray, and has entered into the practice of healing, they have experienced the palpable presence of God in their midst. Diane's warm confession of Jesus as Friend and Guide is common language at Calvin. Many others at the church spoke in equally personal terms about God, Jesus, and the Spirit. They expect God to speak to them; they expect God to answer prayers; they expect God to guide them; they expect God to be in their midst.

To heal, to pray for healing, to work for healing, is to enact God's dream of *shalom*, to participate in God's longing to restore created harmony to the universe. Indeed, one of the Christian titles for Jesus, "Savior," comes from the Greek *soter*, which means both savior and healer. Contrary to what I learned in childhood, Jesus did not just heal a few people in a few odd stories about miracles. Rather Jesus embodied healing, healing for all creation, healing that would bring forth God's *shalom*.

Longing for healing is not flaky, idiosyncratic, or New Age—it is an inchoate human desire to experience *shalom*, God's dream of created wholeness. On my research journey, I learned that many churches seem to be responding to this longing. Calvin's new emphasis on healing was not unusual. In all the congregations visited, I heard similar longings from churchgoers for healing, for harmony, for sensing the touch of God to overcome division, dissolve boundaries, and bring *shalom*.

Many of the churches practiced healing. At both Cornerstone United Methodist in Florida and Church of the Epiphany in Washington, D.C., hospitality is linked to healing. The opening of a congregation's heart to welcoming the stranger led to healing within one's own heart—and a passion for healing between people. At Cornerstone, they even refer to the church as "a spiritual clinic" where "God does the work and we just have to pay attention and be on our toes!" At Epiphany, a church that served as an actual hospital during the Civil War, "it was literally a place of physical healing," their minister points out. Today, they practice regular healing prayer following the weekly Eucharist.

In Memphis, Tennessee, Church of the Holy Communion (Episcopal) offers a wide array of "health and wellness" practices to parishioners
to help them cope with stress and achieve balance in their lives. They
have learned to see ministry as something for "the whole person, not
necessarily for the small time of worship." In Santa Barbara, California,
the people of Goleta Presbyterian Church set aside time in the worship
service for healing prayer offered at prayer benches in the back of the
sanctuary. As Steve Jacobson, their minister, commented, "I embrace a
lot of secular psychology in terms of explaining things, but I really feel
the spirit of God shows up on the subliminal edges of consciousness, and
we can have experiences of healing. Things from the unconscious get
carefully drawn up, spill over, and weave things."

At Saint Mark Lutheran, where a surprising number of people are
nurses and teachers, congregants participate in healing by tending to
one another's needs through acts of kindness and pastoral care. In their
anonymous suburb, the radical practice of friendship heals isolation
and loneliness. At Redeemer United Church of Christ in New Haven,
Connecticut, the congregation has experienced healing in overcoming
divisions of race, class, and poverty. The harder I listened to these congregations, the more I understood that healing, the quest to join in the
harmony of God's universal song, is central to the Christian life. No
more jangles of discord, healing is the music of *shalom*.

Unlike the stereotype of healing from my childhood Methodism, the
Christian practice of healing is neither spooky nor kooky. It involves
growing into a deep awareness of oneness with God, finding healing
within and moving beyond the self to help heal the world. Occasionally,
healing leads us to the unexpected territory of miraculous physical cures
and dramatic conversions. Like Lynne, a member of an Episcopal congregation who survived a near-death experience and was cured of stage-
four melanoma—events that completely redirected her life. Or, like
Marsha, an aged African-American matron at Epiphany, who proudly
testified that Jesus healed her of a life-threatening heart condition. Al-

though some mainline Protestants may be skeptical of physical healing, I heard quite a few stories from smart, well-educated—and clearly not Pentecostal—churchgoers about supernatural healings.

More typical, however, were stories from people who claimed healing as a process of transformation that occurred rather gently, slowly over time. We practice healing, and as we practice it, we learn the quiet dimensions of *shalom*, the unheralded dimensions of salvation, of compassion and charity. Graham Standish says, "Salvation is a healing process in which Christ's healing love heals our souls from the damage and power of sin so that we may be transformed by God to become the stewards of healing ourselves."

Often, healing is not physical but, as Graham said, the healing of "our souls from the damage and power of sin." The people of Epiphany learned the truth of these insights when one of their beloved lay leaders, Jack Harrison, did not experience a miraculous cure for pancreatic cancer. Although struggling with his illness, Jack was scheduled to preach one Sunday. Weakened by the cancer, however, he could no longer make it to church. But he insisted that he could still preach. He wrote out his sermon and it was read for him. From his deathbed pulpit, he preached of Jesus' disciples and healing as told in the Gospels:

> *We learn that people received healing through the laying on of hands and anointing with oil—the first-century forms of the healing arts that we reenact here each Sunday morning—but which take on different forms when we engage in healing, and sometimes even curing, today's real world.... I do think it makes sense to keep in mind why we're doing all "for-the-church" activity. We are always, always working for God's world. What this church gives to us individually through the healing we receive, our own sense of belonging, and a clarity about God's kingdom is the equipment we need to be Christ ... to meet the needs of a world that is calling for relief and seeking the sure and certain knowledge that it has been saved.*

The entire congregation sobbed. But people heard the message of salvation as never before. One person told me that it was the most meaningful "come to Jesus sermon" he had ever heard. "That's right," he echoed, "we need to be Christ." A few weeks later Jack died.

According to this vision of Christian faith, salvation is a process whereby we enter into God's saving work—not a single moment of miraculous transformation through which we are rescued from sin. Rather, salvation is, as Jack Harrison proclaimed to tearful friends from his own dark valley, a lifetime of practice, receiving God's healing grace and power, being changed by it, and offering healing back to the world. The healed heal. The practice of healing traces grace in our hearts and opens us to see the evidence of *shalom* in all creation. Jack Harrison lived this. And, as he died, he reminded a mourning congregation that healing points the way to God's reign.

"Bring your brokenness," said one Florida Methodist. "We're all broken and in need of God's healing. We'll heal right along with you." The church can be, indeed, a spiritual clinic, a hospital for the broken, where sinners find *shalom*.

EIGHT

Contemplation

OPEN FOR PRAYER

Memphis, Tennessee, conjures visions of southern religion. These two words, *southern religion,* evoke images of folks hootin' and hollerin' about God. Eternal damnation and hell. Sweating preachers thundering on about sex, drinking, and Democrats. Southern religion is all heat and fire, the blinding light of Jesus converting sinners to saints in a flash. This is what more reasonable Christians used to ridicule as "enthusiasm."

In Memphis, the Church of the Holy Communion, an Episcopal parish, stands in stark contrast to the fulminations of southern evangelical religion. Situated on a prominent street corner in a prosperous part of town, its white columns and graceful spire point seekers toward heaven, not hell. The genteel brick exterior and clear glass windows bespeak a different southern tradition, one of measured and rational faith.

Appearances, however, can be deceptive. Holy Communion, too, is about heat and fire, about the Spirit's blinding light. Every Sunday

evening a congregation of more than a hundred gathers for contemplative worship. Electric lights are dimmed so that the primary light in the
building emanates from hundreds of candles—on the high altar and
chancel rail, around the lectern and pulpit. A large Celtic cross graces
the altar, icons flank the table, two large racks of unlit votive candles sit
in front of those icons. A small group of musicians is playing an Irish
tune, "Si Bheag Si Mhor," on hammered dulcimer, harp, guitar, and
wooden flute.

A bell rings. The priest enters and draws the congregation to prayer,
using words written by the Iona community in Scotland: "Breath of
God, breath of life, breath of deepest yearning." They respond, "Come
Holy Spirit." The invocation continues:

> *"Comforter, Disturber, Interpreter, Enthuser,"*
> *"Come Holy Spirit."*
> *"Heavenly Friend, Lamplighter, Revealer of truth, Midwife*
>   *of change,"*
> *"Come Holy Spirit."*
> *"The Lord is here."*
> *"God's spirit is with us."*

The congregation sings a beautiful Irish hymn, "How lovely is thy
dwelling place, O Lord of hosts to me!" A reading follows from the
Gospel of Matthew. After the reading, we sit in silence. The priest then
offers a meditation on the gospel. When he finishes, we sit in silence
again—this time for two minutes. Prayers follow. As the musicians play,
people get up, walk to the altar, and light candles in the votive stand as
a symbol of their prayers. Nearly everyone goes forward. And the soft
candlelight glows brighter with each prayer. "See that ye be at peace
among yourselves," offers the minister in a grace, "and love one another. Follow the example of good men and women of old and God will
comfort you and help you, both in this world and in the world which is
to come."

The music carries us to communion, and the leader's words invite us to come forward and partake of the Lord's Supper:

> *This is the table, not of the Church, but of the Lord.*
> *It is made ready for those who love him*
> *And for those who want to love him more.*
>
> *So, come, you who have much faith and you who have little,*
> *You who have been here often and you who have not been here*
> *   long,*
> *You who have tried to follow and you who have failed.*
>
> *Come, because it is the Lord who invites you.*
> *It is his will that those who want him should meet him here.*

It is an altar call, but not like those in other southern churches. Here, the invitation is to dine with God—not to submit to God's gaze of condemning judgment. At this altar, salvation comes through love, not fear. No "Just as I Am" accompanies this call. Rather, a traditional Scottish ballad plays as the congregation goes down the aisle to meet God. As I walked, a picture of Holy Communion's spire came to my mind as I inwardly heard the words of Saint Bernard of Clairvaux, "Continual silence, and removal from the noise of the things of this world and forgetfulness of them, lifts the heart and asks us to think of the things of heaven and sets our heart upon them."[60]

And, as in all good southern religion, there is heat and fire, the blinding light of Jesus pointing us heavenward. The heat and fire of contemplation. Of candles flickering with prayer. The blinding light that shines through silence. The spirit comes in stillness, not the whirlwind. The traces of grace whose footprints southerners intuit always. There we are: walking the sawdust trail, just like our ancestors, only here the way is marked by icons. This is the most ancient "old-time religion" I have ever experienced in a southern church.

The service ends with a hymn to the tune of "Ar Hyd Y Nos":

Go, my children, with my blessing, never alone.
Waking, sleeping, I am with you, you are my own.
In my love's baptismal river I have made you mine forever.
Go, my children, with my blessing, you are my own.

Although I only notice as we sing, I am weeping. I glance around. I am not the only one. Like they do at Pentecostal holiness churches, Holy Communion should probably provide Kleenex at the altar.

In January 2001, I was teaching a course at Wesley Seminary in Washington, D.C. One student asked me what I thought the twenty-first century would be like. Without a moment's hesitation, I replied, "Noisy. It will be noisy." Intense population growth, increased urbanization, the spread of technology. Just think of cell phones on airplanes, I opined. Yes, this new century will be noisy.

Therefore, I was surprised by how much silence I encountered as I traveled through the emerging mainline. When I was a girl in the mainline, I rarely experienced silence—and seldom witnessed acts of prayer. The old mainline, the one in which I grew up, succumbed to writer Richard Rohr's dictum, "When the church is no longer teaching the people how to pray, we could almost say it will have lost its reason for existence."[61] Yet, throughout these congregations I visited, silence, meditation, and contemplation were commonplace, and many new members testified to the spiritual attraction of prayer. Martha, a member of Holy Communion, has come to recognize the "importance of silence." She says, "Not many churches give you real silence, if you think about it. I've come to value it.... Encountering God certainly [happens] in silence." However, the contemplative emptiness of ancient Celtic airs and the deep silence of Holy Communion's liturgy was but a single example.

I witnessed Presbyterians, Lutherans, Methodists, and Congregationalists practicing silence at board meetings, prayer meetings, Bible studies, pastoral care sessions, labyrinth walks, yoga classes, and discernment groups. I sat with Presbyterians doing centering prayer and went on retreat with Episcopalians following the teachings of the monk Thomas Keating. A group of Lutherans, who engaged practices drawn from Ignatian spiritual exercises, told me that they had "learned to listen to God, not just to pray for things." In some congregations, I watched small children in their Sunday school classrooms sit—for a few seconds at least—in God's stillness. Next to my desk as I write is a picture from Holy Communion. It shows a little girl—about five years old with hands folded in her lap, blonde hair tied back with a black ribbon—staring contemplatively at a candle. All these mainline Protestants, people known for their earnest activity, are finding God in silence as if they were seasoned monastics or practiced Quakers.

Some church-growth specialists think that successful churches entertain people during worship—the more activity, the more noise, the more loud music, the better. From that perspective, silence is boring and an evangelism turnoff. Quiet churches cannot be fun churches. Contemplation is not a gift for the whole church but something practiced only by supersaints. As a fellow historian reminded me, "The tradition has always reserved the contemplative life, and contemplation itself, for the very few." After all, contemplation leads directly to God's divine presence. Such "unmediated access to the divine energy" can be spiritually dangerous for novices in faith![62] Following this logic, it is best, I suppose, to keep everyday Christians distracted with overhead projectors, rock bands, and podcast sermons.

In our society, noise actually serves to further disconnect us from others and drive us deeper into isolation, claims David Schimke in the *Utne Reader*. "Surround sound," he says, "is the new, virtual picket fence."[63] I wondered if that was happening in churches with so much noise. Were they actually cutting themselves off from God and each other?

Ironically, people think that noise enables them to find meaning, purpose, and connection. P. M. Forni, a professor at Johns Hopkins University, says that noise "is all part of a phenomenon expressed in ancient

Latin as *horrovacui*, which is abhorrence of the void, fear of emptiness, horror of nothingness. I believe that we often overuse electronic gadgets for the same reason that we spend innumerable hours shopping: We do not want to be left alone with our thoughts." Professor Forni continues:

> One of the most disquieting phenomena of our time is the flight from thinking, meditating, and ruminating. When was the last time we followed a thought where it will take us without our eyes or ears being pulled away by a screen or an artificial sound? In order to do this we need to rediscover silence.[64]

The fourteenth-century Christian mystic Meister Eckhart said, "Nothing in all creation is so like God as silence." To rediscover silence, as these churches are doing, is to rediscover God.

In recent years Holy Communion has come to understand itself as "the sacred center" of Memphis, where God's presence is palpable, where people serve in Jesus' name, and where spiritual growth is a communal hope. Holy Communion, the once-traditional parish church, is becoming almost like an open monastic community with contemplation at its center.

Holy Communion has not always been this way. For much of its history, it was about tasteful worship and doing good works. And its piety was deeply personal and privatized. People did not talk about their faith. For a while, however, some parishioners had expressed hunger for the deeper spiritual life—for example, Robbie and John McQuiston, had long practiced the rule of Saint Benedict with a small group of parishioners. But they found it difficult to connect Benedictine spirituality with the life of the larger congregation. Then, in 2000, the church's longtime and highly regarded minister retired. A year later a new minister, the Reverend Gary Jones, a man with a rich contemplative vision, arrived at Holy Communion.

Gary's first day at his new parish, September 11, 2001, would prove a fateful one. Arriving at church that morning, Jones and his new staff hung out a huge banner in front of the church, OPEN FOR PRAYER. The words would prove prophetic. Indeed, Holy Communion was open—spiritually ready—to pray deeply and differently. Martha refers to it as "*kairos* time, God's time," a unique moment that birthed new possibilities. The good people of Holy Communion were about to embark on a journey in prayer. Not only were they "open for prayer," they were open to prayer. And open to change. The monk Thomas Merton describes that way: "Prayer is then not just a formula of words, or a series of desires springing up in the heart—it is the orientation of our whole body, mind and spirit to God in silence, attention, and adoration. All good meditative prayer is a *conversion of our entire self to God*."[65]

Gary Jones knows about meditative prayer. From the time he was a young priest spending time with the brothers of the Society of Saint John the Evangelist, the crucible of silence has shaped his ministry. By the time he came to Holy Communion, he had led two other parishes in the practice of contemplation and the cultivation of the inner life. I have heard him quote Jung, "If you can't stand to be alone in silence with yourself, why do you inflict yourself on us?" From the earliest Christian thinkers onward, tradition has insisted that faith, rightly understood, is a quest to know oneself in God. To run from the self is to run from God. People need silence to find their way back to interior wisdom. They need a recovery of the contemplative arts of "thinking, meditating, ruminating."

These things, Gary believes, are not reserved for a spiritual elite. Rather, they contribute to the balance necessary for a healthy personal life and a vital congregation. The church offers seasons, like Lent, to draw Christians into "intentional reflection, attention to God, and restraint." He claims that "We need it now greater than ever. Our haste leads us to forget the needs of the soul. We will latch onto anything to feed us. We hope that something—our clergy, a new love relationship—will satisfy our restlessness."[66] Human desire for fulfillment cannot be satisfied by the world. True knowledge of the self, of love and meaning, comes only in silence.

Restraint is not a word that most people associate with contemporary Christianity. But Holy Communion has opened up a pathway of contemplation that entails reflection, attention, and restraint. To them, restraint is not a spiritual avoidance tactic. Instead, it is a kind of balance that leads to a deep personal relationship with God. This emphasis seems to grow out of the traditions of Benedictine spirituality, which encourages sensible engagement with principles of mind, body, and spirit. With such balance, contemplation does not veer into spiritual excess or elitism. Rather, contemplation becomes practical wisdom—a way open for all Christians. As one parish publication puts it:

> *Living in the 21st century at times seems to be all about being connected—to the satellite, to the internet, to the network, to the wireless world. With the demands most of us have on our attention, it's common for our lives to become unbalanced—and for the lasting connections in our lives to become weakened.*
>
> *At Church of the Holy Communion, we work to foster the connections that matter—connections with one's self, with one's community, with one's family and with God.*
>
> *Those links are strengthened not just by Bible study or prayer—not just by trying to love your family or your neighbor more—but by balanced attention to caring for one's mind, body and spirit.*

To achieve personal and communal balance, they follow a model of "sanctuary-house-closet" laid out by Presbyterian minister Charles Olsen. Each component is necessary to the balanced life: "sanctuary" or Sunday worship; "house" or small-group fellowship; and "closet" or contemplation. In this model, contemplation is not some arcane practice but is simply "one's private experience of God" through "healthy habits of private devotion."[67] Indeed, the contemplative life is the connected life. To quote Thomas Merton again, "If you want to have a spiritual life you must unify your life."[68]

Holy Communion's engagement with contemplative and mystical

practices is loosely drawn from the Rule of Saint Benedict, and bits and pieces of monastic practice may be seen throughout the congregation. The church offers a variety of small groups teaching classical forms of prayer. Adult education includes workshops such as "Chant, It's Not Just for Monks Anymore." In addition to the Sunday evening contemplative service, there is a daily morning prayer service modeled after the monastic practice of hearing scripture in community. Gary refers to the service as "a corner of monasticism in the parish." Brothers from the Society of Saint John the Evangelist visit the parish; and members of the congregation make retreats with the monks. Parishioners are clearly expected to tend to their spiritual lives by participating in "closet" activities of prayer and Bible study.

Having observed all these things, I asked Gary if he was trying to create a kind of open, parish-based, lay monastery. He laughed gently, replying with characteristic modesty in his soft southern accent, "I guess you could say that the whole monastic thing is going on here."

If contemplation at Holy Communion is a kind of parish-based monasticism, the practice at Calvin Presbyterian appears far more Protestant—resembling that of a Quaker meeting instead of sacramental mysticism. Whereas icons and incense frame silence at Holy Communion, Calvin's contemplative practice is more simply framed in God's word and seeking God's will.

Calvin's pastor, Graham Standish, also believes that contemplation is essential to the balanced life, a life that connects the physical and spiritual, the personal and communal. He thinks that most mainline churches have fallen prey to a "businesslike functionalism" that causes spiritual "respiratory failure." He quips, "The first sign of openness to the spiritual is the extent to which *Robert's Rules of Order* dominates the proceedings of the church. The more determined the church's leaders are to follow these rules to the letter, the more the spiritual is cut off."[69] In contrast to monastic guides like Saint Benedict's *Rule, Robert's Rules of Order* is the traditional secular guide to meeting procedure used by civic and political organizations. The foundation for a spiritual church, Graham insists, is prayer.

When he arrived at Calvin in 1996, Graham began introducing silence into the congregation. To me, "silent Presbyterians" seemed like an oxymoron. But Graham was convinced that spiritual renewal started not with big programming but with listening to God's word, meditating on scripture, and discerning God's will. He envisioned something distinctly different from the kind of mainline church in which he grew up; he dreamed of "a congregation of mystics." He easily quotes the Quaker theologian Thomas Kelly, saying that at the core of every church lies "a blessed community" made up of mystics centered in prayer. Like Gary Jones, Graham Standish describes this as a church full of people with direct, personal experience of God.

One member recalls how change started to happen at Calvin:

> *As slowly as you can, Graham has tried to mentor us by bringing more silence, more resting in God's presence. Gently, because so many people are uncomfortable with silence. He's introduced this in very nonthreatening packages, a little bit of reflection before we start a committee meeting. We will meditate on scripture as a way of settling down before we do business. We're saying "God, we want you to come in before us, plow this row before we go."*

"Plow this row before we go" reflects the simple, almost Quaker feel to the practice of silence at Calvin. Unlike Holy Communion, whose mysticism tends toward the sacramental and transcendent, Calvin practices a more earthy, pragmatic mysticism of finding God's presence in the stuff of everyday life. Carol, a prayer minister in the church, longs for even more silence in the worship service: "I wish everyone would sit in silence between sections of the service. I think it's like spinach. We all need it."

There are a few candles around the church, a Celtic cross, some decorative hangings. They practice silence at a small Wednesday evening Centering and Healing service. They pray when they knit shawls for those in need. "As we make these shawls," asks the group in prayer, "may we keep in mind that we are surrendering our hands to God's use." Outside, a handmade rock labyrinth offers a path for contemplative prayer. The key to Calvin's vibrancy is linking desire for God with a homey simplicity (indeed, the education building is called Faith House) that mirrors *both* the great Christian tradition of mystical experience and small-town sensibilities of historic American Protestantism.

The church publishes a pamphlet entitled *A Guide to Listening and Hearing God* that includes such sensible advice as reading scripture regularly and learning to recognize God's "voice." On the back is a benediction by Graham, "I wish you God's blessing in your listening." In a way, that describes his ministry to the whole congregation—to model and mentor listening, the power of silence and prayer for all. Business, board, and budget meetings start with silence, and many meetings have an extended time of centering prayer built into their schedules. An elder in the congregation says that the "meetings are like mini prayer meetings," with elections that result in "God's dream team" leadership. The people of Calvin testify to many personal and communal experiences of God's grace through learning to pay attention in silence and prayer.

At Sunday services, silence does not focus on the holy meal as at Holy Communion. Rather, it centers on things having to do with speech: on prayer, singing, the reading of the Word, and preaching. Silence serves as spiritual white space between the words, allowing each person to hear the word within. Kate, a member and the daughter of a pastor, remarks, "The worship service is a hybrid of this 'island' of reverence, quietness, and reflection combined with a dose of what you do with your life now and what God is doing." Calvin opens its services with a "centering chant," followed by a "prayer of humility" that orients the congregation toward a time of silent confession. The music is mostly contemporary, but not in the typical "happy-clappy" style of much contemporary Christian music. Instead, there are meditative Taizé chants and songs like

"The Centering Song" and the old Shaker song "Simple Gifts." Graham and his music director, Bruce Smith, write music, too. Their "Rest in the Bow with Me" provides an unexpected image of contemplative prayer:

> *Storms and high seas crash over me,*
> *Threatening to drown my soul.*
> *Seeking the voice of Christ, I hear:*
> *"Rest in the bow with Me."*

At the early service, they offer communion every week. But at the later worship, they offer it once at month. Although Graham wishes it were a weekly practice at both services, I sense God's presence and recall some words of my Quaker friend Brent Bill, "Worship becomes Eucharist when we sense God present with our group."[70] The congregation of mystics at Calvin Church seems to intuit that. They have made Eucharist without bread and wine. They made it with words and silence.

Listening to God in silence. The simple gift of contemplation. After decades of decline, Calvin Church is growing again. Since they started their slow journey into silence, weekly Sunday attendance has risen from 100 to 240. They have begun a new building program. And Graham loves being their pastor. "There is a strong belief here now," he says with a sense of gratefulness in his voice, "that when you root things in prayer, God actually does answer."

"Praying congregations are not temples of holiness. They are not filled with mystics or experts on prayer," says Jane Vennard, a United Church of Christ minister. "Praying congregations are lively places made up of diverse people who are longing to take prayer seriously."[71] Holy Communion and Calvin are full of normal, struggling people—people who are rediscovering God in silence. The form their prayer takes is as different as the congregations themselves: centering, contemplative, meditative, bodily, healing, thanks, knitting shawls or building Habitat houses, in worship, in homes and small groups, in closets. By themselves and with others. They are finding that the practice of silence, the way of contemplation, is not narrow, strict, or exclusive. Rather, it is a way marked with a large banner: OPEN FOR PRAYER. I stared at that sign for a while. I thought of all the people I'd met in my travels who had invited me into their prayers and taught me through their silence. I figured that "open for prayer" referred to their hearts.

They also reminded me how much I enjoy being in silence with good company—like just sitting in my sunroom on a summer evening with my husband. At those moments, when neither of us says anything, I know we are real lovers, true companions on a lifelong journey. Church, I suppose, could be like that, too. "In communal silence," my friend Brent Bill assures me, "we find ourselves empowered to walk together a bit further down the pilgrim way."[72]

NINE

Testimony

TALKING THE WALK

In the shadow of Yale Divinity School, the Church of the Redeemer appears conventional on the outside with its red brick, clear windows, wood trim, and white steeple. The inside is much the same, unadorned and simple. A pulpit is set off to the left, and a large wooden cross serves as the only ornamentation in the chancel. Redeemer's current building was erected in 1951 and appears as the architectural ideal of New England Congregationalism: understated, restrained, and intellectual. In other words, religion for a blue-state Yankee elite.

The cool exterior, however, looks particularly inviting on June 13, 2004, an especially warm Sabbath. Although university students are gone and the town is quieting down for the summer, a good-sized crowd has gathered at Redeemer to worship and hear God's word. As Congregationalists do everywhere, they eagerly await Sunday's high point: the sermon. Their senior minister, the Reverend Lillian Daniel, is a promising and notable young preacher—although still under forty, she is gaining a national reputation. Dressed in her academic gown, she mounts the pulpit, as she has almost every Sunday for the last eight years.

But today is different. This is one of her last Sundays in the congregation that she has come to love deeply. At the end of June, she will leave for a new call to First Congregational Church in Glen Ellyn, Illinois, outside of Chicago. Today, she will preach one of her final sermons at Redeemer. Farewell sermons are a venerable tradition in New England Congregationalism. Ministers often use them as charges to the congregation—they often recount the church's history and celebrate successes in ministry. Church of the Redeemer is the first church in which she has served as senior minister. Standing in this ancient line of American tradition, this is her first farewell.

There is a lot to celebrate at Redeemer. When Lillian arrived in 1996, the church was divided by conflict and threatened with closure. Only a handful of families remained. The choir was bigger than the congregation. To survive—just to pay the heating bills—the church had been selling off bits of its property for more than twenty years. Not only were these tangible measures of success low, but Redeemer had nearly run out of hope. Lillian once said to me, "I was the fourteenth senior minister called to the church and wondered in my first days at the church, as the two ministers before me must have wondered, if I might be the last."

By 2004, however, Redeemer had become a vital place with many new families, active ministries, and a new capital campaign under way. Today it is a growing, optimistic congregation, full of new energy. Everything—except the always magnificent music—has changed. Lillian credits much of Redeemer's transformation to the Christian practice of testimony. As part of her charge as she begins her leave-taking, her sermon is entitled "The Great Power of Testimony."

She pauses before she begins and looks at the congregation. For a moment, I wonder if she might cry. Although the architecture is restrained, the atmosphere is thick with emotion. She introduces the scripture reading by saying, "Our church's practice is giving testimony, having people talk about their experience of God. We didn't invent it, it was in the early church." Testimony was not just her project and she says, "I hope it will continue. We have learned that speaking strengthens our community." She reads a dramatic passage from the New Testament's Book of Acts in which the new Christian believers pray for boldness in speaking about God.

"Words are like an earthquake," she proclaims as she begins to recount Redeemer's practice of testimony. In the late 1990s, the leadership realized that Redeemer's people wanted to talk in church and they identified this as a "desire for testimony," to speak about faith in the context of Sunday worship. In a reserved culture like New England's, "we took a risk on these testimonies." Over five Sundays in Lent, the church heard five different testimonies, each powerful and moving, that opened their imaginations to telling stories of faith. As a result, they adopted a regular practice of testimony. And soon most people—even the most private of these Connecticut Congregationalists—were boldly and ably speaking of faith. "People are changed by giving their testimonies, and we can see the Holy Spirit moving them along," Lillian continues. "I have been changed, too. The practice of testimony was a process of releasing control and risking that testimony could outshine the sermon. The Holy Spirit uses all of us."[73]

Lillian's words drew me back to the first Sunday I had visited Redeemer, some six months earlier in January. The snow had been deep then, thickly covered with ice. I remember how lovely the music was at that service. And I remember thinking that Lillian's sermon was very good. But, surprisingly, I cannot remember what it was about! Instead, I remember the testimony. On that frigid day, a young Yale student offered her testimony. She had grown up without any kind of faith tradition and, upon arriving at the university, had joined an evangelical group as she searched for a "spiritual home." There, she encountered Jesus and became a Christian. After a while, though, she began to sense that the evangelicals' view of Christianity was somehow incomplete. She was uncomfortable with their politics, their lack of diversity, and their way of interpreting the Bible. She wondered if there was a different way of being a Christian—one more open, yet still vital as a "daily way of life." Someone told her about Redeemer. She visited and stayed. "God rings in my ears here," she said. "Redeemer is my spiritual home and you are my family."

"God rings in my ears here." Back in January, that young woman's testimony—simple, honest, earnest—outshone the sermon. It was risky, I thought, for a minister to open space for people's words, authentic and deeply personal, in the midst of worship. It takes a lot of trust to let go, to create safe space for the spirit, to help people speak what is in their souls. It can even be dangerous when "the Holy Spirit uses all of us."

Lillian is ending her sermon, still talking of the risk of testimony: "Many churches would be afraid to try this." Testimony changed her preaching and reshaped the community. "It gave voice," she says, "to our diversity." Yet, at the same time, in listening to and respecting that theological and racial diversity, "the Holy Spirit knits us together." Through the stories of our lives "we are and are being transformed."

Around me in the pew, people are nodding and smiling in agreement. Although I have known them only a short time, I know many of their stories. In coffeehouses, at the church, and in offices at Yale, they have shared their testimonies with me. Bits of their stories ring in my ears: They love Lillian. They love her family. They love Redeemer. They love one another. They love the city of New Haven. They love the poor and outcast. And mostly, they love God. When the sermon ends, a professor from nearby Hartford Seminary rises and awards Lillian her doctorate in ministry. The congregation stands and applauds with warm enthusiasm. Many people are hugging each other. This was the joyful charge, the celebration of an amazing eight years in which Redeemer found new life, new boldness in speaking faith. Two Sundays from now will be Lillian's last. Tears can wait until then.

A few months after my time at Redeemer, the United Church of Christ, the denomination of which the church is a part, started a national advertising campaign entitled "God Is Still Speaking." I chuckled when I saw the ads; I wondered if the producers had visited Redeemer! Certainly, there I witnessed God *still* speaking through God's people. The reality of the Christian story, of the power of biblical faith, was not the stuff of distant historical events. Rather, their own stories vibrate with the Spirit's wisdom—of discovering faith, of living faith, of struggling faith, of risky faith. Yes, I thought: God continues to speak.

And it was not only at Redeemer. At most of the congregations I visited, I heard people speak of faith—offering their testimonies to the power of God in changing their lives and their communities. Daniel, a fifty-something member of a progressive Episcopal church in California, was born to a fundamentalist family, rejected Christianity, became a Buddhist, and then returned to the Christian faith at that Episcopal congregation. He confessed to "having a horror of talking about my faith" after having grown up as a fundamentalist. "But," he said, "now I can't help myself. I go to work and colleagues ask, What did you do this weekend? And I start telling them about some fantastic sermon or liturgy at church on Sunday. I can't hold it in. I've just got to share."

Daniel's comments were like many I heard from mainline Protestants who could not stop speaking about faith, "testifying" to God's work. Indeed, encountering silence was a surprise because the people I met on this journey were so extremely talkative! What a contrast to the mainline practice of my childhood. Back in the 1960s, both parents and church school teachers taught us Methodist children that it was impolite, rude even, to talk about religion in public—even among people you knew. Faith was inward and private, something between you and God. Like sex, it was something you were not supposed to talk about. Religion as a whole, and one's own devotional life specifically, was a personal matter.

We recognized that some people did talk about faith: African-American Protestants and white evangelicals. I never heard anyone comment on testimony in African-American churches (perhaps no one in my immediate circle had ever seen it), but I heard plenty about testimony in white evangelical churches. I remember hearing it called bad taste, poor manners, and indiscreet. The words *Holy Rollers* pretty much summed up mainline Protestant attitudes toward excessive, emotional, and experiential religion. Years later, when I was a teenager, I worshiped in an evangelical church and learned that this was a caricature of the practice of testimony. The people at Scottsdale Bible Church talked about their experience of God ably and naturally—in a way rather like what Daniel would later say to me, "I can't help myself." And it was there, at Sunday night youth-group meetings in suburban backyards, that I would learn the practice of testimony for myself.

In many ways, testimony is the most democratic—and empowering—of all Christian practices. The entire New Testament is a testimony, a record of experiences that early Christians had with the transformative power of God. Those early believers wrote down their testimonies, their experiences of sharing their testimonies, and the impact of their testimonies on the people around them. This basic structure underlies almost every book in the New Testament—most of which claim to "witness" or "testify" to the love and grace of Jesus Christ. Indeed, the Book of Acts asserts that the church itself started with the apostle Peter's testimony on the day of Pentecost: "This Jesus God raised up, and of that all of us are witnesses" (Acts 2:32). From that point onward, famous disciples, like Peter and Paul, and regular converts and believers spread the good news of Christian faith across the Roman Empire through their testimony. Their stories of experiencing God were so powerful, so personally transformative, that many were willing to die rather than recant their testimony.

After the emperor Constantine legalized the Christian religion in 313 C.E., the practice of testimony began to wane. Once the faith had achieved a certain level of respectability, people became Christians for a variety of reasons and in a variety of ways—sometimes for political or social advancement, or by being born to Christian parents. The need to talk about faith became less urgent, and more pressing needs—like building churches, educating children, and training clergy—took its place. Testimony developed into a practice for the spiritual elite, who recorded their experiences of God in theological memoirs, such as Saint Augustine's famous *Confessions*. For most of the Christian Middle Ages, testimony was practiced largely by monks and nuns.

As Europe changed and new, more democratic impulses grew during the time of the Reformation, the practice of testimony reemerged. People testified to their embrace of the new Protestant faiths in church gatherings, in town squares, and in print. Indeed, for some Protestants, testimony served as the portal to the new community. Acceptance, and in some cases, even baptism, depended on one's ability to witness to God's power in one's life. Testimony shifted the authority to tell the Christian story away from the learned elite, from the ordained clergy, theologians, and magisterium of the Roman Catholic church, to the people. Testimony emboldened all God's people to speak of faith.

In the seventeenth century, however, New England Puritans elevated testimony to dramatic democratic expression. They required anyone seeking church membership—a coveted status in New England society—to be able to testify publicly to the works of God in his or her life. This meant that everyday people had to discern the impulses of spiritual awakening in their own souls, and offer evidence of their salvation to the whole congregation. From these humble New England beginnings, testimony would become an indelible part of American religion. In the eighteenth and nineteenth centuries, evangelical revivalists picked up the practice. As testimony became widespread in revivalism, however, middle-class Protestants began to shy away from it. Evangelicals, like those in my high school youth group, maintained the practice and taught it to their children. At Scottsdale Bible Church, everybody testified. By the middle of the twentieth century, more "respectable" Protestants—including the Congregationalist descendants of the New England Puritans at Church of the Redeemer in New Haven—had all but abandoned their democratic birthright of testimony.

It was not easy introducing the practice of testimony to Redeemer. Lillian remembers their first response to reading about the practice: "an intriguing description of what other people did." Yet she noticed that announcements and prayers had turned into "small testimonies" and that people were eager to share. The word *testimony* seemed awkward, however, carrying connotations that might be misunderstood by the congregation. So the deacons agreed to try the practice in worship under the guise of "Lenten reflections."

Darrell Carpenter, then the church's moderator, offered the first testimony. "The Spirit moves you when you think about having to do a testimony," he later told me. "It works on you, it changes as you discern about it, and pray and ask for the Lord's help. It isn't just a story on a piece of paper. You get tapped into the whole Spirit and it carries you." When the people of Redeemer talk about testimony, everyone mentions Darrell's story. On the first Sunday of Lent in 2000, his testimony astonished the congregation:

> *I grew up in an agnostic household, where Lent was an exotic part of other people's lives, but I'd like to relate a time in my life, much longer than forty days, when I was in a kind of spiritual wilderness, cut off from connections between my true self and the people around me.*
>
> *In 1983 at the age of thirty-four, I came out as a gay man, first to myself, then to my family and friends. Loyalties were stretched, some toppled, most survived. I divorced my wife and struggled to find what it meant to be a gay father to our five-year-old daughter.*
>
> *I was in church every week, singing in the choir, but not a member of the church, participating in but not connected to worship. I served on the missions committee, and when I was invited to serve on a search committee for an interim minister, I figured it would be a good time to join the church, but I was still in the wilderness.*
>
> *One Sunday afternoon in August 1997, I was back in my office, working alone against a long-term deadline. There was a church leadership meeting at Lillian's home at 5:00, and for reasons I don't understand, I decided to go.*
>
> *It was hot. I didn't feel comfortable with the people there. I didn't know what would happen. We started with a simple exercise: Lillian read a passage of scripture about the transforming power of the Holy Spirit.*

Good stuff. Then she asked each of us to write about a transformation in our own lives.

I couldn't think of a "safe" example, so I wrote about the personal transformation I experienced in coming out, in accepting myself as a gay man. No one had to know: I was writing this for myself.

But when Lillian asked if anyone wanted to share their story, the Spirit moved me to volunteer. I didn't know what would happen. There was a lump in my throat, my palms were sweaty. I took a leap of faith. It was a leap back from the wilderness into a new relationship with God, one based on my true nature. It didn't hurt that no one gasped or avoided me: in fact, I felt affirmation. In moving me to speak from my heart, the Spirit had also transformed my relationship with the congregation.

I felt radiant, lighter than air. I felt I had found home.

I hope we can learn together how to call others from the wilderness to a home in this church.

Lillian recalled that "After Darrell offered his reflection, he rejoined the choir to sing the offertory anthem red-faced. There were people in the church in tears." She laughed: "My sermon that day was on spiritual practices, but I could have thrown it out and no one would have noticed."

Kurt Mounsma, an active lay leader in the congregation, said, "That was incredible, it really was. All the testimonies were meaningful and inspirational, but some were epiphanies. I remember Darrell Carpenter talking about being gay. And he talked about how he was accepted. There wasn't a dry eye in the house." Darrell's courage helped lead the congregation toward becoming "open and affirming," a church hospitable to gay and lesbian persons.

Few people understand testimony as well as Kurt Mounsma, who has attended Redeemer since 1989 and served on the search committee that called Lillian. Kurt holds a doctorate in American religion with expertise in New England Puritanism. He points out that there is more "change than continuity" in Redeemer's practice of testimony from the Puritan way. "It used to be very much a profession of the central points of religion, and you did it to be able to join the church," he says. "Now testimonies are almost post facto. They are something you do after you become a full member. It is almost like a mark of maturity or a rite of passage." With the Puritans, Kurt notes, testimony was rather doctrinally "formulaic," and then he says, "Nowadays they're more individualistic, there's more self-revelation. It is much more wide-open."

There is a good reason for the change. The Puritans used testimony as a way of stepping into roles that were already decided for them—by God, their families, their community. For them, testimonies were a mark of adult responsibility, the acceptance of their place in the social order. Wrestling with God typically meant submission to his will based on the conviction of one's inadequacy. Now testimony is, as Lillian put it, "who we are and who we are becoming." Our stories no longer tell tales of spiritual acquiescence and conformity. Rather, they tell of finding meaning, finding unique selves, and finding God in a confusing and chaotic world.

Contemporary thinkers have noted the change—and the new role that storytelling plays in our lives. Sociologist Anthony Giddons claims that our identity is found "in the on-going story about the self" and further asserts that "each of us not only 'has' but *lives* a biography."[74] Moral philosopher Charles Taylor says that we understand life as an "unfolding story" in which "we grasp our lives as narrative."[75] Put simply, we become ourselves as we tell our stories. We cannot know ourselves apart from our stories—stories in which we are both author and actor.

The practice of testimony at Redeemer sharpened this sense of life as story. As one woman at Redeemer said, "Looking where I was and seeing it as a faith journey, I would have never used those terms about it before. But thinking about it that way transformed how I thought about myself, and how I thought about the congregation." Thus, ancient Puritan stories testified to how God had already changed them, a completed past action. At Redeemer, the congregation testifies to the power of stories to change us, a continuing work of the Holy Spirit. Like Darrell's story. By testifying to acceptance, he inspired the congregation to open their hearts wider, accepting him more deeply and accepting others. Testimony reminds us of where we have been, helps us see where we are, and directs us toward unanticipated paths.

In Washington, D.C., Epiphany practices testimony, too. Once a month, a member gets up and shares a "faith story" about how he or she met God at Epiphany. One Sunday morning, Gregg Browne testified about unanticipated paths, those turns in our journeys. The tall, well-spoken African-American lawyer stood up and told of his surprise at hearing God's call at Church of the Epiphany:

> *I don't remember how I first came to notice the church, but I'm sure it happened during a walk around the area at lunchtime. I have to admit that what first "called" me to the church was the 12:10 weekday communion. I grew up going to church every Sunday morning and getting up was often difficult. I was attracted to the possibility of fulfilling my church obligations during the week at lunchtime. But fate and Randolph had other things in mind for me. Randolph invited me to come to church on Sunday. I resisted the invitation for a while but finally gave in and came one Sunday.*
>
> *I got here at what I thought was a respectable time—8:20—only to find a service going on already. I figured I would wait around for the next service, which surely had to be starting right afterwards. But, to my surprise, the next service did not begin right away. Instead, someone came into the sanctuary from the side door and began calling off names from a list. [Although Gregg did not know, the list was a sign-up for homeless people who planned to attend breakfast that morning.] One by one, every person in the room, upon hearing their name called—left and headed off to somewhere in the back of the church. Eventually, I was alone in the*

sanctuary because my name was not on the special list and, therefore, I had not been called. But looking back on that morning, I realize that although my name wasn't read aloud I had nonetheless been called.

I did not know it at the time, but I had just had my first encounter with the Welcome Table, one of Epiphany's oldest and most successful outreach ministries. As I watched each person rise and head to the back, I realized that this was not the type of congregation I had grown up in. I realized that a significant portion of the congregation was likely homeless and/or poor. Most were wearing old clothes; there was a lingering smell that indicated bathing was not a regularity; many were awakened from sleep when their names were called; many were carrying every possession they owned. To paraphrase a line from an old car commercial, "These were not my parents' Episcopalians." But they were Epiphany's Episcopalians—or Buddhists, Muslims, Catholics, atheists, or whatever. They were Epiphany's family and the choice was mine as to whether to join the family or not. I could walk through the door to the Parish Hall or walk out the door to the street.

Well, I did not go through the door to the Parish Hall that morning, but I did walk through it after the 11:00 service. And, in time, I became a full member of Epiphany. I've been a Welcome Table volunteer for the past four years and it has been an incredibly rewarding experience for me. If there is a moral or lesson to be taken away from this, it is that we should all be aware of the many ways in which we are called.

Gregg came to Epiphany intending to fulfill his "church obligations." But he found a family, and now serves its most humble members. In the process, he became the leader of the church's outreach committee "to respond to human need and touch the pain of the world, ministering with the poor, and working for systemic change." He could never have anticipated God's call that morning, nor could he have anticipated the ways in which being a member would change him. By telling his story, he invited the congregation into his surprise—seeing themselves as a newcomer might, affirming their practice of doing justice, and welcoming participants into a deeper life of service. Testimony gave him a chance to confirm his own call to outreach and to strengthen his connections to the larger congregational family. By remembering his own transformative moment in a faith story, he opened the way for others to experience the unexpected presence of God.

For Christians, telling stories invariably includes that practice of testimony. In some cases—as it was for the New England Puritans—testimony may follow formulas of acceptance and submission to God's will. I have been at many revival meetings where I knew exactly what the speaker would say before the testimony began: "I once was lost in sin, but Jesus saved me." But in the mainline churches I visited, testimonies did not take a single, rehearsed form. Rather, they were unexpected—individual stories of being surprised by God's love and transformed in unanticipated ways. Like a young woman who finds hope in a liberal church. Or a gay man talking about the power of the Holy Spirit in his life. A lawyer waiting alone in a sanctuary to hear his name called.

Ernest Kurtz and Katherine Ketcham refer to such personal storytelling as "the spirituality of imperfection," a practice that is "eccentric and unexpected" as well as "unconventional and iconoclastic."[76] Although they studied the practice of testimony at AA meetings, it occurred to me that they were also describing a larger cultural phenomenon—one that I observed at Redeemer, Epiphany, and other mainline congregations. "This particular story is more of a *pilgrimage*, a wandering, digressing sort of journey." What they call the "spirituality of imperfection" was everywhere obvious on my own journey—"a spirituality of not having all the answers."[77] It appeared to me as a spirituality of living the questions.

Testimony is not about God fixing people. Rather, it speaks of God making wholeness out of human woundedness, human incompleteness. Still questioning whether to stay Roman Catholic, Katrina, who regularly attends Redeemer, says, "Though I have not felt ready to take the leap of converting, my experience of the worship and community here have effected a very significant conversation within my heart and mind. I look forward to further exploring where God is leading me."

Unlike the stories of Puritans and revivalists, mainline testimony is not a spirituality of arrival, of the certainty of securing eternal life. Mainline testimony is the act of getting there. Pilgrimage stories. Testimony is not a formula of salvation; rather, it is a way of being, a map to an undiscovered country. And, in telling the stories of our lives, we find we are not alone on the journey. Other pilgrims are on this road, too. Pilgrims have always told stories along the way. And, in those stories, we may well hear God ringing in our ears.

TEN

Diversity

MAKING COMMUNITY

North of Santa Barbara, California, the Goleta Valley lacks the glitzy allure of its neighbor. But it possesses a real sense of place. Here, the distance between mountains and ocean widens, and rich flatlands replace scenic coastal charm. For much of the valley's history, agriculture was its business and Goleta was an unincorporated town—essentially a western ranching village populated by a diverse assortment of native Chumash Indians, Spanish settlers, midwestern Anglo exiles, and Mexican immigrants. In more recent decades, but when land was still relatively cheap, Goleta served as both a radical student mecca and a middle-class suburb for Santa Barbara. Today, sky-high real estate costs are driving another change: the displacement of the students and the old middle class by the super-rich, a change that has intensified the divide between the haves and the have-nots. Although many of the old farms are gone, Goleta's remaining strawberry fields, avocado trees, and citrus groves still testify to its fertile soil and perfect climate.

The valley remains a patchwork of this diverse history, of many peoples inhabiting a place and forming community. The visitor still sees rolling hills populated by wineries, small farms, and ranches—but the valley also includes subdivisions and government-mandated "middle income" housing developments, a funky "downtown" strip of mom-and-pop shops, the University of California at Santa Barbara with a crowded student "ghetto," a posh five-star resort, the local airport, a small industrial zone, and a high-tech corridor. Despite its small-town agrarian roots, Goleta is now pure California; it is ethnically, socially, and culturally diverse—and completely post-Christian.

In this unlikely setting, behind a modest strip mall, sits Goleta Presbyterian Church. The congregation meets in a new sanctuary, noted for its simple—almost austere—beauty. Founded in 1960 by midwesterners who came to Santa Barbara to work in the new aerospace industry, Goleta Presbyterian stills reflects its unassuming roots. With 275 members, it is not a large church. And it has struggled as Goleta has changed. Beginning in the 1980s, the church lost 170 of its members as the founding generation died. At the same time, however, 200 new people filled its pews, numerically replacing the losses. Most of the new members, like the earlier ones, are white. Although they look alike, they are very different from the founding generation. Pastor Steve Jacobsen estimates that three-quarters of them did not grow up Presbyterian. Like the pastor himself, many were born into other traditions. And some were brought up with no religion at all. "For centuries congregations were formed around ethnic identities," Steve says. "People shared a native language, customs, and well-defined theology. But all that has changed."[78]

Of the five members of Steve's leadership team, only one was born into a Presbyterian home. One was raised Roman Catholic (but left that tradition for Buddhism as a young man), another was reared Methodist (and became a charismatic), and the other two were brought up in nonreligious homes. Of the five, three underwent extended periods of spiritual searching. "If you were in conversation with this group," Steve comments, "you'd find that they have different views of how to interpret scripture and the significance of other faiths. They have different political views and opinions about key social issues. They have differing musical tastes. They represent the eclecticism that California is known for." He continues:

> *But despite their differences, they have two things in common: they have come to the door of this particular church and stayed, and, if you listen to them tell their stories as I have, you would be persuaded that God's Spirit has been leading them and forming them for a very long time.*

Some Protestant pastors look at such diversity as a problem, bemoaning the decline of denominational identity and the rise of theological chaos. But not Steve Jacobsen. As a native Californian, he has been shaped by the ideal and practice of diversity. He believes that "the loss in homogeneity leads to a richer diversity" and thinks that communal variety is a source of "complex wisdom," a quality that Christians should value. He even has a name for congregational diversity: "a polyculture of the Spirit—different ways of being Christian, each with an inherent integrity and vitality." Unlike those who think that diversity sounds the death knell for Christianity, Steve says confidently, "When we create programs, study groups, and worship services, we intentionally seek to reflect the diversity we have in our midst."

Randy, a member of the congregation, states: "One of our hallmarks for a long time has been an ability to hold creative tensions, different places on the theological spectrum, different tastes in music." He believes that the theological and political division evident in national issues is dangerous and worries that single-party views could "manifest more within our congregation." But Goleta Presbyterian remains committed to practicing diversity. As Patty, the director of family ministries, explains, "There are very conservative people politically and theologically as well as very liberal people. So, here's an opportunity to have real community—a challenge to elucidate issues and communicate instead of all of us getting together and saying, Isn't it wonderful that we understand

and *those* people over there don't." Jeannie, church secretary and long-time member, says, "This is a church full of difference but not a lot of division."

Although some might speculate that political diversity offers the biggest challenge to Goleta's "polyculture of the Spirit," it does not. The most troubling division comes from the tensions within the Presbyterian denomination between the church's traditionally more liberal theological constituency and its vocal evangelical minority. At Goleta, located in a particularly conservative presbytery, this can sometimes be problematic. For example, Tamara, a new member who "takes the Bible fairly literally," was preparing to teach Sunday school when another parent admonished her class, "I just want you to remember, boys and girls, that these are stories. Like a metaphor. Not literal truth." Tamara was offended and the two teachers were at odds. In congregations, people are more likely to argue about theological perspectives than political issues.

Instead of allowing this to fester into a full-blown conflict, Steve and the children's educational director brought the differing parties together and opened a conversation about what Presbyterians really teach about the Bible. Neither the parent nor Tamara had accurately presented the denomination's tradition. Each side left the discussions having learned new things about scripture. As Katie, the church's evangelical youth director, says, "Nobody felt like they were a bad person or that their opinion wasn't valued or honored." The Sunday school was not ripped apart, and the content of children's education was actually refined through the disagreement. Unlike in evangelical churches—where doctrinal uniformity is considered nonnegotiable—theological diversity shapes the daily life of most mainline churches. Steve confesses that holding diversity together "can be tricky at times." But the congregation keeps at it. "We believe when we do a scripture reading that everybody has a piece of the puzzle," Steve explains, "and when we all come to the end, we are blessed by the encounter. To me that is when I feel God present."

Perhaps not surprisingly, given Goleta's history, Steve bases his understanding of "polycultures of the Spirit" in farming. In a very real way, people's souls are the soil of God's spirit, the congregation a kind of ecosystem of faith. Drawing from scientist Wes Jackson, Steve says that "polycultures are ecological systems that include many species of plant and animal life within a particular region. They have evolved slowly over a period of time." Polycultural systems can withstand "many swings and changes in climate and many kinds of pests and disease." In such an environment, "various life-forms depend on each other, drawing from each other in many intricate ways." Steve argues that monocultures, such as those fostered by industrial farming, yield large harvests but lack the "wisdom and subtle integrity" of polycultural complexity. As he explains this, I immediately think of evangelical megachurches, with their huge congregations complete with doctrinal statements and Republican voting guides. Big yields, yes. But where is wisdom?

In 2004, a year of fractious social and religious division in national politics, Goleta tested its polycultural resiliency when the congregation rewrote its mission statement to include citizenship concerns, politics, and "a moral perspective to issues" such as human rights and environmental justice. Randy confesses that he was concerned that "redoing the mission statement" during an election year might foster conflict. But, he recalls, "the congregation and Steve handled it really well." Their renewed sense of vision begins: "Goleta Presbyterian Church is a place where people of many backgrounds and ages encounter a God that is alive, personal, powerful and full of love for all people." The congregation commits itself, among other things, to active participation in God's work in the world and "the creation of a healthy, multicultural community." While some Christians in 2004 seemed committed to dividing the country along religious lines, the people at Goleta walked another path. As one woman told me, "It's such a variety, and yet it's all lovingly held together as a church."

Like their ancestors, the people at Goleta Presbyterian are good farmers. As the world changed around them, they might have lost their little church. But they did not. Instead, they sowed seed for a new kind of congregation, a polycultural one. And the church has grown. After all, the valley soil is fertile.

*   *   *

All along my journey through emerging mainline congregations, I found people who cherished diversity of every kind—political, theological, cultural, and racial. They appreciated, as Geoffrey Chaucer wrote of his medieval pilgrims, "sundry folk" along the journey. For people on this way, diversity serves as a sign of God's love for all humanity. The churchgoers I interviewed proudly proclaimed their own diversity, even if their congregations looked relatively homogeneous. Like the good people at Iglesia Santa María in Falls Church, Virginia, who told me—in Spanish—that they wanted their new Episcopal congregation to be "for Latin people, but also the American people, all people." In an effort to understand Christians from other cultures, they befriended people at the local Korean Presbyterian congregation. The folks of Santa María envision church as "God's house" filled with "a big family" that embraces all races, ethnicities, and cultures. All the congregations I visited were actively pursuing diversity—for spiritual and theological reasons.

Yet, I have often heard leaders of the religious right attack diversity as "political correctness," a kind of affirmative-action liberalism. In my own denomination, the Episcopal Church, conservatives eschew diversity (along with the related "inclusion") as evidence that secularism has invaded the church. To them diversity is merely a form of popular relativism, an "anything goes" attitude. From their point of view, it appears that God wants us all to be the same—believe the same things, worship in the same way, and vote for the same political candidates.

As a Christian, this surprises me. A Christian practice of diversity is not secular relativism. Rather, it is the active construction of a boundary-crossing community, a family bound not by blood but by love, that witnesses to the power of God's healing in the world. Throughout the scriptures, God is a God who delights in diversity. In the beginning, God created plants and animals of "every kind," and human beings in God's own diverse image: male and female. God looked out over this dizzying variety of creation and pronounced it "very good." Eventually, God called Abraham and Sarah to birth the nation of Israel, a people who

will worship God and keep God's promises. But even Israel is not sin-
gular—they are a people made up of twelve tribes. And those tribes are
further commanded to bless all the earth's peoples, "Declare his glory
among the nations, his marvelous works among all the peoples!" (Ps.
96:3). Indeed, the central vision of the Hebrew scriptures is God's love
redeeming all nations "as the waters cover the seas."

For Christians, Jesus embodies the love of God for all peoples. Jesus
welcomed children, sinners, tax collectors, fishermen, women, thieves,
traitors, Roman soldiers, faithful Jews, lepers, those who were deaf and
blind, the poor and the outcast. Indeed, the New Testament depicts Jesus' followers as one of the most diverse groups imaginable. And, when
Jesus called people, he never said, "Come with me, and you will become just like the rest of us." Jesus never issued a demand for uniformity. Rather, he beckoned people to follow with a promise of healing,
transformation, and love—that he would make known to his disciples
"the way of life." He did not say that his followers would be alike; he
said that despite their differences, they would be changed by love: "As
the Father has loved me, so I have loved you; abide in my love" (John
15:9). Love would open the way for people who were different to be
reconciled—brought into harmony with one another—and model the
dream of God's *shalom*.

Jesus' earliest followers gathered into culturally diverse congregations where Jews, Gentiles, Samaritans, and Africans worshiped and
served God together. Besides being racially and ethnically diverse, early
Christians held a variety of theological views and created varied spiritual practices that shaped the new religion. Christianity thrived in the
multicultural cities of the Roman Empire, and the faith reflected this environment. Yet, in the midst of this variety, the practice of love bound
together the Christian community into a kind of oneness that honored
diversity while, at the same time, fostering harmony and unity—creating a new kind of family, "an inclusive table fellowship that emulated the
social practices of Jesus."[79]

Of this, the apostle Paul would say, "There is no longer Jew or Greek, there is no longer slave or free, there is no longer male and female; for all of you are one in Christ Jesus" (Gal. 3:28). Paul did not imply some sort of spiritual flatness here. Instead, he would remind early Christians that "there are varieties of gifts, but the same Spirit; and there are varieties of services, but the same Lord; and there are varieties of activities, but it is the same God who activates all of them in everyone" (1 Cor. 12:4–6).

Although he is not usually credited as such, Paul is the great apostle of diversity. Paul said, "The body does not consist of one member but of many" and God intended that "there may be no dissension within the body, but the members may have the same care for one another" (1 Cor. 12:14, 25). Paul did not depict the Christian life as one of uniformity. Rather, he envisioned a community of unity-in-diversity: "Now you are the body of Christ and individually members of it" (1 Cor. 12:27). From the heart of God's diversity, Paul argued, comes the wisdom, the "still more excellent way," of love.

When Christians elevate uniformity, "alikeness," over Paul's dream of unity-in-diversity, shunning, excommunication, heresy trials, inquisitions, schism, crusades, and religious warfare are among the predictable results. As a historian of religion, I never cease to be astonished at the prevalence of this theological mistake—and its tragic consequences. The Christian West has been marked by a twisted insistence on sameness—especially in belief—that has led to a sadly ironic result: vast numbers of people who doubt or reject Christianity on the basis of its hypocrisy. How can a religion that speaks so eloquently of love so brutally destroy its questioners, its dissenters, its innovators, and its competitors?

In this framework, diversity is not a capitulation to political liberalism. Rather, it is a deeply biblical and profoundly theological Christian practice—one that is desperately needed in today's world. Some people think that diversity is simply a condition of history, while others argue that it is a kind of politically correct multiculturalism. For Christians, neither of these is true. The scriptures witness to the command for Christians to do something more—to make community that purposefully includes multiplicity in order to overcome the hatred that issues from differences. Like the early Christians, mainline pilgrims embrace diversity as part of God's dream for the world, and are actively constructing their communities as, to use Steve Jacobsen's term, "polycultures of the Spirit." Diversity is more than a political condition; it is something Christians do. Christians pursue diversity because it models creation, embodies love, and through the related practice of reconciliation, aligns our lives with God's dream of harmony. As the people of Santa María know, God wants us all to be family.

At the clearly upper-middle-class Episcopal Church of the Redeemer in Cincinnati, the Reverend Bruce Freeman explained, "We may not look terribly diverse, but we're a 50/50 church." Half Republican, half Democrat. He shared this with me in October 2004. I had been in Ohio only a few days, but long enough to know that the airwaves were full of political attack ads, as well as local-news stories about a gay neighborhood (of John Kerry supporters) that had been vandalized. Leading the church through the fractious Ohio election—in the racially divided city of Cincinnati—was not easy. Redeemer decided not to ignore the tensions. They offered a multiweek adult education course on religion and politics. Speakers came to the church to discuss controversial issues from a variety of viewpoints. "It was a real challenge," Bruce confessed, "but people listened to one another and treated each other with respect. We believe that arguing can be productive, and we are committed to conversation and discussion." He refers to the church as a "theological university, a school of ministry, where all perspectives are welcome."

Like Steve Jacobsen and other mainline Protestant pastors, Bruce Freeman thinks about diversity. Church of the Redeemer understands its political, theological, and religious diversity as a part of its calling to be a place of conversation, discussion, vision, and action. Bruce believes that the congregation's ability to "hold diversity in prayer" makes "us the church we are supposed to be." He confesses that he is influenced by Archbishop Desmond Tutu's *ubuntu* theology. According to Bruce, *ubuntu* roughly means "I cannot be without you." At Redeemer,

"We're not going to throw anyone out for their theological opinions." The church, he insists, is "passionate" that the process of talking with each other, of being in community, is more important than a winning outcome. "We believe that without all points of view, without different kinds of people, we can't be the kind of church we are called to be. By living into our diversity, we are making room for the kingdom of God."

Although he is a surprising source of inspiration for an Ohio pastor, Archbishop Tutu suggests that African Christianity may help us better understand the biblical vision of diversity. Tutu explains that Africans believe "a person is a person *through* other persons." Fundamental to our humanity is that "we are set in a delicate network of interdependence with our fellow human beings and with the rest of God's creation." Tutu says, "The truth is we need each other. We cannot survive and thrive without one another." He continues in words reminiscent of the apostle Paul:

> *In God's family, there are no outsiders. All are insiders. Black and white, rich and poor, gay and straight, Jew and Arab, Palestinian and Israeli, Roman Catholic and Protestant, Serb and Albanian, Hutu and Tutsi, Muslim and Christian, Buddhist and Hindu, Pakistani and Indian—all belong.... God's dream wants us to be brothers and sisters, wants us to be family.... In our world we can survive only together. We can be truly free, ultimately, only together. We can be human only together, black and white, rich and poor, Christian, Muslim, Hindu, Buddhist, and Jew.*[80]

In contemporary America, we may as well add "Republican and Democrat."

As unlikely as it may seem, Bruce Freeman is helping his Episcopal congregation to practice *ubuntu* in suburban Cincinnati. A few months after those divisive elections, Martha, a member of Redeemer, commented, "Even though we have very diverse opinions, we all go to the altar together." In language that reminded me of Steve Jacobsen's "polyculture of the Spirit," she continued, "It is because we are a community that we weather all these difficult and challenging times."

And, back at polycultural Goleta Presbyterian, the congregation models the hope of *ubuntu*, a contemporary non-Western version of the apostle Paul: one body, many gifts, interdependent in love, God's dream of human family. As Katie, the youth minister, says, "There's not a sense that you have to believe this exactly or you can't be a member, or you can't get to heaven. For all our differences, our church knows they are family." Her words remind me of Archbishop Tutu's: "Jesus said, 'I, if I be lifted up, will draw all to me.' Not some, but all. And it is a radical thing that Jesus says that we are members of one family. God says, All, all are My children. It is shocking. It is radical."[81]

On Maundy Thursday, in 2005, the people of Epiphany in downtown Washington gathered in silence for the solemn Holy Week service. After a few minutes of quiet reflection, worship began with an African folk song:

> *Jesu, Jesu, fill us with your love,*
> *show us how to serve the neighbors we have from you.*
>
> *Kneels at the feet of his friends,*
> *Silently washes their feet,*
> *Master who acts as a slave to them.*
>
> *Neighbors are rich and poor,*
> *Neighbors are black and white,*
> *Neighbors are nearby and far away.*
>
> *These are the ones we should serve,*
> *These are the ones we should love.*
> *All are neighbors to us and you.*

They sang with heart. No wonder, I thought. The congregation reflected the words! In mainline Protestant churches, diversity is often invisible. But not at Epiphany. The pews were filled with white and black people, rich and poor, Washington lawyers and the homeless, immigrants and native-born, gay and straight people. Here is a robust vision of God's family. "We work to be more inclusive," one church member told me. "It's not just a matter of tolerating differences or accepting differences; it's appreciating differences for the richness that they bring to our community."

While theological and political diversity is common in mainline churches, racial diversity is much less so. Indeed, much of the history of American Protestantism is a history of racial exclusion. As late as 1959, African-American theologian Howard Thurman could comment, "There was not a *single instance* known to me in which a local church had a completely integrated membership. The color bar was honored in the practice of the Christian religion."[82] The "color bar" in most Protestant churches is a sad commentary on our lack of faithfulness to the good news of God in Jesus Christ.

Although Church of the Epiphany had black members at the time of its founding in 1844, it would take a long time—until the mid-twentieth century—for the church to be truly diverse. It, like so many other congregations, reflected cultural patterns. That changed, however, during the civil rights era, when Epiphany made strong public stands in favor of the movement, often providing food and shelter for marchers and protestors during demonstrations. The congregation's support was rewarded when, during the race riots that destroyed their neighborhood in the 1960s, African-American activists protected the church building from mobs. Epiphany's early commitment to civil rights created a congregational passion for diversity as a sign of God's justice—and opened the doors for a truly inclusive parish. Today Epiphany is a 50/50 congregation—50 percent white, 50 percent black. And the current members agree that "the diversity of our parish is what drew many of us to this church to begin with."

One parishioner described a scene that explains the power of Epiphany's diversity:

Imagine an outsider opening the door of the Willard Room and listening to about a dozen people participating in a forum that seeks to understand the meaning of a passage from the Gospel of Luke. The participants are from all walks of life, black and white, middle class, homeless, and formerly homeless, and from Asia, Africa, and the Caribbean, talking about the Bible metaphorically and literally; all trying to understand each other's viewpoints.

From one angle, this scene might appear as a contemporary Tower of Babel. But the New Testament Book of Revelation clues us to another reality. The author, caught up in a vision of heaven, says, "There was a great multitude that no one could count, from every nation, from all tribes and peoples and languages ... they fell on their faces before the throne and worshiped God, singing, 'Amen! Blessing and glory and wisdom and thanksgiving and honor and power and might be to our God forever and ever!" (Rev. 7:9, 11–12).

This throne-room vision grounds the practice of diversity in mainline churches. I heard it from nearly everyone and witnessed it nearly everywhere. As one member of Downtown Presbyterian Church in Nashville recalled, "The diversity of this congregation is one of the things I love most about this church. At one of our Christmas pageants, Joseph was played by one of the wealthiest men in Nashville while Mary was played by a homeless woman. Singing 'In Christ There Is No East or West,' I shared my hymnbook with a black woman with AIDS. It reminds me that in heaven, we will find such a diverse congregation gathered with the Lord." As Methodist pastor Roy Terry, in Naples, Florida, put it so succinctly, "We are all about breaking down the walls between people. If you don't want to break down walls, you really can't call yourself a Christian."

Besides the fact that diversity is a deeply biblical and profoundly Christian practice, it is just more fun to go on pilgrimage with interesting people. I grew up in a congregation that treated spiritual, political, and racial conformity as an ultimate goal. It was, frankly, boring. Now, especially after this journey, I find it hard to imagine a church where everyone looks alike, thinks alike, and acts alike. Diversity is, after all, a foretaste of heaven. God's dream here and now.

ELEVEN

Justice

ENGAGING THE POWERS

"As Martin Luther King said, we are called to be the church that is maladjusted," proclaimed pastor Roy Terry at Cornerstone United Methodist Church. "We are to work for reconciliation. In our baptisms, we made a promise to stand against injustice!" He asks the congregation, "Do you agree that is important?" People in the crowd nod, saying "yes" and "amen."

It is a beautiful January day in Naples, Florida. It is also the day that many Protestant churches celebrate the legacy of Martin Luther King, Jr., and the civil rights movement. Instead of a traditional sermon, Roy offers reflections on how Martin Luther King "is key to Cornerstone's theology and identity." To underscore the centrality of King's vision, the worship service opened with a powerful African-American anthem, "Lift Every Voice and Sing."

> *Lift every voice and sing till earth and heaven ring,*
> *Ring with the harmonies of liberty.*

Let our rejoicing rise high as the listening skies;
let it resound loud as the rolling sea.
Sing a song full of the faith that the dark past has taught us;
sing a song full of the hope that the present has brought us;
facing the rising sun of our new day begun,
let us march on, till victory is won.

After the hymn, members of the congregation read scriptures paired with selections from King's writings. Behind the readers, pictures and images from the civil rights movement flash on the screens to the left and right. Photographs of people at prayer. Men and women walking across the bridge at Selma, Alabama. King preaching. A bombed church. A lynching. In his remarks, Roy challenges the church: "We need to break down the most segregated hour in America!" He stresses the need for hospitality, of caring for the "strangers at the margins of the city." He concludes by saying, "This is serious church work; if you don't want to be a part of it, well ..." He pauses and smiles. The congregants smile as well, and nodding, they agree that Cornerstone is, as Roy says, "about breaking down the walls" so that God's justice can flow forth. A few minutes later, Roy offers communion, "This is not my table or Cornerstone's table, but the Lord's table. All are welcome here."

Cornerstone is a diverse congregation, especially in terms of class, where all people are welcome at God's table. Yet, they do not cultivate diversity for its own sake. Rather, they pursue diversity as a way of justice—of practicing reconciliation that will, as Roy says, "address worldly wrongs." Martin Luther King, whose influence is evident here, once said, "The end is reconciliation, the end is redemption, the end is the creation of the beloved community." Indeed, before his death, "Dr. King caught a glimpse of a new social order" that would be brought about by a spiritual journey of drawing together those who had been divided by oppression and hatred.[83]

In some ways, it still surprises me to sit in church and hear perspectives like this. During my Methodist childhood, some preachers did attempt to address these issues from their pulpits. But, although a few white churches may have heeded the challenge, many more resisted calls for social transformation and the breaking down of walls. Christianity was about being polite, not about God's politics. Indeed, most of the adults in my church thought Martin Luther King was a Communist and a heretic. During my white, middle-class Methodist upbringing, I never heard one good word said about him. When he was assassinated, I heard some of my relatives say that he deserved it. And my congregation ignored the events that took place in Memphis in April 1968. Back then, they would have run a preacher like Roy Terry out of town on a rail.

Almost forty years later, however, Cornerstone's people listen to King's message and nod in agreement. It is an unlikely change—a white-majority, southern congregation being formed in African-American theology. There is another difference here from the 1960s, a difference not so immediately obvious to outsiders. At the time of the civil rights movement a few white mainline churches, even some southern ones, supported integration and voting rights for blacks. However, they typically did so on the basis of political liberalism, drawing from the language of fairness, equality, and rights. While fairness, equality, and human rights are very good things, they are also primarily secular ideals. As shocking as the discovery may be to many American Christians, that secular language is not found in the Bible or in the vast consensus of Christian tradition. Instead, those ideals emerged during the Enlightenment, the liberal philosophical movement that has shaped Western thought for the last three centuries. By the 1960s, Enlightenment liberalism dominated theological thinking in white mainline churches. During my Methodist childhood, it was hard to figure out what God had to do with what was happening in Mississippi or Alabama. "Justice" had more to do with the courts than with the Bible.

Unlike white Protestants, African-American Christians spoke a different language of justice—one that was deeply spiritual and tapped into the stories of the Bible. King talked of justice as a spiritual journey, as doing the work of God. Although some white liberals agreed with his cause, many found King's religious vision, with its implicit criticism of secular politics, hard to take.[84] At Cornerstone on Martin Luther King Day, political liberalism is notably absent. They celebrate King's vision of diversity and justice as biblical ideals, as part of their spiritual journey. For them, justice is not about backing a secular political agenda— whether that be liberal or conservative. Rather, justice is part of the faithful life of being a Christian; justice is spirituality.

Every week during the school year, thirty Cornerstone parishioners meet for the Sojourners group, an intensive newcomer course in Christian formation. Designed jointly by Roy and his associate, the Reverend Lisa Lefkow, the twenty-eight-week course introduces basic Christianity and Methodist spirituality. At its core is a diagram, a four-quadrant grid arranged in the shape of a cross. Marking the quadrants are the four key aspects of a Methodist way of life: acts of worship, acts of devotion, acts of compassion, and acts of justice.

One evening, Roy explains this cross-shaped way of life to the class. The group easily understands worship, devotion, and compassion, but they fumble with justice. Roy confesses that "acts of justice" are the "hardest" for Christians. Acts of justice can be hard. Maybe they should be. After all, the world is mostly a place of injustice. But Roy says the reason runs deeper: "As Christians, we are against the powers and principalities of the world; we are not talking about forgiving wrongs against you but rather addressing worldly wrongs." At its heart, he insists, justice is a spiritual struggle.

Roy's comment reminds me of theologian Walter Wink, who has written extensively on the "powers" of this world:

> *The Powers That Be are not, then, simply people and their institutions, as I had first thought; they also include the spirituality at the core of those institutions and structures. If we want to change those systems, we will have to address not only their outer forms, but their inner spirit as well.*[85]

Doing justice is much more than supporting a particular political party and its policy agenda. Doing justice goes beyond fixing unfair and oppressive structures. Doing justice means engaging the powers—transforming the "inner spirit" of all systems of injustice, violence, and exclusion.

Wink refers to oppressive powers as the "domination system." Christians, by actively being the beloved community, enact justice through practices of hospitality, prayer, discernment, testimony, and diversity. As such, says Duke University theologian Stanley Hauerwas, the church stands "within the world witnessing to the peaceable kingdom." Hauerwas continues, "The gospel is political. Christians are engaged in politics, a politics of the kingdom." God's politics are those of authentic justice—not causes, power, and control—and find their "true source in power of servanthood rather than domination."[86] Roy, a graduate of Duke Divinity School, is deeply influenced by this theology and has shaped Cornerstone in it.

At Cornerstone, doing justice means that, as members frequently say, "we are the hands and feet of Christ" who embody the virtues of the servant community in the world. They embrace the Methodist ideal of "social holiness," that "God does have something to say about the way we treat the world, our neighbors, those different from ourselves, nations, our environment, and our ruling authorities."[87] Acts of justice may well be hard, and sometimes hard to talk about, but the congregation is busy trying. For them, doing justice means being a faithful church. Thinking their congregation should be more welcoming, more diverse, they hired a Haitian minister and have started a new worship service for refugees and immigrants. They recognize the vast injustice in their community, unimaginable wealth existing alongside the squalor of migrant-worker poverty. They initiated the Amos Center, an institute "to restore a prophetic and broad moral vision into the body politic," to train clergy and address the issue of poverty in southwest Florida. As one woman at Cornerstone told me, "We are to help to fight injustice in any way that we can."

*   *   *

Seattle is about as far away from Naples as you can get and still be in the mainland United States. Yet, more than three thousand miles from Cornerstone the people of Phinney Ridge Lutheran Church also understand the connection between Christian spirituality and social justice. Sitting high on a ridge above the city, the church has commanding views of both the Olympic and Cascade mountains. On a clear day, you almost feel like you are floating. "It's kind of symbolic," says Susan, a member of the church. "We're up on a hill."

The symbolism may be even more powerful than Susan suspects. The idea of the church as a "city upon a hill" is an ancient American ideal. Aboard the ship that had carried Massachusetts Bay colonists to the New World, before even setting foot on land, Puritan governor John Winthrop preached a sermon, "A Model of Christian Charity," that laid out a religious vision for the settlers. God had called New England to be a model Christian society, he said, one shaped by justice, compassion, and charity. The test of American faithfulness would not be purity of doctrine; rather, God—and the world—would judge the colonists on the basis of how they cared for one another. "There are two rules whereby we are to walk one towards another," stated Winthrop, "Justice and Mercy."

Winthrop reminded the settlers that, in the early church, believers shared everything in common, remitted debt, freed the oppressed, gave bread to the hungry, and clothed the naked. This, he claimed, was the way of justice as evidenced by love. And he equally insisted that if the settlers failed, God would withhold blessing their land. "Now the only way to avoid this shipwreck and to provide for our posterity," he advised, "is to follow the counsel of Micah, to do justly, love mercy, and walk humbly with our God." Justice would be the church's primary witness to the world: "For we must consider that we shall be as a city upon a hill. The eyes of all people are upon us."

Governor Winthrop linked entry into the new land, the beginning of a new life, to the biblical practice of justice. So, too, Phinney Ridge

Lutheran links entry to the Christian life, the beginning of a new way of life in baptism, to doing justice. Like Cornerstone in Florida, they have a year-long newcomer process, something they call The WAY, that emphasizes four disciplines: worship, prayer, scripture reflection, and ministry in the world. The last few weeks of The WAY, ministry in the world, "provide time to reflect on what the Christian calling means in everyday life." As pastor Paul Hoffman says, "If we are really new beings in a new life in Christ, how exactly do we live that out?"

Occasionally, the answer to that question has surprised Paul Hoffman. He recalls a tense time, a few years ago, when the church was asked to host a Tent City for the homeless. People worried that inviting the homeless to live on the church's front yard would split the congregation. "We held congregational deliberative meetings," he says. "As a staff, we were prepared for people to say, 'If you bring Tent City to this congregation, we will leave; we will have to find someplace else to worship'." He laughs. "We were ready to hear that and we were ready to respond in ways that I think were pastoral, faithful, and appropriate." But, he says, the church staff was not prepared for what happened: "We weren't prepared for the newly baptized to say, If you don't bring Tent City to live on our front lawn, we're afraid we won't be able to stay with this congregation. Because on our way into the baptismal waters, you told us that we would be washed to serve the world and if we can't do that in this place, then we believe God will call us to another place where that is possible." The newcomers insisted the church be, as Susan recalls, "a spiritual community that actually walks the walk." Needless to say, they hosted the tent city. The experience changed the way the congregation practices justice.

Setting up a tent city on the church's front lawn marks a change for mainline congregations in the practice of "Christian charity." When I was a girl, Christian charity typically meant sending money to the poor, taking care of people's needs at a distance. We thought of the church as a kind of United Way with prayer. On some occasions, when the denomination reminded us, practicing justice meant contributing to the national church offices in Washington, D.C., in support of some political policy. The most committed people in a congregation might attend a protest rally (but they probably would not tell the rest of the congregation about it). These were worthy endeavors, but everything happened far away from the congregation. Essentially, we practiced charity and justice by paying professionals, who often took largely secular political approaches to social concerns, to do it for us.

Throughout my journey with emerging mainline congregations, I encountered people doing justice that involved hands-on service, linking social concerns and spirituality in local mission and activism. At Phinney Ridge, the emphasis is obvious—posters throughout the building invite people to enact justice in a variety of ways, from supporting the poor to participating in interfaith activities. Susan explains the difference between the older mainline approach and Phinney Ridge's commitment to doing justice: "Our church is very progressive, but it is progressive in the best ways, not just politically. When we say we're going to help people, we're going to follow what the Bible tells us to do. We just do it and we go out there." Susan and other members of Phinney Ridge talk about "connecting" people "within" with people "outside," and about "connecting" faith with the larger community.

In post-Christian Seattle, where 80 percent of the population claims no religious affiliation, attendance has risen in recent years at Phinney Ridge. "People are looking for a place that will enable and encourage meaningful service in the community," says Paul Hoffman, "a way to live out the faith that they hope to espouse." Evidence of that is everywhere in the congregation. On a warm Easter Sunday, people start arriving at the church at 8:00 A.M. Some wear dress clothes, a few wear shorts. A young couple, with Starbucks cups in hand, enter the sanctuary and sit down in a pew. They listen to the organ and begin to hum the tunes of the old Lutheran hymns. People gather around, and they introduce their friends. One woman in her twenties smiles broadly and says, "This is the best place in Seattle!" Little do they know that they also are, to use John Winthrop's ancient phrase, a model of Christian charity.

*   *   *

"As the door clanged shut," recalls the Reverend Lillian Daniel, "suddenly I could only see light through a tiny window that was barred." Arrested at a protest in support of locked-out health care workers, Lillian was in jail. "If there's one thing the earthy call and hospital visits give you," she says of one of the minister's main tasks, "it's a fierce respect for health care workers and a sense of shame at how our society treats them."

Police arrested four clergy that day as "hundreds of locked out, striking workers gathered in the Connecticut capitol building and sang 'Amazing Grace.'" They put her in a paddy wagon by herself, "surrounded by trash and the smell of vomit." Lillian did not mind going to jail. She expected that. She did not, however, expect that so few of her clergy colleagues would risk themselves for the sake of justice. She confesses to a "moment of self-indulgent bitterness" as they drove her to the prison. "I wondered," she says, "how the church of Jesus could produce so many ministers willing to fall on their swords over issues of sexuality, but unwilling to notice the demonic gap between the rich and the poor."[88]

Lillian also confesses that she acted before thinking. "I was angry at myself. I had failed to warn my church members of my actions." Indeed, some people at Redeemer were offended by the idea that their minister had been arrested in a labor strike. Ethan, an active lay leader, recalls, "During the strike, there was division almost down the center of the church with people who worked on both sides of the union issue." After the pastor was bailed out of jail, Madeline, the church's moderator, called a congregational meeting to discuss the situation. Redeemer held such meetings regarding the war in Iraq but, Ethan says, "this one was tougher." People said what they wanted to say, and some were very angry, but, as one participant said, "There was no effort on the leadership's part to come away with any one consensus that the church had to follow." After airing the emotions that had been simmering under the surface, "almost to the person, they felt better about it." Ethan explains,

"We knew that we were a church that could disagree and still hold each other up in the arms of Christian fellowship. That was a powerful moment in our history. That was a remarkable thing."

Ethan, who came to Redeemer a few years ago seeking "authentic community," participates in Elm City Congregations Organized (ECCO), an interdenominational group, "a rainbow of people who work for positive change in the New Haven area" that forms churchgoers as "disciples in public life." Begun by Pedro Curbelo, a retired industrial engineer, and his Roman Catholic parish, Saint Rose of Lima, ECCO now comprises nineteen congregations in New Haven—including Redeemer.

One Sunday afternoon, Ethan, Madeline, and her husband, Aaron—all active in ECCO—drove me around to explain Church of the Redeemer's public ministry work. When we began the drive, I thought it would be a short trip highlighting the tourist sites of this historic university town. Instead, they took me on a social justice tour of New Haven. For more than two hours, they showed me neighborhoods reclaimed from drug lords, told me about the growing immigrant communities, and recounted the history of the civil rights movement in New Haven. Aaron proudly pointed out ECCO housing projects—including the massive site of a $2.5 million, five-hundred-house restoration and new home construction project. They also shared with me their experience of being in reconciliation groups through ECCO, small groups that met to form friendships and learn from each other across racial and class lines. They regaled me with stories of their own spiritual lives, the things they have learned from serving the poor and seeking justice.

In the process, I saw New Haven through their eyes. The city was no longer just a university town but rather a complex interweaving of cultures, classes, and race, a microcosm of twenty-first-century America. And, the most surprising thing was how much they loved it—they loved the place, they loved the people, they loved its past and its possible futures. As I listened to them, I began to realize that they saw New Haven through the eyes of faith, and I suspected that God saw the city in much the same way. By the time they dropped me off at the train station, they had convinced me that the Christians in New Haven, like their Puritan forebears, are seeking to build God's "city upon the hill."

That afternoon only provided a small glimpse, however, into Church of the Redeemer's commitment to social justice. Lou, Lillian's husband, who is also a labor organizer, was the first member of Redeemer to tell me about Doc Edmonds, the retired pastor of Dixwell Congregational Church, and a hero of the civil rights movement. Doc now attends Redeemer. Like Lillian, Doc participated in the New Haven labor strikes. But, as Lou recalls, "When the police reached Doc, they refused to arrest him. I remember Doc fighting, really angry, demanding to be taken down to jail with the other protesters." Lou credits Doc with teaching him about the "liberator God," who "challenges us to engage in struggle [and] fight for God's kingdom of justice and peace."

Just as at Cornerstone, the civil rights movement provides Redeemer's members with a powerful vision of justice that is political and spiritual. People also credit Doc Edmonds with "long spiritual coattails," saying that his vision has proved compelling in transforming Redeemer. "He's just amazing," says Kurt Mounsma. "When he talks about Martin Luther King, social justice, and God's kingdom, all the little kids gather around just spellbound." Doc's stories of the past, and their "synergy," as Kurt says, with Lillian's passions, are paving the way to the congregation's future.

According to the Reverend Sam Dexter, Lillian's associate, Redeemer has always been "a socially prominent and active kind of church," but it no longer has an "old-fashioned understanding of itself as a civic church." Once, a certain style of public involvement was an expected part of New England Protestantism, but Sam insists that has changed and a "new-fashioned activism" has taken its place. That new-fashioned activism melds historic Protestant civic faith, the African-American experience of justice based in the Bible and prayer, and the spiritual longings of a pilgrim generation. "I think people are interested in their own individual journey and they see their work in the community as an extension," Sam explains. "They're not doing it out of a sense of civic responsibility, although they might have civic responsibility. They are doing it out of a desire to be changed by it, and have a more meaningful life, and be rewarded by the things they do." At Redeemer, this is linked with worship and scripture. Sam says the congregation now understands that "faith is something you do all week, and not just on Sunday." Being a Christian means being in the world—and working for justice.

Kurt, an active lay member of Redeemer, grew up in a church he describes as "confessional and conservative," what he calls "the Big C's." For him the most powerful aspect of Redeemer is the link between "the social vision and the theological vision," which ties his own journey to the struggle for God's justice in the world. He says that in his childhood church:

> *Life on earth doesn't really matter so you don't have to worry about the earth, you don't have to worry about people living in slums, you don't have to worry about anything as long as you support missionaries. As long as you've sent people out to preach the word, you'll be okay.*

He sighs, mixed emotions visible on his face. He says that he and his wife are now "these progressive individuals and people of faith," something he once thought impossible. "But Church of the Redeemer has opened me up to seeing the world and the role of faith in the world very differently, and I think I'm much more liberated in an enabling sort of way." I ask if he is happy for the journey. He says definitively, "Yes. Very happy."

At the new congregation of Santa María in Falls Church, Virginia, one woman told me of her vision for the church: "Since we belong to the Latino community, I want to see people who can help and help is in lessons. English, computer, anything." The man sitting next to her agrees, "How can we help people? Give more opportunities, like language and computers. This is the point of church, to help the community." Another woman chimes in, "Also our goal is to create some activities for teenagers and for other kids because as Spanish people we like to work too much and we sometimes forget about our children. We do not want the kids to be in the streets or in gangs or other things."

They share their excitement about their congregation, being a new mission, having their "first home" in America. Throughout, there is talk of justice—something that grows naturally from their experience of being immigrants. "We are Latinos," one man tells me. "Many of us don't qualify for the salary that people from other churches have. You know, this is America. Money talks. But we help our own. We're fighters." At Santa María, justice is not celebrated in special services and acts of political protest. Rather, daily acts of justice—from selling sandwiches to pay the church's bills, to contributing to one another's down payments on homes, to repairing the church kitchen—frame their lives. Listening to them, I think, *It is hard to live justly in a society that treats them so unfairly.*

Just when I am tempted to romanticize the plight of the poor, however, one woman calls me back to reality. "I just want to say that after I came here I felt that my life is changing," she confesses. "I feel more compassion for others. Before, I saw people in the same way. Everybody was the same to me." As a younger woman, she explains, she held others, especially people who were successful or wealthy, in contempt because she felt like such an outcast. She did not really care about others. "I came here and I felt compassion. I love the elderly, children, and I think the church is doing it. God is doing it."

Compassion enacted. Back at Redeemer, Roberta, an African-American woman, told me, "It is love. And that is radical." A senior member of the congregation nodded in agreement, "Church isn't comfortable anymore. We have to reach out." I thought of Jesus. "He looked at the crowds and had compassion on them." Seeing with compassion led to healings, forgiveness, acceptance, and forming a new community. Mercy is the beginning of justice, the first footsteps toward God's kingdom. No wonder African-Americans refer to justice as a spiritual journey—"we're going to the promised land." From this angle, justice is more than a noun, a place we go or a reward we get. Listening to these voices, I have learned that justice is also a verb, something we do to get there—the acts of envisioning, marching to, and embodying—the promised land. Justice is not a program, a political platform, or a denominational position on social issues. No, justice is the pilgrimage of the beloved community, "the journey toward the establishment of the Kingdom of God."[89]

TWELVE

Worship

EXPERIENCING GOD

Scottsdale Congregational United Church of Christ is a low-slung block structure framed with large overhangs and covered walkways that screen the relentless Arizona sun. Like so many mid-twentieth-century Scottsdale buildings, the church blends into its surroundings with muted earth tones and desert landscaping. Founded in 1959, the church is a western version of its parental New England Congregationalism, the tradition that stretches back to the Puritans. Indeed, from the outside, the building is as spiritually spare as its white clapboard ancestors back east—simple and austere.

Those early New England buildings served as meeting houses for spiritual refugees escaping the cold formality of the established English church—the structures were sanctuaries of communal grace in a hostile world. Puritan settlers often described them in nautical terms, as safe havens or harbors—and sometimes even built them to resemble ships. At Scottsdale, perhaps surprisingly, the aquatic vision remains, although here the church is not a ship. Rather, it is an oasis in the desert.

Oases are strange things. Sometimes they are nothing but mirages. Only when you reach an oasis can you discover what is really there. Scottsdale Congregational is much the same way. Inside, against the simple template of white walls and tan blocks, the church explodes with color, texture, and sound. Artwork decorates the walls. There are hangings, table covers, and multicolored candles. A large cross is mounted to the wall behind the communion table, and two contemporary stained-glass windows of the burning bush frame that cross. To the left and right of the platform, large screens project film clips. On this day, as the congregation enters, the video is that of a mountain stream and waterfalls. A jazz band plays the kind of cool improvisational music that is usually associated with a coffeehouse or a wine bar. A skilled saxophonist lays down his instrument and begins singing, "Jesus in the house, in the house, in the house. Jesus in the house." The congregation joins the refrain. Icons flash on the screens beyond the band. This is not my parents' mainline religion.

As at Redeemer UCC back in Connecticut, the people at Scottsdale testify. But here, testimonies often take the form of question-and-answer sessions with the pastor, Eric Elnes. A woman comes forward and Eric asks her to share her spiritual journey. She talks about growing up in a particularly rigid form of fundamentalism and, eventually, finding the presence of a loving God at Scottsdale Congregational. Next, Terry, a middle-aged man wearing a black shirt and with a large cross hanging around his neck, rises. Eric tells the congregation that Terry grew up in a mainline church. They make a few jokes about fundamentalism. He asks Terry, "Would things be great if everyone joined mainline churches?"

Terry laughs. Although he faithfully attended church as a teenager, he confesses, "I found bumps in mainline denominations. I was bored. My heart was always in worship, but it didn't seem like worship or God could get in my heart." Mainline churches were cold. So Terry found his way to a fundamentalist church. Eventually, however, he discovered that despite their lively worship, he could not truly be himself there. His search for a vital worshiping community that was also open and thoughtful led him to Scottsdale Congregational. Here, he assures those gathered, "I could connect my inner life and my outer life."

It was not so long ago, however, that Scottsdale Congregational fit Terry's description of a boring mainline church. As a teenager, I lived down the street from this church. My best friend, who is now an ordained minister, struggled as a high school student to maintain a vital spiritual life there. Evidently, she was not alone. For a generation, Scottsdale Congregational had trouble holding on to its young people. When Eric Elnes arrived in 1995, he tackled the problem by creating something he called the World's Most Dangerous Bible Study (WMDBS). WMDBS intermixes rock music with scripture reading; the teenagers loved it and responded by getting more involved in church. "Yet despite our youths' newfound enthusiasm for seemingly everything having to do with church," Eric recalls, "there was one place they absolutely would not go. Worship. They avoided worship like you or I would stay clear of nuclear reactor meltdown."[90]

This realization led Eric into a period of introspection about the nature of worship. During one summer study-leave at a lakeside cabin on the Oregon coast, he sat on the dock thinking about the question "What is the basis of worship?" As he stared at the water, the largest bass he had ever seen swam past, leaving the water rippling in its wake. "I stood up," Eric said, "and gasped as a sense of awe and wonder provoked a surge of adrenaline through my body."

A moment later, Eric had an insight about worship. "This is the foundation of worship. If you can take an hour on Sunday morning and open people to experiencing just a quarter-second of awe, wonder, and surrender you just experienced, it is accomplished." Although the early Puritans based their faith on a sense of divine wonder, Congregationalists have long since abandoned religious experience in favor of more sedate, intellectual approaches to faith. Opening people to experiencing God? Eric could not imagine how to do this without manipulating people or "tugging people's emotions and pretending it is a God-experience."

Back in Scottsdale, with guidance from his congregational leaders, Eric realized that the object of worship "is not to *create* anything." Rather, he says, "the goal is simply to invite people into a sense of openness and attentiveness akin to sitting at the edge of that dock in Oregon. You never know whether or not a bass will swim by, but if one does, you want to be ready for it." Although Eric is an intellectual (he holds a Ph.D. from Princeton in Hebrew Bible), the church began an alternative service "centered more around experience than message." Instead of creating a "churchy" experience, Scottsdale takes the material of everyday life—art, music, film, and reflection—and assumes that it is the entryway to the sacred. Combining elements of jazz, performance art, film clips and video, multimedia reflection, live-camera feed, testimony, readings, silence, contemplative prayer, and journaling, they christened this service The Studio.

The teenagers loved it. So did the unchurched people who found their way to the congregation. In the five years since The Studio began, the church has grown by a third. And, perhaps surprisingly, folks who attended the "traditional" service loved it, too. Eric is uncomfortable with the division between traditional and contemporary worship that rips apart so many mainline congregations. So, instead of jettisoning traditional worship, he and the worship team applied the principles of experiential worship from The Studio to the other service. Instead of jazz, however, they opened the congregation to experience through classical music, and also wove art, multimedia, and contemplative prayer into the traditional structure. Eric says that it is fast becoming as experiential "in its 'traditional' format as The Studio is in its more 'contemporary' form."

The people at Scottsdale are excited by the changes. Eric has noticed that "by bringing everyday life into worship and centering worship around experiencing God in our lives, the effect is that Spirit ultimately takes on flesh and blood, much like a sculptor's armature is ultimately covered in clay." Bill Davis, a church member for forty-five years, says, "It's a lot different from the old service that I used to know. I still go to the traditional service, but this service has a better appeal.... It has done a lot for the church."[91] Others agree. As one thirty-something mother says, "My husband and I used to come just for the sake of our kids. Now we come for us." And Terry? Well, he is never bored now. As Eric says, "Truly, worship has changed everything at Scottsdale Congregational."

As I think back on my journey through the emerging mainline, I recall how many times I saw the ripples on the lake, how many quarter-seconds of awe and wonder God sent my way. In every congregation I visited, from simple silence to exquisite music, from improvisational to elaborate ritual, I experienced the Spirit and I felt God. Perhaps more than anything else, the expressiveness, the emotive quality of mainline worship surprised me. I certainly expected the new mainline to be good at practices like hospitality, diversity, and justice. But the practice of worship? I never really expected them to be skilled at opening people's souls to transcendent experiences of God.

In the 1970s, while my best friend valiantly struggled with boring mainline religion at Scottsdale Congregational, I left my Methodist church in favor of a lively evangelical congregation. There, former mainline Protestants ridiculed their old churches as God's "frozen chosen" and congratulated themselves on having found a new church where faith was vital, exciting, and transforming. When I first heard the label *frozen chosen*, I thought that it perfectly summed up my childhood experience of Christianity. After discovering the heartfelt faith in my new evangelical congregation, I was always trying to drag my girlfriend to the church. She came occasionally, humoring me in her gracious way, but she remained loyal to her childhood church. I could not figure out how she could grow in faith in such uptight and chilly surroundings.

In recent years, however, it appears that some mainline churches have been thawing out. And, as with Scottsdale Congregational, worship is changing mainline congregations. For much of the history of American Protestantism, worship primarily meant going to church to hear a sermon.

Author Anthony Robinson, who is also a UCC minister, refers to this as a "head-first" experience. He says that

> *Our historic respect for the mind and the intellect is a strength and a virtue. But like all virtues, when pushed too far or too single-mindedly, it becomes a vice. Worship becomes arid, abstract, and disembodied. For the Hebrews, the heart was the center of the human being. It represented not only the emotions but the whole person—intellect, emotions, will, and senses.*

Worship, Robinson concludes, needs to be an "experience *of* God," rather than a "reflection *about* God."[92] In the congregations in my study, mainline worship had moved eighteen inches: from the head to the heart.

Around 1700, when Protestantism was in its fourth or fifth generation, the once-lively movement to reform Christianity became ossified under the weight of rationalism. Although the first Protestants had ridiculed medieval Roman Catholicism as "dry" and "scholastic" and urged Christians to experience God's saving power for themselves, by the 1700s Protestant fervor had all but vanished. In this arid climate, revival preachers like George Whitefield urged their flocks to get "born again," to have an experience of God in prayer and worship that would change their hearts. These revivalists assailed traditional Protestant worship practices as sterile and deadening. By 1740 their "religion of the heart" had become a movement called evangelicalism that swept through the English Protestant world. The new evangelicalism echoed the impulses of early New England Puritanism and took hold of the young nation's soul. As a result, much of American Protestantism was shaped by the ideals of devotional piety and experiential faith. In many denominations, worship was the place where people encountered God.

Heart religion is, however, very hard to maintain across the centuries. The encounter with God is always set in the frames of human culture. What proved meaningful, transcendent, and life-transforming to one generation may leave the next generation cold. Although God may be the same, human beings experience God differently through time, opening up styles of worship and liturgy that vary wildly through the centuries. When any one form becomes codified, a kind of chilling effect sets in. "That's the way we've always done it," say the founders to their children. "If it worked for us, it will surely work for you." In the process, once-vibrant worship becomes stilted and, very often, becomes increasingly a matter of the head (beliefs about God) rather than the heart (experiences of God). Once this pattern sets in, it can be difficult to change.

Among emerging mainline congregations, I met people who used the language of feeling, experience, and mystery to talk about worship. I cannot recall how many times I heard comments like those of Paula, at Epiphany in Washington: "The way everything is put together allows me to sit and be closer to God. I come and I really feel it. I feel God when I walk into church and I part. The liturgy's wonderful; the hymns we sing. It's amazing. Sometimes we just sit here, together, and we all just smile because it feels so good." And I heard often about experiences like that described by Marge, a lifelong churchgoer in her sixties, "When I left worship at Scottsdale Congregational the first time, I felt happy. I never knew that church could make you feel happy."

At its core, worship is an experience that transforms the heart. But it is not just any experience. For Christian pilgrims, worship celebrates the life, teaching, and acts of Jesus. The *Oxford English Dictionary* defines "celebrate" (a verb—something people do) as to "commemorate an event with ceremonies or festivities." Christian worship, though graced with appropriate reverence, need not be solemn. Instead, Christian worship embodies the full range of emotions any person would experience in celebration, from sorrow to mirth. As such, Christian celebration is merriment, as in "to make merry," because it participates in God's festival of life and *shalom*.

The English writer C. S. Lewis referred to this as the "great dance," wherein justice and mercy clasp hands, and the universe moves in rhythm to God's intention for creation. Worship is right harmony, all sounds of discord gone, all injustice banished. Every act of worship, no matter how private or public, how discreet or elaborate, enacts God's dream for the world. By learning to look for it, by opening ourselves to sensing the awe and wonder of the dance, we might glimpse the ripples of God. Worship is much more than something Christians attend on Sunday morning—it is something pilgrims make together. By making it, we join in the dance. This is what Christians mean when they refer to "mystery," seeing that which lies beyond human knowledge to the passions and purpose of creation.

The theologian R. Kevin Seasoltz has written:

> *The experience of God's mystery is discovered above all when we are conscious of God's presence and have centered our lives on God. That experience flourishes in a climate of hospitality, of welcome, in which people are present to one another as the body-persons they are, as members of the body of Christ, comfortable with one another, gathered together with one another.... An attractive beauty in all that is said and done, used or observed is the best way to facilitate the experience of mystery, for God is not only goodness and truth; God is also beauty. We should be able to sense a transcendent reality in everything that is seen, heard, touched and smelled in the celebration.*[93]

Hospitality, beauty, celebration. Awe, wonder, mystery. Communities making merry. For too long, mainline Protestants equated worship with thinking about God. Now, in at least some places, their hearts—the whole capacity of being human—are learning to experience God.

New Testament scholar Marcus Borg states that faith is the "way of the heart," the act of "beloving" God, of giving one's whole self to God.[94] When I read this, I always think of the Christian Middle Ages, the great age of faith, a time in which the universe seemed enchanted, when the natural and supernatural joined together in the dance. Before the heart and mind were severed by modern dichotomies, beloving God made more sense. Such a vision is not just the product of my overactive historical imagination. Scholars actually refer to the older world as an "enchanted universe," and argue that the Enlightenment and the scientific revolution whittled away the sense of the supernatural in the West. Beloving God devolved into believing things about God. Is it possible to *reenchant* the universe? Can we move back to a holistic way of apprehending God? Can we heal what has been torn? Can we belove God?

On Palm Sunday in 2005, I stood in the light-filled entry portico of Saint Mark Lutheran Church in Yorktown, Virginia. The congregation mills around the breakfast tables and the courtyard fountain, waiting for the service to begin. They hug one another, laugh, and talk; they busily chase toddlers and share local news. The people of Saint Mark's are delightful—friendly and kind—the sort of middle-class people who inhabit most American suburbs. Ushers hand out palms and bulletins to the waiting crowd. The service is about to begin.

Pastor Gary Erdos, dressed in elaborate white and gold vestments, gathers the congregation. He raises his palm branch high, and the sense of expectation grows. Children stand on tiptoes or peer around their parents' legs to watch. Acolytes stand on either side of Gary, holding their candles as he chants the liturgy. A young man waves incense as Gary blesses the palms. They sing the ancient Christian song "All Glory, Laud, and Honor" as they process into the church.

Such ritual may not be uncommon for Roman Catholics, Eastern Orthodox Christians, or even Episcopalians, but it is not the norm for Lutherans. Until Gary arrived at Saint Mark, the church practiced "middle of the road, low Lutheran worship," and would have been considered a "pretty ordinary mainline church." But Gary's liturgical sense is not that of the "ordinary mainline." He is deeply schooled in medieval spirituality and shaped by liturgical renewal in his denomination. Passionate about worship, Gary believes that the Eucharist, the celebration of the Lord's Supper, is central to the Christian pilgrimage. In his first months at Saint Mark, he instituted weekly communion at all Sunday services.

Gathering around God's table, he insists, "is at the heart of what we do—of who we are." And, from that heart, people are finding a deeper sense of spirituality and new connections with one another and God.

Parishioners appreciate the new style, with its incense, vestments, weekly communion, and close attention to liturgy, as important to their deepened sense of God's presence in their lives. They experience holy drama, a sense of participating in a story larger than themselves. June, a longtime member, says, "Our services are meaningful and uplifting." Pam and Jack, a married couple, tell me they are pleased that Gary does not "dumb down" the worship. "We appreciate the return to tradition." One man recognizes that "We've moved toward the Anglican/Catholic side of Lutheranism. It was strange at first, but now I love it." Many people said they joined Saint Mark because of the worship, citing the beauty of the liturgy, the meaningful music, and their conviction that "God speaks through the sermon." In the last seven years, the church has doubled in size. Worship has changed their church. But more important, the people understand the link between worship and life; worship is changing them. As we waited in the courtyard that Palm Sunday, a senior member told me, "We used to be snake-belly-low Lutheran." Incense wafts through the courtyard. She laughs. "We're not that anymore."

Through Saint Mark's distinctly high-church Lutheranism, with its mystical and experiential forms of liturgy, the congregation is rediscovering tradition. There is no PowerPoint or multimedia here. Nothing improvisational. Only banners, candles, robes, crosses, processions, and incense. Here, they are reclaiming the territory of the heart through tradition. Ancient prayers. Lutheran music. "What if those ancient mystics were right," asks Gary rhetorically, "and this style of prayer really does move our soul? What are we to do? Make a generational decision about whose music is better?" He laughs. "Instead, we went back to something even older." In the last five years, they have redesigned the worship space to communicate the power of ancient faith for today. "The joke is that we don't use Latin or German," Gary says. "So, this is contemporary!"

Into this fabric of the past, Gary weaves the word of the sermons.

He stands in front of the congregation (not behind a pulpit) and unpacks scripture. His sermons are masterworks of mainline preaching, thoughtful and well crafted. But they are also exceedingly spiritual and practical. I have listened to Gary preach more than a dozen times, and I am not sure how he does it. Perhaps because of his deep attachment to prayer, the words of his sermons actually become gateways to experience God. To use Anthony Robinson's phrase, Gary does not preach *about* God but preaches *of* God.

The core of Saint Mark's recovery of ancient Christianity is the practice of Ignatian spirituality, a form of prayer developed in the sixteenth century by Saint Ignatius of Loyola. When Gary graduated from seminary, he went on a thirty-day Ignatian retreat, an intensive process of scripture reading, discernment, prayer, and spiritual direction. "Those thirty days," he recalls, "have sustained my entire ministry. I always wanted to serve a church where I could share that with the congregation." At Saint Mark, Gary formed an Ignatian spirituality group. June was part of that group. "I finally began to articulate my faith," she says. "I learned to communicate with God; I learned talking with God. God was really present." For her, and for the others involved, Ignatian prayer opened an experience of God that served as the "seedbed" of congregational change and vitality. "The biggest change," she tells me, "is from being content and complacent about faith to being all that we can be to the glory of God."

At Saint Mark, tradition opens the way for experiencing God in the heart. They heeded the advice of Lutheran theologian Gordon Lathrop, who suggests that "We only impoverish ourselves if we forget that ancient symbols, such as the language and actions that have originally filled the meetings of all the churches, are among the richest resources to us in our need." In Yorktown, behind a used-car dealership in an industrial-looking building, these Lutherans are creating what theologian Robert Webber once referred to as an ancient-future church. There, they are taking ordinary things—making music and eating a meal—and weaving new patterns of faithfulness. They both receive and reinterpret tradition, allowing for "deeper participation of heart and mind."[95] By linking the past to their hopes for the future, they are reenchanting their universe.

For more than thirty years, mainline Protestants have fought bitterly about worship. Typically, the argument is about the use of "contemporary" versus "traditional" music, art, and liturgy in church. Yet, as I journeyed through the mainline, I observed that the particular style of music did not necessarily matter to congregational vitality. Some churches, like Scottsdale UCC, worshiped in jazz and contemporary idioms; others, like Saint Mark, used traditional music. And still other congregations, like Goleta Presbyterian Church near Santa Barbara, blended styles, borrowing from three or four kinds of music and liturgy in a single service. I have witnessed mainline Latinos singing hymns set to the tunes of 1960s folk music; white Episcopalians making music in African drumming circles; Presbyterians performing Broadway show tunes; Congregationalists playing medieval recorder music; Lutherans singing Latin chants; Methodists rocking to their own locally written praise songs; African-American Episcopalians sitting in silence to Bach.

In mainline churches across the country, I listened to music from a dizzying number of traditions: African, Caribbean, Native American, African-American, classical European, Celtic, jazz, southern folk, gospel, American country, contemplative chant, rock and roll, techno-pop, and even rap. I sang old hymns and new ones, standby praise songs and Taize chants. Songs in Spanish and English, French and Latin. I even struggled to learn a couple in Swahili. People played organ, piano, guitar, brass, violins, drums, lutes, mandolins, lyres, fiddles, flutes, and harps. Once, I stood with a congregation while we created a tune by humming. After a while, it all blended together for me—creating a symphony of mainline spirituality in my memory. I realized that the kind of music and art did not matter in worship. Rather, innovation and experimentation mattered. New music or old music in new ways—people making music everywhere, playing and celebrating God in their midst. All the people

I met and worshiped with linked music and art to spirituality, a way of opening the heart to God.[96]

On a warm June evening, I participated in prayer service with a group of Episcopalians in Virginia. They came from various churches, yet we did not meet in a church. Rather, we met in a conference room at a seminary. The chairs in the room were arranged in the shape of a Celtic cross, four rows intersecting with a circle. Small votive candles marked the aisles between the straight rows. At the center of the circle, several dozen pillar candles resembled an indoor campfire. As I entered, a gentle chant was being played from a CD. "What is God calling you to?" asked the leader, who sat off to the side of the room in the last chair in one of the rows. We read scripture and poetry, reflecting together as a group and in pairs, and we prayed for both ourselves and justice in the world. We learned a new song. During the last part of the service, the leader passed out cardboard boxes. We placed them on our knees and we learned how to drum, in what he called the "Afro-Celt" way. We drummed. Single-handed, two-handed, rolling our fingers, making different patterns with our left and right hands. We drummed and drummed. We added humming and musical shouts. Someone picked up a tambourine and maracas. "Music," he shouted, "we are God's music!" We moved all the chairs to the side of the room and danced around the candles in the center. People were smiling, laughing, and shouting, cheering one another in the dance.

The leader, an English priest named Philip Roderick, calls it "contemplative fire."[97] It has been a long journey from the frozen chosen to a dancing-drumming circle. I call it a miracle. As I shook my tambourine, I thought of other pilgrims on their journeys. Like the pilgrims in the *Canterbury Tales.* Gathering around the evening fire, making music, singing, eating and drinking, telling tales. Making merry. Wanderers, "sundry folk," falling together in good company along the way.

THIRTEEN

Reflection

THINKING THEOLOGICALLY

Now in her midfifties, Lynne Thornton, a member of Church of the Redeemer in Cincinnati, is a child of the old mainline. The niece of an Episcopal bishop, with active Episcopal parents, she grew up in Akron, Ohio, in a lovely, and very proper, church founded by the Firestone tire family. Being an Episcopalian was important to her family—she describes them as "very religious"—but church left her cold. Although she sang in the girls' choir and fulfilled her familial religious obligations, she recalls her childhood church as "something to be gotten through." She says that "church was about going to church or the pretense of going to church." She dropped out as soon as she left home, attending only occasionally after she married and had a daughter.

At about the time she reached her fortieth birthday, Lynne went back to church: "You know, middle age kind of creeping up on you, the fact that the party will be over someday." She liked Redeemer for its excellent liturgy and music—and especially the dynamic preaching of the minister—but confesses that she was still a "disappearing" sort of Christian, a churchgoer who wanted to stay in the background.

Lynne's intuition about her own mortality proved eerily correct. Following complications from emergency surgery, Lynne went into toxic shock and doctors induced a coma in a desperate attempt to save her life. While in the coma, she had three experiences of God in which Jesus appeared and assured her that everything would be "okay." Although the doctors later told her that she had had only a 17 percent chance of survival, Lynne pulled through the crisis. When she awoke, "I realized I had two choices: that I could go on living my life the way I'd been living it, or I could honor the experience of God by finding a different way to live my life."

For a few months Lynne tried to be "some Mother Teresa type," but she struggled with her new commitment to "saving the world." She could not figure out how to be a saint. Finally, she realized that although she had been a Christian her whole life, she did not really know much about God. She decided to join an evening Bible study offered by a young assistant priest at Redeemer. "I was stunned to find out that Episcopal churches had Bible studies," she laughs. "Honestly, I had no clue. That tells you about the spirituality of my upbringing. Bible study wasn't something we did. But I thought that would be a good way to find an entrance."

The young priest opened the door of scripture for Lynne, with his "love of God, the church, and scripture." She remembers his profound acceptance of his own humanity, and his "openness." As she became increasingly fascinated with the Bible and theology, Lynne's hunger to learn became a pathway to God. Admittedly a "head person," Lynne says, "If I could spend the rest of my life learning stuff I would be thrilled." When the church offered an intensive class in theology called Education for Ministry (EFM), Lynne jumped at the chance.

Education for Ministry is a national curriculum offered in many Episcopal churches that is, essentially, a four-year seminary education for laypeople. "I joined it thinking I would find the 'big answer,'" Lynne recalls, "and of course what I found is there is no big answer. There's just lots of questions and, in fact, sometimes you have questions, then you find bigger questions. The first questions don't even matter anymore. They are different questions." Lynne and her fellow students studied the Bible, church history, theology, and ethics, learning the solid content of a theological education in much the same way that ministers are trained. "It was fabulous," she says of learning so much about Christianity. But it was about more than information. "The other thing we did in EFM was a thing called theological reflection."

She explains that it is a "way of reflecting on life. You learn how to think theologically." Each week, the group would examine "an experience someone had had during the week" by using language, metaphor, and insights in scripture, hymns, sermons, poetry, art, or literature. They would look for theological themes—ideas like sin, redemption, mercy, and reconciliation—and connect the themes with their own lives. At its core, theological reflection is a way of seeing the world, of being able to imagine life in relationship to God's story, of linking the intellectual content of faith to its everyday practice. Theological reflection taught her that learning *about* Christianity was not enough; you have to *learn* Christianity. "You do that for four years," Lynne states, "and you just start to look at life differently."

Church of the Redeemer is not an evangelical Protestant church, the kind of place usually associated with intensive Bible study. Yet, as a congregation, Redeemer is deeply schooled in scripture. For more than twenty years, their former minister, the Reverend Dr. Jim Hanisian, emphasized the teaching of scripture and theology. "We did everything," he says. "Hot button issues ethically and morally, the lives of theologians, scripture from soup to nuts. One whole year on the Book of Romans." On Thursday mornings, dozens of people attended his weekly Bible study, arguing with and questioning scripture. One former member recalls, "It was Bible study as I had never experienced it before. It was almost rabbinical; it took years to finish a book." Eventually, every meeting at the church started with an abbreviated form of the Thursday morning Bible study. Across the congregation, Redeemer's people engaged scripture, talked about theology, and argued about faith. This intellectual liveliness became—along with prayer—the spiritual glue that holds them together. Over the years, Redeemer has come to understand itself as a kind of experiential seminary, an intellectual and spiritual training ground for lived Christianity, a school of faith.

Lynne emphasizes that Redeemer's practice of scripture is *"not* a Holy-Roller" sort of thing. Unlike conservative evangelicals who read the Bible literally, seeking out proof-texts for narrow moral or ethical readings of scripture, the Episcopalians at Redeemer approach the Bible "seriously, but not literally."[98] At Redeemer, teaching and Bible study are not concerned with dogma and doctrinal facts; rather, they immerse themselves in the biblical stories, attempting to connect their lives with the text's ancient wisdom. They explore the Bible using the tools of contemporary scholarship, never eschewing difficult questions. Indeed, for them, the questions, along with their arguments, are essential to understanding—not unlike Jewish Talmud scholars bickering over a biblical passage.

As Lynne recounted, the process is not intellectually arid nor does it reduce the Bible to scientific analysis. Rather, Bible study is a practice of thoughtful faithfulness, one that blends Christian commitment with openness. As such, learning moves beyond information and becomes spiritual formation in a way of life, a life, as Lynne had hoped, that nurtures compassion and justice. From this perspective, Bible study emerges as spiritual inquisitiveness, a "pathway" through the mind that transforms the heart. "I just know," Lynne testifies, "that I am a different person than I was before Education for Ministry." And not just Lynne. Bible study changed Church of the Redeemer. Unlike the well-educated but theologically vapid congregation of Lynne's childhood, Redeemer embodies the faithful intellect. Heart and head, spirit and intellect, tradition and questioning—all of a piece.

*   *   *

Many people do not realize that places like Church of the Redeemer exist. William, who was once a Southern Baptist, is now an Episcopalian attending Holy Communion in Memphis, related:

> *What I did not find pleasant about the Southern Baptist Church was that they were so literalist, so fundamentalist. There was only one way to look at scripture. And I didn't like that. That's when I quit going. I thought that no church out there was going to say that there is more than one way to look at things. It took about twenty years after I left to find that there were churches out there that said you don't have to take everything literally.*

Over the course of my study, I heard other testimonies like William's. Most came from former Southern Baptists, former evangelicals, and former Roman Catholics who had felt intellectually constrained in theologically rigid churches. Until they "found" a vital mainline church, they had given up hope that any form of religious faith could also engage their minds.

Unfortunately, church people often pit the mind against the heart. Some simply ignore the mind in favor of experience; others reduce intellectual endeavor to memorizing approved dogma or Bible verses. In many religious circles, the life of the mind is deemed dangerous because of its potential to challenge authority or reject church teachings. Being a "good" Christian, whether Protestant or Catholic, means that asking the wrong sort of question is off-limits. Thus, Christian education is often a closely guarded process—geared to provide approved answers and protect Christians from thinking too hard about complex issues. Many churches encourage thinking—as long as you think like everyone else. As a result, much of American religion has a strangely circumscribed intellectual character, a sort of anti-intellectual intellectualism. A cursory glance at the *New York Times* proves the point. On any given day, it reports on evangelicals in Kansas attacking evolution and insisting that

public schools teach "intelligent design," on Christian parents calling the
Harry Potter books "satanism," or on some preacher urging politicians
to overturn secular law in favor of biblical law.

Strands of American Christianity have long resisted this temptation
to theological narrowness and instead emphasized intellectual openness
as a practice of faith. This tradition of inquiry has generally been called
liberal Protestantism, a theological movement going back to the sixteenth century that emphasizes the free conscience of the individual in
matters of faith against all forms of authoritarianism. Today, the word
liberal is much maligned and misunderstood, mostly defined by politics
and political language. From the perspective of history, however, religious liberalism was an intellectual and spiritual disposition rather than
a specific set of political beliefs.

Several years ago, an English friend gave me an eighteenth-century
print. It depicts a muse crowning a baby with a wreath and the phrase
"Liberality excites genius" emblazoned under the picture. The print is
the eighteenth-century equivalent of a business motivation poster. In the
language of the twenty-first century, the caption might read, "Generosity
fosters creativity" or "Open-mindedness breeds innovation." Once, not
so long ago, *liberal* was a good word meaning generosity and openness. It
implied a host of positive things: reform, freedom, toleration, thoughtful
inquiry, and lack of prejudice and absence of bigotry. In its most classical
sense, liberal meant opposition to dogmatism, authoritarianism, inquisi-
tion, religious bigotry, and theological intolerance. Historically, religious
liberality—theological generosity—sparked much of the energy, passion,
and intellectual liveliness of American Protestantism.

Despite its robust history, Protestant liberalism essentially collapsed
in the mid-twentieth century. After the 1960s, liberal churches began to
lose members and more conservative churches attracted large numbers
of people. Critics blamed the decline on liberalism itself. Too much freedom, too much openness is a bad thing, they argued. People need religious authorities to tell them what to think and how to act. Dozens of
books appeared attacking religious liberalism as a bad thing, detrimental

to true faith. Faithful Christians, their authors suggested, must always submit to traditionalist teachings and church dogma. Liberal churches decline because they are liberal; conservative churches grow because they are conservative. People hunger for order and authority in a confusing world. People need answers.

However, this dictum does not work in the vital congregations on my journey. In these churches, people identified liberality—what I call theological generosity—as one of the most attractive qualities drawing them to the congregation.[99] They rarely used the word *liberal* (fearing, I suspect, that it would be misconstrued; some people had replaced *liberal* with *progressive*), but they consistently praised openness, tolerance, and generosity as marks of mature Christian character.

Everywhere, mainline pilgrims insisted upon the importance of intellectual openness to vital spirituality. A Seattle mother told me that she joined her congregation because "church engaged my brain." A man in another congregation proudly claimed, "Our church has a lively climate of inquiry into faith." In Connecticut, a college student defined faith as intellectual curiosity: "What is faith? Where does faith come from? Tough, important, and vital questions mark pivotal movements when a child listens and learns." In Memphis a woman testified that "one of Elaine Pagels's books fed my brain and reintroduced me to the Gospel of Mark, and also helped me see that the controversy of today is really an age-old debate about orthodoxy." "You know," said an Arizona man, "God didn't ask us to check our intellect in the parking lot when we drove in and the service started."

These mainline pilgrims linked intellectual curiosity with humility, however. For the people I met, thinking theologically did not mean arriving at certain conclusions. One Memphis woman, who was taking a philosophy class at a local college, laughed as she said, "I think there are answers out there. I want the big picture, but I don't think I'm gonna get it!" She thought of church not as providing answers but of opening people to "glimpses" of truth. In Ohio, an Episcopalian said that his church had taught him that "it was okay to question things and there is not always one right answer." The adult education director of one large church talked about "biblical literacy" rather than "biblical literalism." Over and over, people echoed the comment of a person in Memphis who said, "It is okay for people to disagree, not everything is totally clear-cut." Back in Seattle, the same young mother who came to church to engage her brain said, "It is more gray than black and white."

Being liberal in this sense was not the problem. Hundreds of people made comments like this to me—extolling free intellectual inquiry in matters of the spirit and longing for theologically generous communities of faith. They did not want to be part of a congregation that insisted on a single or literal interpretation of the Bible. They worried about movements in their denominations to push their churches toward narrow viewpoints. As I listened to them, realizing that they actually appreciated spiritual liberality, I began to wonder if the problem was that midcentury liberalism had lost its sense of humility, becoming overly institutionalized and politicized, and in the process sacrificed its sense of wonder.

In the early twentieth century, liberal religion became "establishment" religion, with its beliefs and practices dominating pulpits, seminaries, religious studies departments, theological journals, and even the pews. Back then, William would not have had any trouble finding an open congregation. But, as establishment religion, it became politicized, and liberality gave way to liberal*ism*. Until Protestant liberalism was challenged by conservative evangelical religion in the 1970s, it was the only game in town. Humility was not its strong suit. When liberality hardened into hubris, Protestant liberals traded open questions for easy answers—their own. As soon as certainty replaces humility, it leaves little room for the intellect to transport the faithful to awe. It does not much matter if certainty is that of the "left" or the "right." By the 1960s, Protestant liberalism was self-absorbed and secular. Like Lynne Thornton and many others who grew up in that tradition, I found it both cold and spiritually deadening. For a while, I gave up on it, too. A lot of people did.

Perhaps surprisingly, the people I met had rediscovered the humility of spiritual liberality. They stitched new connections of heart and head, creating an entirely new pattern out of the old liberal tradition in their congregations. They had lost all their illusions of religious grandeur. Maybe they had to. After all, evangelical Protestants are the new establishment with all the press, people, and political power. Vital mainline congregations are giving up liberal*ism,* but finding their way back to liberality—that genuine openness which reminds us that in the economy of the universe, we are only human and, despite our marvelous intellectual capabilities, there will always be things we cannot know. In that gap God breathes, and there, we experience awe. In some mysterious way, the sundry folk on my journey managed to create a space for theological generosity in the gap and, in doing so, to catch glimpses of God.

The Christian life of the mind is not, however, merely some disembodied or mystical experience. "What got me excited when I first came [to this church]," said one Florida Methodist, "was that God was very real here, that it wasn't just words. People really, really meant what they were doing." Along with theological generosity, the practice of reflection in the congregations on my journey expressed the active intellect. The people I met clearly loved words and ideas, but they strove to connect words with action, to authenticate words by works of mercy and justice.

Scottsdale is not known as a haven for the intellectual life. Arizona is a physical place where sports and recreation occupy its residents more than philosophical contemplation. Yet, Scottsdale Congregational Church is growing by, as one member said, "making people think." Laura, who began attending five years ago, says, "We are not spoon-fed anything, and you often leave thinking more about what was going on. We are very purposeful in having people examine their faith, their beliefs, what they think, and how we practice it out in life."

Her friend Elise agreed. In making people think, "it brings the message, the Christian message, and makes it real in our life today." She observes that some people in the church remain timid of reading the Bible, but "all the messages are from the Bible" and are "made relevant to pres-ent-day issues." Every week Elise asks herself, "How can I live my faith today in a way that is relevant versus just being stuck in a book?"

Although Elise downplays the use of scripture, Scottsdale Congre-gational is biblically literate, just not biblically literal. Indeed, most of the members appear to be escaping more literalist traditions. Gary, a congregational trustee, talks ably about "trusting not only our hearts but our minds in the integration and use of our intellect." He compares con-servative Protestantism to Jenga, the game in which someone can pull a block and the tower tumbles. "If something was to be proven untrue, then your whole system falls down. If there is a literal thing in the Bible that you believed and it turns out not to be correct, does your faith com-pletely disappear?" he asks rhetorically. "Science actually expanded our faith and it didn't take away from it," he claims. Like Gary, Elise agrees that "science and faith go together" and says, "I look at Christian theol-ogy now more as metaphor. Things in the Bible are more metaphorical than literal."

Elise's literary interpretation of scripture does not, however, dimin-ish its power in her life. Rather, understanding the Bible as metaphor strengthens her faith. As Elise stated, "It is much more exciting because it makes it more relevant to today when you look at things that way." She related how the "Phoenix Affirmations," a faith statement being writ-ten by the congregation, were changing the community. "The Phoenix Affirmations are one of the most exciting things that we have been do-ing over the last few months," she said. "They are the foundation and groundwork of being able to state—in a concrete way—what our theo-logical basis is, why we are Christians, and why we do what we do as Christians." Ron, another member of the church, called it "reclaiming the message of Christianity." They are attempting to describe a kind of Christianity that is "not fundamentalist" to people "who have precon-ceptions about what a church is."

The Phoenix Affirmations are a set of twelve beliefs that articu-late what members call progressive Christianity. Based in scripture, the twelve points elaborate the themes of loving God, loving neighbor, and loving the self. Together, they spell out the theological basis of Protestant liberality: being open and humble, yet grounded in the biblical story of God's dream for humankind. The Affirmations take the form of a pledge whereby members commit themselves to living "the way of Love" in counterdistinction to a Christianity based in fear and violence. But the Affirmations are not just about beliefs; they are also a call to action, with each affirmation beginning with an "-ing" word: walking, listening, celebrating, expressing, engaging, claiming, and caring.

The people at Scottsdale Congregational worry that, in the minds of many (if not most) Americans, the word *Christian* is interchangeable with the word *fundamentalist*. They claim that "the public face of Christianity in America today bears little connection to the historic faith of our ancestors." The Phoenix Affirmations are the congregation's "voice" because "we will be no longer silent." So the Affirmations are more than a creedal statement or a pledge. Members of the congregation are working to turn them into a movement to challenge both the religious right and what they call the secular left. From Easter to Labor Day in 2006, they intend to walk three thousand miles across the United States, preaching and teaching along the way in dozens of congregations. The walk will end at the Lincoln Memorial, where they plan to post the Affirmations on the "nation's front door" as a call for a new Protestant Reformation.

God is not just words—especially not just literal words from the Bible. These pilgrims think about God, in metaphor, story, poetry, and history. They embrace the languages of science and culture but have not succumbed to secularism; they remain distinctly Christian. By connecting God's word and the words of the world, they express their biblical faith in the active intellect. Christian reflection is not done in an ivory tower; it is not the quiet contemplation of the monastery garden. Rather, reflection is the pathway to a life of awe-filled action.

On a lovely Sunday morning in May, a dozen people gather for the pastor's class at Phinney Ridge Lutheran Church in Seattle. They sit at a round table with their Bibles open. At the center of the table, a candle is burning. It smells of incense and serves as a gentle reminder that this is more than a classroom. God is in our midst; we are in sacred study. In addition to their Bibles, most people have three or four theology books stacked at their elbows. The books are highlighted, and several have Post-it notes marking select passages. I recognize the books—they are substantial texts. I have required all of them for college classes I have taught over the years. The topic today is the problem of suffering. A difficult subject at best.

Pastor Paul Hoffman opens with prayer. He talks about the Christian understanding of pain. "The resurrection," he says, "is the crux of the matter. Before the resurrection, Jesus had to die first." Any theological reflection on suffering begins there—and moves backward to the crucifixion.

A woman protests, "It depends on which Christians you're talking about." Faith communities have different interpretations of suffering. "Like evangelicals," she says. "Evangelical Christians have a spin on this subject. They are so certain about God having a plan. There's no mystery to suffering. They know every answer." Others around the table chime in. Not everyone wants to start with the crucifixion. Some say the starting point is compassion, others say forgiveness, one insists on grace. Finally, an older man speaks up. I do not know his story, but people stop and listen to him. "Suffering *must* be part of the deal," he states with a touch of emotion in his voice. "Christ asked for the cup to be taken from him, but it wasn't."

His comment redirects the conversation. A man sitting across the table starts talking about the "nonviolent" life of Christ as the answer to suffering. "We are called to imitate that," he says. "Most Christians don't understand suffering," adds the woman who talked about evangelical spin. "Most seem to think God promises prosperity. That's what the radio evangelists talk about."

As the conversation unfolds, they refer to scripture and theology. I am amazed at how well they know the Bible—and that they ably paraphrase theologians like Martin Luther, Søren Kierkegaard, C. S. Lewis, and Martin Marty. Pastor Hoffman enters the conversation again as he reads from an article in the *Christian Century* about the "ecological understanding of humanity and the earth." He has the group open their Bibles to the Cain and Abel story in Genesis. He teaches them a few words of Hebrew to help them understand the text. This story, he says, shows us that sin is about more than us—more than our need for personal salvation. The Cain and Abel story teaches that sin has disordered the whole of creation; it reveals "the brokenness of the world and the disintegration of nature."

The people are very quiet, listening to their pastor teach from God's word. "We often distill this issue down to why human beings suffer," he says. "But what about the possibility that this is a larger story? A larger issue of suffering, of disorder? What does that mean for us? For understanding God? For our calling in the world?" Clearly, the perspective he offers is new to them. Around the table, several take notes while others seem to be digesting the questions. Suddenly, one woman asks with astonishment, "Are you blaming the tsunami on sin?" He laughs, "Not in the same way Pat Robertson did!" They launch into a vigorous discussion of the relationship between sin, suffering, and natural disasters.

Fifty minutes fly by. Suddenly, Pastor Hoffman looks at his watch. "Sorry," he says. "We have to wrap up today. I've got to get ready for the service." The group looks disappointed. They do not want to stop. As he leaves the room, he assures them that they will pick up next week. A man turns toward me, "Did you enjoy the group?" I reply that it was a really good Bible study. He smiles, saying, "This is the reason I go to this church. I'm a questioner. And Pastor Paul asks great questions. He doesn't always answer them. That's encouraged—asking questions in faith."

His words reminded me of a testimony by Deanna, another member of Phinney Ridge, who had come to faith as an adult. "I was skeptical bordering on cynical," she confessed. "I considered myself a very unlikely candidate for any organized religion, especially Christianity."

But after attending Phinney Ridge for a time, she began to participate in The WAY, the church's process of learning Christianity. There, she said, "I was fed dinner, dessert, words, and scripture." Eventually, she concluded, the people of Phinney Ridge "killed me with kindness and conquered me with love." She wanted to become a Christian.

But one thing nagged at her. She knew that "my so-called intellectual friends will make fun of me if I become a Christian. They might think I've gone back to the dark ages." So, she asked questions. "Here," she recalls, "my questions were allowed and encouraged. . . . I brought more and more questions." Eventually, she decided to be baptized and entered into a Christian faith journey. But she remains a "rebellious Adam" or "doubting Thomas," whose "dogged need to understand and get my questions answered kept me coming back."

Not many churches welcome doubting Thomases. Instead, they discourage questions, offering easy answers *before* people have a chance to seriously engage doubts, the difficult, complex, and conflicting possibilities opened by exploring life's perplexing dilemmas. But the churches I visited were full of questioning Christians. I think about all the congregations I have been to in the last three years—their book groups, Sunday forums, adult education courses, Bible studies, film discussions, guest lectures, and pastor's classes. Groups with names like "Popcorn Theology," "Soul Food," "Rocking Chair Theologians," and "Novel Faith." I remember the people—many of whom had switched to mainline congregations from Southern Baptist or Roman Catholic churches—who shared with me their questions, and their gratitude for open Christianity.

I speak to a lot of clergy groups about spiritual trends and growing churches. Occasionally, someone will comment, "Don't people want answers? Aren't they looking for someone to tell them the truth?" Some people, perhaps. But not the people I met on my journey. Most of those folks were only looking for a place to ask questions, where they can rest comfortably with few answers, learn new questions, and to be accepted by others in faith community. In the emerging mainline, questions—the gap between human knowing and God—are an essential part of the pilgrimage. Intellectual engagement takes pilgrims to the edge of the gap where, unexpectedly, theological reflection melds into the Spirit. At that place, believers glimpse God, and the vision can empower—as it did for Moses when he saw only God's back—acts of faith. Head, heart, hands. Connected and integrated.

It is hard to imagine that the always brainy but often arid mainline could ever make the leap of faith into that gap. Yet, in some places, they appear to be jumping. As one Episcopalian in Memphis told me, "It's not just studying God and the Bible sort of abstractly. It's the whole emphasis to experience God. I think that's a big change for a lot of us." As I write, I stare across my office at the print given to me by my English friend. I remember Lynne and William, the people at places like Scottsdale Congregational and Phinney Ridge Lutheran, the scores of folks who testified to the power of theological openness in their lives. I do not know if liberality excites genius, but it sure seems to excite faith.

FOURTEEN

Beauty

TOUCHING THE DIVINE

My first visit to Redeemer in New Haven was on a very cold day. The chill wind cut through my down coat. The snow was deep, and topped by a thick crust of ice. The starkness of New England's winter impressed me anew. The same quality that haunts the season also marks New England Congregationalism, the region's native Protestantism, that unyielding Puritanism of early America. Especially in deep winter, the white clapboard Congregational churches add to the season's sense of spiritual void, the bleak beauty of a world frozen, as if perpetually awaiting the arrival of spring.

Unlike many of its sister Congregationalist churches, Redeemer is not white against the snow. It is brick. Although the color appears warmer than the traditional white, its architecture still exudes a familiar sense of Puritan austerity. I make my way up the stairs—careful to avoid any ice patches—and enter. The outside may be reddish-orange, but here, in the vestibule, everything is white. Through the doors, I see the large sanctuary, also white. Its plain interior replicates the older world of colonial New England. Clear glass windows, tall white columns, simple

wooden pews, and a massive pulpit blend harmoniously. A large cross
hangs in front of a curtain in the chancel. This is religion unadorned,
just like Puritanism of the past. The architecture exists to frame the sermon, not distract from hearing the word of God. Only the light fixtures
provide decoration—brass atomic-age chandeliers looking a little like
UFOs hang above the pews. I try not to judge what this may mean to
others, but it is not really my taste.

People enter quietly and take their places in the pews. The congregation is not big. I cannot imagine that a frigid January Sunday would
draw a large crowd. From my seat, I count about one hundred resilient
churchgoers. The organist plays Bach. From the rear of the sanctuary,
the choir prepares the congregation for worship with a short piece called
"Gathered Here." They sound professional, although I later learn that
they are not. As they process to the front of the church, the congregation
stands to sing. The hymn is "Joyful, Joyful, We Adore Thee," set to the
tune of Beethoven's "Hymn to Joy."

> *Joyful, joyful, we adore thee, God of glory, Lord of love;*
> *Hearts unfold like flowers before thee, praising thee, their sun*
>   *above.*
> *Melt the clouds of sin and sadness; drive the dark of doubt*
>   *away;*
> *Giver of immortal gladness, fill us with the light of day.*
>
> *All thy works with joy surround thee, earth and heaven reflect*
>   *thy rays,*
> *Stars and angels sing around thee, center of unbroken praise.*
> *Field and forest, vale and mountain, blooming meadow,*
>   *flashing sea,*
> *Chanting bird and flowing fountain, call us to rejoice in thee.*

The sanctuary, so tranquil just a moment ago, explodes with music.
Suddenly, the wintry space thaws into images of spring. The sparse con-

gregation, its voices filling the space with song, seems at least twice its size. There will be many good words in the service—prayers, announcements, testimonies, and a sermon—but the words are interlaced with astonishing music. A piece called "Meditation" draws the congregation to quiet contemplation after the confession and pardon; a traditional hymn, "Fairest Lord Jesus," acts as a sung prayer; a Handel anthem offers praise to God; and, finally, an exquisite Telemann piece concludes the service. Played by a student who grew up in the church, the medieval music creates a sense of timelessness, as if the congregation is suspended in God. By the time the music ends, I am surprised to find myself gently crying.

In describing Redeemer to me, the Reverend Lillian Daniel said, "We are a church that cares about liturgy and music." That did not particularly surprise me. After all, the church sits right downhill from the Yale Institute for Sacred Music. Sitting and singing with them, however, I realized that more is involved than just caring *about* music. As the choir sang, many listened with closed eyes, seeming to experience an almost mystical sense of God's transcendence. And I was not crying alone; the medieval recorder brought a few other people to tears. These people *live* music.

Redeemer congregants are skilled at testifying. Yet, they struggle to explain what happens to them in music. Although it is hard to imagine in this brainy-Yale group, perhaps it is beyond their vocabulary. One woman fumbles a bit as she says, "It's not about performance; it's about drawing people to another place." Daniel, a member of the choir, says, "I came as a singer and then gradually came into the life of the church. That was a transformation as well, because the music was important to me but it began to take on another dimension." Natalie, an active member of the church, confesses that she "wouldn't be here if it weren't for the music." Congregants ably connect the music to the biblical story, extolling, as one woman says, the way "the music fits the scripture." She continues, "It's not just the choir, but the music that we are singing as a congregation." Madeline, who has served as the church's moderator, says quite simply, "I love the music here at Redeemer. I love listening to it, I love rehearsing it, and I love singing it."

Many churches have excellent music, with concert-hall quality organists and choirs. Sometimes, though, fabulous church music can devolve into performance, with the congregation reduced to an audience and all the "action" happening with the musicians. In these cases, music becomes, to use an old phrase, the tail that wags the dog, undermining other church ministries. In contrast, at Redeemer music, liturgy, and word were completely one, as were the choir, minister, and congregation. Indeed, the congregation appeared to be inside the music, not just watching a performance. It was a kind of grace-filled dance. And it was doing something spiritual to them. Together, they enacted the music, transforming their plain room with auditory beauty. In every sense, music at Redeemer is, as Kurt Mounsma told me, a Christian *practice*—they work on making beautiful sound in community.

People attribute the power of the practice to the leadership of Marguerite "Maggi" Brooks, the music director whom one member called Redeemer's "soul." Maggi has been at Redeemer for twenty years, long before Lillian arrived. Under some circumstances, this might prove awkward for a new minister. However, the two women, who share a similar sense of liturgy and music, developed a genuine liturgical partnership. And, says Lillian appreciatively, "she's a fantastic musician." Maggi is indeed that—as well as professional and dignified. She also understands church music and the purpose of a worshiping community. Church is not just about the sermon or the music (or, as at some churches, the two competing). Rather "it's a total focus of the service which, if you do it right, the whole thing begins here," she says pointing at her heart, "and takes you out there." Like a conductor, she moves her arm gracefully heavenward. How do she and Lillian make that happen? "The Spirit drives us," she says gently.

Maggi grew up an Episcopalian and attended a church school where music was an important part of worship. Like other members of Redeemer, she easily relates her own spiritual journey and connects what happens in church to her gifts and passions. She has no formal theological training and, as she says, laughing a bit, "I spent a long time *not* in church." She mostly attended church to sing. Music shaped her. In recent years, she has studied the Bible and theology in more depth, but she insists that choral singing and studying at the Yale Institute helped her find God. She has wide experience of congregational music, and talks of experiencing God through the songs at a Jewish seder, in improvisational jazz, and in the music of a gospel choir. She speaks easily of "the beauty of simple songs" and says, "I hear [God] with a different sort of ear."

Maggi's ability to listen led her to realize that not everyone hears God in the same way—that variety reflects the diversity of God and God's people. Although the overall style at Redeemer is classical, she draws from European, African, African-American, Native American, and other ethnic traditions. "I think to only do one kind of music is treating the congregation as a one-dimensional entity," she insists. "There is more to musical style than one style, regardless of what that is." She aims to touch the heart of every person in the congregation: "I try to aim for hymns that, at some point during the year, people will say, 'Wow, that's really the hymn for me!'" Her emphasis is on paying attention to God's spirit, on maintaining excellence while being flexible and open. "Our music is not always musically of a piece," she confesses. "It would casually look pretty random to a musician." She smiles as she says, "Sometimes it really works."

It worked one Sunday in January. As I remember that day, I think of theologian Don Saliers's words, "Whatever people can say with passion and in heightened speech they will end up singing in some form." Redeemer's people can certainly talk about faith, and in their practices of justice, they deeply live faith. No wonder they can sing! "When life is deeply felt," Saliers continues, "music gives shape and voice to the very pattern of our experienced world, through pitch, rhythm, and intensity, through lyrics and harmony. So, the act of singing together of life lived and felt binds heart and mind with ordered sound."[100] When connected to experience, pitch, rhythm, intensity, lyrics, and harmony create beauty. Redeemer's music painted that plain sanctuary with verbal image and vibrant color. The beauty of sound transformed the church into sacred space, as spiritually moving as any great medieval cathedral. We moved beyond austerity to the viridity of God. The people at Redeemer may be the heirs of New England Puritanism, but they know the power of beauty.

A few years ago, I led a two-day workshop at an elite mainline seminary, renown for its intellectual prowess, and stayed at the seminary's guest house. When I checked into my two-room suite, I could hardly believe my eyes. Everything was beige—walls, carpet, upholstery, bedspread, and towels. The chairs, pillows, and bed were hard. There was no television, radio, or CD player. No icons, no crosses, not even a cheesy Bible-verse poster. Absolutely nothing in the room was warm, comfortable, or visually pleasing. The suite was plainer than any Roman Catholic monastery in which I had ever stayed, and its complete emotional and spiritual emptiness was appalling. God seemed utterly absent. Just one piece of art hung over the sofa: a large photograph of snow—with six shoots of wheat standing heroically amid the frozen tundra. I wondered if that was their vision of church—or, even worse, the Christian faith! If so, I thought ruefully, it would certainly explain their denomination's decline.

People expect mainline Protestantism to be intelligent, but few expect it to be beautiful. Despite the fact that I was taken aback by the cold guest house room, perhaps others would expect such bleakness. After all, beauty is not the point. Knowing about God, thinking about God is the point. That is, after all, why people call us the frozen chosen.

For two centuries, American Protestantism has struggled between the poles of rationalism and mysticism—with rationalism most often winning. For most of the twentieth century, mainline religion has been associated with the life of the mind: learned theologians and Ivy League–educated clergy. Beauty has not been its strong suit. But that has not always been the case. In the late nineteenth century, against America's expanding industrial and technical culture, Protestantism exploded into a frenzy of romantic arts, music, and architecture. Mainline Protestants were taken by the mysteries of beauty, building vast neo-Gothic churches filled with jewel-like stained glass and intricate sculpture and carvings. The Protestant imagination went through a renaissance of poetry, painting, and the visual arts. Protestant theology emphasized emotions and ethics, moving toward ideals of beauty and mystery. These mainline ancestors were fascinated by history—especially that of medieval Europe and ancient Egypt—and by tradition. Across the country, congregations replaced or renovated their buildings, erasing all traces of early American rationalism in favor of the new emphasis on beauty.

In the early twentieth century, however, the trend reversed. Protestants began attributing all this exuberance to Victorian sensibilities, regarded as tasteless by the new generation of Christians. Protestantism defaulted to its historic rationalism. And any emphasis on beauty as a way to God was muted in favor of cool intellectualism. The beige utilitarianism of the seminary guest room only mirrored the aesthetic sensibilities of most midcentury Protestant modernism. But, on my journey, I had discovered that the tide was turning again. In the vital congregations I visited, rationalism was giving way to new expressions of beauty and finding God beyond words.

"I've only just recently come to the conclusion that I'm an artist and I can actually say that, and that's weird to me," said Alice Connor with a laugh. "Like many artists, I don't want to call myself an artist. But I do see, I understand things visually." She may feel awkward about the name, but she looks like an artist. Alice is a recent seminary graduate, still in her twenties, with closely shaved red hair, dangling earrings, numerous piercings, and a visible tattoo. She is ironic, mildly sardonic, edgy, and hip; her husband is a writer.

She may well be an artist, but she is also the Reverend Alice Connor, an Episcopal priest. At Redeemer in Cincinnati, she serves as assisting clergy working with youth. "I'm a big fan of reasoning things out and trying to make connections," she says. "I'm right there, but we need more than that. For me, aesthetics are part of it and I can't live without it. To me, God is beauty, and God created us in God's image. I can't live without that beauty." I wondered what she would have thought of the seminary guest room's beige God.

I heard remarks like Alice's all along my pilgrimage. In every congregation I visited, there was a growing emphasis on beauty, on knowing God through art, music, and drama, on engaging more than just the mind. Alice considers herself an intellectual and enjoys philosophical speculation—especially arguing about theology and politics. She says that although many people think that "we can reason God out in our minds and that's enough," she believes there are some things "our big brains" cannot figure out. Instead, she insists, "words and pictures speak to me." She says that she finds paradox "beautiful," and that certain ideas about God speak to her only "on a physical level."

For Alice, one such idea is the Christian doctrine of the Trinity, that God is both One and Three at the same time. (Thomas Jefferson once referred to this as the "incomprehensible arithmetic of the Trinity.") "I was opposed to the doctrine of the Trinity for so long." She laughs. "It is still difficult," she confesses rather boldly, "but the best argument I've heard is that rather than One of two—or One of eighteen—or 653 in One—we have One in Three because it's so elegant." She laughs again. "After this huge argument in seminary and after reading the church fathers and mothers and reading all this theology and not getting it—just arguing and being angry—my professor said that. It is elegant. And I said, 'Ah! I get it. That makes sense.'"

For Alice, beauty is the doorway to understanding. And she is not alone; the impulse toward melding beauty and speculation is strong among younger Americans. Indeed, they may well be creating a new way of thinking theologically—a way that springs from the experiencing of beauty. Alice's testimony reminded me of a similar story that I heard from the writer Phyllis Tickle.

Phyllis was speaking at a large southern cathedral. About five hundred people, mostly baby boomers and older, attended her lecture. During the question-and-answer period, someone asked what she thought about the Virgin Birth. As such questions invariably do, this one devolved into a discussion of whether the Virgin Birth was a matter of scientific and historical fact.

As the discussion got more heated, Phyllis noticed that a young man, about seventeen years old, who was helping set up refreshments in the back of the room, had stopped his work to listen. She could see him on the steps leading to the balcony, listening intently to the exchange. When she closed her lecture, he came up to talk with her privately. "Ma'am," he said politely, "there's something I don't understand."

In her enormously generous way, Phyllis asked him, "What don't you understand?" She was ready to expound upon the complexities of the Virgin Birth with the young man.

His response, however, forestalled her explanation. "I don't understand why everyone is so upset about this," he said. "I believe in the Virgin Birth. *It is so beautiful that it has just got to be true—whether it happened or not.*"

Later, Phyllis told me that she felt as if the universe had shifted. "It is a whole new world," she said to me. "He had moved beyond mere facts to understanding based on apprehending beauty. I felt like I was standing on holy ground."[101]

Some people refer to this turn of intellectual events as "postmodern," a shift away from Enlightenment reason toward more experiential forms of knowing. I have heard some church leaders decry this development as somehow threatening to faith. However, both Alice's and the young man's remarks are rooted—perhaps unawares—in an ancient thread of American Christianity. At the height of theological rationalism in the eighteenth century, the much-misunderstood Puritan theologian Jonathan Edwards suggested that the apprehension of beauty, what he called "the divine and supernatural light," was the pathway to true Christianity, and the only possible antidote to intellectual and spiritual aridness. Although early American theologians revered Edwards, few substantially developed this aspect of his thought. Except for its flirtation with romanticism in the nineteenth century, much of American Protestantism walked straight into the trap laid by Enlightenment reason—a universe with no God, devoid of the Spirit's supernatural touch. By the time I was growing up, mainline Protestantism amounted to little more than secular church.

Perhaps unexpectedly in this highly technological age, young adults may well have found their way back to an untapped stream of American theological mysticism. Postmodern and ancient at the same time, new and old, innovative and traditional. One of Alice Connor's paradoxes. Truth is moving beyond the categories of Reason, beyond provable facts to a different realm. Christianity is changing—from being the Truth of rational speculation to being an exploration of the exquisite truthfulness of beauty.

All this reminds me that God is, indeed, elegant. And, as scientists, physicists, and philosophers are now teaching, God's universe is equally elegant—a quality that Christians believe creatively bespeaks God's being. Moreover, there is a remarkable elegance to those mysterious Christian things like the Trinity, the virgin birth, and resurrection. They may or may not have happened, but they certainly are beautiful.

In Asheville, North Carolina, Molly Easton testified about coming to deeper faith. In the 1980s, when she was still in her thirties, her husband died. In the midst of personal crisis, she sought out the comfort of church. Through a friend, she found her way to All Souls Episcopal Cathedral, a small church that sits on the edge of the old Biltmore estate, right in the center of quaint Biltmore Village. Built in 1896 by the noted architect Richard Morris Hunt, the building is considered one of the prettiest churches in the country. Shaped in the form of a Greek cross, the interior is literally a masterwork of stained glass, painting, and carving—all carefully designed to convey the romantic vision of the late nineteenth century, with its passion for beauty and its recognition of the medieval ideal of apprehending God through the heart.

Molly confesses that she became "hooked on all things All Souls," starting with the people, then the liturgy, the music, the furnishings, and the architecture." She said:

> *It makes little difference whether the church is filled to overflowing on Christmas Eve or if I am the only one in the building, I find a sense of communication with the Holy One; however, when the choir is playing and singing and the sun is shining through one of the stained glass windows, that conversation is raised to a higher level. I have been close to tears at the visual impact of the colors rippling through a newly commissioned banner or the flood of light from the west sun turning Charity's halo to gold.*

In sum, Molly says, "I find the whole aesthetically pleasing and I find peace in a not so peaceful world." She believes that many of her fellow parishioners share her experience: "Art and architecture, you might say, helped to lead us to All Souls and opened the doors to a deeper spiritual life."

All Souls is known for hosting notable arts events and for its creative use of the arts in congregational worship. Todd Donatelli, the priest who currently serves the cathedral, believes that the arts create an environment that is "safe enough" to allow people to listen to God. Quoting a noted Quaker theologian, Todd says, "I think that is what Parker Palmer means when he speaks of 'hearing things slant.'" We can "hear," Todd insists, because the arts "speak afresh" Christianity's ancient texts in physical, embodied ways. In this way "the arts can also speak and connect us to the divine when we are too weary or simply have no words to offer," says Todd. People seem to natively understand this approach to faith. "I am continually amazed," says church member Tom Allen, "at the ability of hymn texts and anthem texts to move me to tears, slipping around every defense I possess and rocket right to my heart." Or as Douglas Hart, another member of the parish, says more simply, "I think art is a refined form of prayer."[102]

At All Souls, the arts frame the spiritual life. As at Redeemer, though, they are not just performance or show. The arts link to other Christian practices, things like prayer and hospitality. Perhaps most surprising, however, is the relationship between the arts and social justice. All Souls was instrumental in founding the Church of the Advocate, a nongeographical "worshiping community" for homeless persons. Advocate is not a conventional church in any sense of the word, partly because it meets in shelters across Asheville. One of the ways in which Advocate works to support its members—and local homeless ministries—is through artwork and music. All Souls supports the homeless congregation by showing and selling its art, including a music CD produced by Advocate members. Thus, at All Souls, beauty is not just a practice of personal spirituality or tasteful worship. Rather, the arts connect All Souls' people to both God and their neighbors—providing a way, to use Todd Donatelli's words, "to enact in our bodies what we proclaim with our lips."

There is more than a little irony in all this. Their beautiful building was constructed as a church for Cornelius Vanderbilt, the industrial baron of the Biltmore estate. The little gem of a church was originally conceived as a romantic English-style chapel, an exquisite worship space filled with arts and decor suiting the Vanderbilts' European tastes and refinement. Today, however, the people at All Souls insist that theirs is an inclusive community where the arts are "not the luxury of a few, but the best hope of humanity to experience joy on this planet." Art points the way to joy, the joy of touching the divine.

From the earliest days of Christianity, when new believers painted signs of their faith on the walls of Roman catacombs, art has pointed the way to God. Creativity is at the heart of every spiritually vital religious movement.

Sometimes, however, art can be contentious. Christians have long worried that the arts are so seductive that people might be tempted to worship the art or artist rather than the divine presence. So, Christian history is riddled with arguments over icons, paintings, stained glass windows, and statues. In some sad periods of the faith, Christian icono-clasts destroyed the beauties of the past. Today, that tendency is largely muted—and Christians of all sorts are engaging the arts. However, there is still a rift in the ways that Christians view art. Some, usually those in evangelical churches, understand art instrumentally. Art is important because it proclaims a message, usually intended to convert people to the faith. Such congregations often offer elaborate Christmas or Easter programs, or put on religious plays or film series, with the sole purpose of convincing the audience to believe in Jesus. Art is important for what it can accomplish.

Other Christians, however, engage art for the sake of mystery in-stead of a message. Art reaches toward God, where humanity touches divinity, and where the intellectual fades to apprehending beauty. Art is important because it is a pathway of mystical experience with God. One Seattle Lutheran said that beauty "raises [people] out of the mun-dane, media-blitzed, cubical-induced lives that they live every day and somehow gives them a glimpse and hope of eternity." In Memphis a woman told me, "Part of what we do is theater. It is ritual and myth and things that are more important than anything.... It is something that transcends the ever-changing world." As a California Presbyterian said bluntly about art, "It helps move people away from blind literalism" to what is "truly there."

Although the arts are, indeed, mystical, they are not entirely ethe-real. Throughout my journey, people taught me that beauty is a faith practice—something people *do* that can be learned, rehearsed, and en-acted—in our lives and community. In their churches I saw art shows, artist studios, art programs for children, and summer art camps. There were piano lessons, artist seminars, book signings, poetry readings, and web design classes. From seniors to preschoolers, from the homeless to the prosperous, all sorts of people engaged the arts together. I saw min-isters play guitar, do cartwheels, and dance. They wrote liturgies and composed hymns. In worship, they employed a range of arts—from traditional choirs singing to potters spinning, from painting icons to projecting PowerPoint images on walls. With only a few exceptions, their churches were elaborately decorated with candles, crosses, flowers, paintings, prints, pottery, banners, sculpture, weavings, embroidery, icons, and fountains. There were film series and craft workshops, knitting groups and drama troops. Liturgical dancers and shape-note singers. Madrigals and rock musicians. Most of it was good. All of it was done with heart. They made me think of Genesis: "And God saw everything that he had made, and indeed, it was very good."

Of his congregation, Todd Donatelli said, "It is a community that believes that for those created in the image of God, a sign of their faithfulness, a sign of their engagement with the Spirit, will be creativity." Todd's observation held true in all the congregations along my way. They were a symphony of creativity! From them I learned that congregations can craft beauty through the arts, faithfully employing skills and gifts that opened the way toward helping them understand God beyond words. Through the arts, human beings embody God by imitating God's creative life—shaping the clay of their experience with voices and hands. In that place, everything becomes new as we participate in God's continual creation of the universe. Or, as one Congregationalist said of his renewed joy at being Christian, "I didn't realize it was so beautiful."

PART III

From Tourists
to Pilgrims

Not long ago I was at Trinity Church, Wall Street, one of the oldest churches in the United States, and the church that sits at the edge of the World Trade Center site. Since September 2001, more than two million visitors a year have passed through its historic doors. The clergy and I were talking about spiritual tourists, the throngs of people who journey to the church to understand the devastating events of September 11. They are the unmoored, nomads in a fractured world trying to make spiritual and theological sense of the changes—the violence, suffering, and war—that have engulfed us.

"I've got tourists galore," sighed the Reverend Dr. Jim Cooper, Trinity's senior clergyperson. "They come. They come in droves. But I don't want them to leave as tourists. I want them to become pilgrims. I want them to connect, to know that there is something more."

Although not many other churches have two million tourists a year, Trinity is not completely unique. In effect, Jim Cooper's words speak to all religious communities. Every church, synagogue, mosque, and temple in the United States sits among a throng of tourists; each is surrounded by people on a journey of self-discovery and meaning. But simply being on a spiritual journey does not necessarily mean that people will find meaning. Rather, as Jim suggested, they need to "connect," to discover that journeys can become pilgrimages. Tourists can become pilgrims.

Trips and journeys are wonderful things. Every year I joyfully anticipate my family's summer vacation at the beach. However, that trip lasts only a week, and its sole purpose is to remove us from the stress of life in Washington. We are not trying to find a new way of life. Rather, we seek a change of scenery that gives us a perspective on our normal lives; rest and play that strengthen us for things back home. Being a tourist takes us outside of daily life, and when we are at the beach, we know that we experience the place in an entirely different way than do the locals, the year-round people.

But what if, instead of making a yearly trip, we moved in? Becoming a pilgrim means becoming a local, a year-round person, who adopts a new place and new identity by learning a new language, rhythms, and practices. Unlike being a tourist, we embark on a pilgrimage, not to escape life, but to embrace it more deeply, to be transformed wholly as a person with new ways of being in community and new hopes for the world. Being a tourist means experiencing something new; being a pilgrim means becoming someone new. Pilgrimages go somewhere—to a transformed life.

Nora Gallagher, a member of one of the churches I visited, once wrote that she came to her church as a "tourist" and wound up "being a pilgrim." For her, becoming a pilgrim meant walking through the seasons of the congregation's life, celebrating each of its festivals, living through its ordinary times, suffering at the dark moments. Although it was initially hard for her to imagine settling into a community, the quirky beauty and quiet passions of the congregation caught her imagination. She knew she could never really understand Christianity unless she lived it. As she connected to the church, she connected to the larger Christian tradition, and she changed. Settling in was not, however, dull or boring. She found that not only was she changing but the church was changing as well, and they were touching the larger community with God's transforming love. Becoming a pilgrim taught her that change is not just a journey of self-discovery and personal meaning. Rather, pilgrims find that transformation is communal and corporate. Changing the self empowers pilgrims to change the world.[103]

Throughout my own pilgrimage, I met people like Nora whose lives had been transformed by embarking upon Christian pilgrimage. They testified to change—the transformation of the self, of their congregations, and of society by connecting to God, connecting to a story, a language, religious rhythms, and faith practices.[104] By settling in, they had gone on a different kind of journey, one they would never have experienced had they remained tourists, one that became increasingly less self-directed and increasingly aimed toward God's love and *shalom*.

FIFTEEN

Transforming Lives

Although Bernard had been born into a Roman Catholic family, he was essentially a nomad, a man wandering through life with no grounding in a faith community. His family had stopped attending church when he was in elementary school, and he grew up with only a "cursory knowledge" of Christian faith and religious practice.

He also confesses that, as a young adult, his way of life had been self-indulgent. As a well-paid member of a distasteful profession that has "only negative impacts on the world," Bernard enjoyed financial success, but he was ashamed of his work and felt trapped. When he and his girlfriend, Catherine, had a son, the child's birth inspired him to seek a "meaningful positive life." As a couple, they began looking for a church that might help them become better people and found their way to First Presbyterian, down the street from their house.[105]

It is hard to imagine what most churches would make of this family, an unmarried couple with a baby, who benefited financially from an unsavory occupation. But the congregation, schooled in the deep practice of Christian hospitality, welcomed Bernard and his family into its midst. The church's pastor, Mac Wilson, came to their home and did not "judge harshly" their lifestyle. Bernard says Mac's warm encouragement to pursue being Christian surprised him. The acceptance by congregation and minister, Bernard says thankfully, "laid the foundation of trust" that his family needed to take the steps of joining the church and having their son baptized.

Joining First Presbyterian was not easy, however. Unlike many mainline congregations, the church asks that people go through an extended process of Christian formation in scripture study, prayer, discernment, and reflection before they join. Although somewhat intimidated by these requirements, and still feeling shame, Bernard and Catherine committed themselves to the journey of faith offered at the church. In the process, they became more than members. Their lives were transformed in authentic Christian community. Bernard says that he found "new perspectives, role models whose example of faith and Christian life" taught him that change was "indeed possible." They experienced the love and mercy of God, learned the Bible and prayer, sang new songs of faith, entered into the church's liturgical life, asked questions, and developed the ability to "bring religion out of Sunday morning and into everyday life."

Bernard and Catherine married. As he pondered the state of his own soul, Bernard realized that "if we know God will forgive us, we can begin to forgive ourselves." He also reflected on the Christian call to serve others, to give to the least among us, to "change and grow toward the potential that God sees in us." After spending months in community immersed in the practices of Christian faith, Bernard returned to his original dilemma. He was finding a more meaningful way of life, but could he find an "occupation that would be a benefit rather than a detriment to the world"? Catherine suggested that perhaps he was called to serve people, and to comfort those in distress—she sensed that God was calling her husband to be an undertaker. Bernard knew she was right. The man who had once made money by dishonoring the living would now honor the dead.

Like the early followers of Jesus, who left their nets by the shore when called by God, Bernard and his family left their comfortable life and moved to another city so that he could attend a school for funeral directors. While there, they lived in a small house in a "pretty bad part of town" and on less than half of Bernard's previous salary. After a few years of "poverty and difficulty," he received an offer of a position in another part of the country. The family moved to a nice city where they have an entirely new life. "I have found that funeral service is a very meaningful calling for me," Bernard says. He tells the story of being called in the middle of the night to embalm two bodies at a local hospital. "As I spent the whole night carefully preparing these people, I certainly wished I was home in my warm bed. But I did my best, as I always do. They are treated with all the respect and care that I would want my loved ones given. It gives me a wonderful feeling of goodness." Although he has been gone from First Presbyterian for several years, he is deeply grateful that God, through that congregation, changed his life. "I am in a position to serve others and this service enriches me and fills me with great peace."

Once Bernard had been a nomad, wandering alone through the waste of society, covering guilt and shame with possessions. Now he is a pilgrim transformed by a hospitable community of Christian practice. Bernard is still on a journey. But unlike the nomadic travels of his youth, on this journey he continually finds meaning, deeper purpose, renewed identity, and greater love.

Bernard changed. Christians call change conversion, a change of heart that revolutionizes the whole of life. The biblical word for this is *metanoia*, a radical encounter with God that turns life around. The paradigmatic *metanoia* story in the Christian tradition is that of Saint Paul. In the years after Jesus' death, Paul, then a zealous Jew called Saul, persecuted Christian believers. On the road to Damascus, Saul heard Jesus call to him, "Saul, Saul, why do you persecute me?" Struck to the heart, Saul fell to his knees and dedicated himself to Jesus' service. He took on a new name, Paul, and a new mission—instead of persecuting the church, he would strengthen it and help it grow. Paul's road-to-Damascus experience was *metanoia*.

More than any other biblical character, American Protestants venerate the apostle Paul. Perhaps because of Paul's special place in the American pantheon of saints, Americans have long cherished dramatic conversion stories. Beginning with the great colonial revivals, we have celebrated spiritual change through encountering God in Jesus. Generations of people walked "the sawdust trail" to give their lives to Jesus, making their way to the front of revival tents and churches to get born again. American Christianity has often been a road-to-Damascus sort of religion—full of instantaneous, miraculous, and complete personal conversions.

This American interpretation of Paul, however, misses something in the biblical story. After the powerful encounter on the road, which leaves him blind, Paul is rescued by some Christians who take him to the city and heal his blindness. He says that he "went away at once to Arabia," where for three years he learned about Jesus and his way. Only after this intense time of reflection, prayer, and preparation was Paul ready to engage in public his new calling of being the "apostle to the Gentiles." Paul may have been stopped in his tracks on the road to Damascus, but it took three years of living in Christian community and learning its practices for him to be fully changed. Even the biblical story, with all its breathless enthusiasm, regards change as a process that happens in a community of practice.

Bernard's *metanoia* story is not all that different from Paul's. Struck by the beauty of his newborn son, he sought a different way than the one he had been living. For many months, he made himself a learner in Christian community, being changed by the practices of hospitality, prayer, worship, and reflection. His conversion was not a split-second decision at a revival meeting; rather, it was a process of transformation, a change of heart that is still occurring for him even today. Bernard changed from a person taking advantage of others to a man who serves.

*   *   *

During my journey, I met hundreds of people—former nomads—whose lives have been transformed through practicing faith in community. Although often not as dramatic, many of their stories resembled Bernard's. They shared a common sense of being spiritually lost, of seeking meaning, and of religious dissatisfaction. The ways of being Christian that had suited their parents and grandparents had failed them. Many had been Roman Catholics or conservative evangelicals—renderings of faith they felt were too narrow or authoritarian. Yet, they did not want to reject Christianity. They craved a form of faith that offered them an authentic and meaningful way of life.

Contemporary Western culture is marked by a sense of dislocation, the feeling of being lost in the universe, unmoored, without direction, without hope. In different ways and different places, the people I met refracted the traits of nomadic existence: radical individualism, aimlessness, consumption, fragmentation, and forgetfulness. In recent decades, these characteristics have reshaped our world, making customary forms of religious faith and practice increasingly less tenable. Some contemporary philosophers suggest that this cultural reorganization constitutes a nearly complete break with the past, and that people must construct entirely new ways of navigating life. One theorist has even argued that the only "rational" choice is to give in—"to be a vagrant or a tourist, or to act as one."[106]

At times of intense social change throughout their history, Christians have responded in various ways. In some cases—the Amish come to mind—they reject change and choose to separate from the world and "freeze" faithfulness in a particular frame of the past. In other cases, like that of fundamentalists, they actively resist change, seeking to overturn new ways of being and return society to a safe and orderly religious and political world. In still other cases, some religious people, like Protestant liberals, simply accept all the implications of cultural change and remake religion accordingly.

The people I met on my journey had adopted none of these strategies. They did not separate, resist, or accept. Instead, they recognized the basic conditions of social change while responding to the challenges they posed to their lives. They were selectively adapting to the cultural changes that are pressuring the practice of Christian faith. To overcome the fracturing of contemporary life, the people I met had reached back toward the historic Great Tradition, what Houston Smith calls "the voice of peace, justice and beauty that emanated from the Christian soul."[107] By reaching back and drawing out wisdom for today, they responded (sometimes overtly, sometimes intuitively) to the five traits of nomadic existence, in effect inverting a potentially destructive cultural pattern into a faith-filled way of life. And, in doing so, they offered a path of transformation for nomads to become pilgrims. They opened the way for change, for the transformed life promised by Jesus.

Radical Individualism: From Wanderers to Pilgrims

Joan Henderson readily admits that when she first arrived at Phinney Ridge Lutheran Church in Seattle, she only wanted to get her children baptized so they could attend a Catholic school. "I didn't want to be changed. I wasn't looking for community." Yet, like First Presbyterian, Phinney Ridge insists upon an extended time of Christian formation, which they call The WAY, before baptism. So Joan's children could not be, as she wanted, "baptized on the spot." The rite had to wait until she had completed the learning process of faith. Although it confused her, Joan stayed with it. At every step, the congregation asked if she wanted to continue. Joan said, "I found this to be both wonderful and frustrating. Wonderful, because it taught me about the power of continuing invitation in the Christian life. Frustrating, because I thought this 'thing' had an end and I wanted to get to the end and get out!"

As the months unfolded, Phinney Ridge marked the path to Christian conversion with a series of liturgies designed to draw individuals closer to God in Jesus Christ. Joan recalls that one of these rituals—when those learning to be Christians are marked with crosses of holy oil—actually changed her. "One of the most meaningful steps in The WAY was when I was marked with the sign of the cross on my hands, eyes, ears, forehead, heart, and feet. It was downright shocking. Crosses traced all over my body. Safe touch. Good touch. Healing touch. It seemed as though with every trace of the cross on my body, meat tenderizer was being applied to my heart."

What was happening to her? she asked. "My get-the-kids-baptized-and-get-out plan was in serious jeopardy. Something big was happening. I could feel it and I couldn't stop it." Joan was becoming Christian. She said that the people of Phinney Ridge, with their patient practice of faith, were the "light of Christ" for her. "I didn't even know it was dark; it had been so dark I couldn't believe there was any light." That was in the early 1990s. Now, Joan understands that being a Christian means following the "stirrings of the Holy Spirit." She describes it as "To invite as we have been invited. To be hospitable with the warmth and lavishness of Christ. To show up to be Christ in the world and in each other's lives." It took being found for Joan even to realize that she had been lost. Without really trying, she went from being a nomad to being a pilgrim.

One of the dominating characteristics of contemporary life is that of wandering—moving from experience to experience for the sake of experience alone. Of necessity, wandering is an individualistic activity, with occasional "joining," "networking," or "hooking up" with other individual wanderers for a limited period and for a particular experience. Like Joan, people may seek religious services for a certain reason for a short time—this is part of the terrain of spiritual nomads. Radical practices of individual autonomy mark contemporary spirituality, with each person serving as arbiter of personal ethics, moral choice, and religious preference. As two British scholars describe it, "The goal is not to defer to higher authority, but to have the courage to become one's own authority. Not to follow an established path, but to forge one's own inner-directed, as subjective, life."[108]

A 2005 *Newsweek*/Beliefnet poll in which 24 percent of Americans claimed to be "spiritual but not religious" demonstrates the turn toward spiritual individualism.[109] Indeed, philosopher Charles Taylor claims that all contemporary changes can be related to a single process, "the massive subjective turn of modern culture."[110]

Such trends trouble many mainline pastors and church leaders. After all, traditional denominations like those of mainline Protestantism are organized communally—usually along lines of family, class, and inherited customs and traditions. Indeed, recent studies suggest that increased spiritual autonomy directly—and negatively—affects mainstream religions.[111] How can traditional churches survive in a "spiritual but not religious" culture?

During my journey, I found that congregations able to link the longings for spiritual experience with the Christian tradition not only survived but appeared to be thriving. Instead of condemning or fearing individual spiritual autonomy, they welcomed it as a precondition for renewed Christian faith.[112]

Perhaps the clearest example from my travels is Phinney Ridge Lutheran Church. In Seattle, where more than 80 percent of the population does not attend church, Phinney Ridge invites spiritual wanderers into The WAY. Modeled on ancient Christian baptismal and formation rites, the process requires a year of worship, study, theological reflection, prayer, and service before a person can join the church. At Phinney Ridge, they recognize that individual longing acts as the entryway to a deeper life of faith. Over the fourteen years that the congregation has invited people into The WAY, it has transformed the lives of hundreds of individuals—former wanderers who now follow Christ.

Aimlessness: From Busyness to Vocation

A few years ago, Foster, a member of Calvin Presbyterian Church, in an economically depressed area near Pittsburgh, was downsized from a good but demanding job. With little money and a family to support, he and his wife decided that she would go to work and he would become a stay-at-home dad. Although he confesses that he has "these ups and downs," he also believes that, through losing his job and being with his children, he has found new meaning in his life. "The church played a significant role in that," he says. "I spent time talking with Graham [the pastor] about it, speaking about what's my purpose."

One day, while he was working on his home computer, Foster's youngest daughter wanted his attention. When he told her that he needed to be on the computer to find a job, she replied: "You're my dad, that's your job. You don't have to do anything else." Foster remembers that as a "turning point" for him. "I now focus less on having to go out there and find a job. Now I focus more on the girls." Through prayer, he has discovered a greater sense of vocation—he now believes that God is calling him to become a teacher, and he has gone back to school to make that happen. "I can spend more time with the girls when I'm teaching," he says, "because I get summers off, and I have the same schedule they do."

At Calvin, people readily speak of finding a new sense of vocation. Unlike the Roman Catholics who speak of vocation as a special call to the religious life of a priest, monk, or nun, the Presbyterians at Calvin speak of vocation as meaning God's call to all of us to discover our place in the world, to do that which God desires us to do, and to do our work with purpose, passion, and pleasure. They talk about making leaps of faith, taking risks to do God's work, and following the "whisperings of the Spirit." As individuals, they often talk about moving from a vague directionlessness toward God's intention for their lives. Figuring out who we are in God also means figuring out what God dreams for our lives.

Calvin's prayer minister, Diane McClusky, lived aimlessly through much of her early adulthood. Although raised in the church, she left it as a young woman—literally moving all over the United States—and confesses that she "began to look outside the church for God." She recalls, "I practiced meditation and alternative approaches. I explored crystals, spirit guides, rebirthing, Wicca, Eastern religions [such as] Taoism and

Buddhism." Occasionally, she took her daughters to church out of deference to family tradition. All the while, though, she felt that she had a "duty to protect my daughters from religion while exposing them to God." Eventually, she and her family moved to Pennsylvania. After trying out several churches that seemed "dusty and dry," they found Calvin Presbyterian.

Through the people at Calvin, Diane began to explore her real calling—to be a healer. She trained in Reiki and reflexology, and as she explored these ancient healing practices, she became increasingly aware of Christ as a healer and of Christian practices of healing prayer. She remembers walking Calvin's labyrinth with Graham, the pastor, burning a list of her sins at the center, and having him serve her communion. "I felt empty and weak," she says, "but I also felt filled with the body of Christ, my Jesus. I had confessed my sins, exposed my sin, and I was forgiven and washed clean by the blood of Jesus. Immediately, I started to sense Jesus as a true, real, and living person—my sweet, sweet Jesus. I guess I had to go into the wilderness to find the home of my soul." Not long afterward, she was commissioned as a healing prayer minister for the church.

Now Diane spends most of her time in pastoral care—visiting and praying for the sick, overseeing a growing prayer-shawl ministry, teaching people a practice of "Christ-guided Reiki," and helping develop Calvin's evening healing service. "What I do know is that I am not the healer," she says. "I am nothing more than the delivery system. Still, I feel grateful and blessed every time I am used by Jesus for healing."[113]

Like Foster and Diane, most contemporary Americans possess no stable identity. Nothing is inherited from the past, few family ties bind, and all forms of personhood must be chosen and, often, chosen again. It is not uncommon for an individual to live in several states, marry more than once, change religious traditions one or more times, and switch jobs or even careers. Because of this open-ended quality, life is an unfinished and unfinishable project, which leaves many wondering if meaninglessness is life's ultimate meaning. Human beings might be, in essence, homeless wanderers, aimless and without final direction. And this wandering, the constant roaming for identity and vocation, fuels random busyness—doing tasks, burying oneself in work, or becoming addicted to hobbies and sports to cover the sense that life may well be without purpose.

As a counterpoint to wandering, Christian pilgrims have a dynamic role and ultimate destination. Pilgrims find identity in baptism, the sacrament that draws them into the body of Christ and defines the self in relation to God's story and the story of God's people. Baptism also calls pilgrims to other practices—things like hospitality, peacemaking, justice, and charity—that deepen a sense of Christian identity.

Across the country, at Goleta Presbyterian Church near Santa Barbara, California, pastor Steve Jacobson describes how an eclectic group of questing individuals can ground themselves, through the very diversity of their wanderings, in Christian tradition. Goleta regularly witnesses "nomads" who stay. "They exchange their nomad identities (wanderers without a home)," writes Steve, "for pilgrim identities (people on a journey who believe they have a home)." He continues, "That 'home' is a reverence for God founding the practice of reverence for one another, as exemplified in Jesus' ministry." And, although they find "home," that home is not a fixed place or predetermined identity. It remains a continual quest, but now a Christian quest, for meaning and authenticity through Jesus Christ, to find God's purposes, and the community of the church."[14]

It intrigued me to see how many of the congregations I visited had ministries serving the homeless. Many people mentioned that, despite the fact that they lived in houses, they too "felt homeless" and experienced a surprising kinship with the actual homeless people they befriended. Because of their own sense of dislocation, they felt that the homeless people had "taught" them about the spiritual life, trust, stewardship, healing, and commitment. I regularly heard mainline churchgoers refer to themselves as wayfarers, sojourners, and pilgrims—all images that conjure a sense of spatial dislocation and spiritual relocation in God.

Their renewed sense of identity gave them a new sense of vocation—faithfully living out the practices that compose a Christian way of life.

Consumption: From Consumers to Practitioners

During Lent 2004, near the midpoint of my mainline journey, Mel Gibson's blockbuster film *The Passion of the Christ* was released. Targeted by robust marketing, the churches and pastors I had come to know found themselves the most desired audience share in the country! One of my friends, Lutheran pastor Gary Erdos, reported that his church received substantial advance publicity on the film, discounted bulk tickets, and a voice-recorded thank-you message from Mel Gibson after a group had viewed the movie. Gary said that although he found much of the film's theology off-putting, it was the marketing of Christianity's holiest week that most deeply offended him. Gary was not alone. Unlike the evangelical Christians who flocked to the film, mainline Protestants more thoughtfully engaged *The Passion* in its theology and as a spiritual product. In the congregations along my way, people struggled to decide whether to see the movie—and what they thought about being a market for a Christian product.

From *The Prayer of Jabez*, television revivals, Christian theme parks, and *The Purpose-Driven Life*, to *The Passion of the Christ*, Christians are a target audience for spiritual products—all promising to lead the religious consumer into a more meaningful life. "In its spiritual life," says pastor Ken Carter, "a congregation is sometimes called to say yes or no to the culture." Ken is no fundamentalist. He is the minister of Providence United Methodist Church in Charlotte, North Carolina, a prominent and successful congregation that seriously engages Christian practices. Ken believes that things such as Bible study, prayer, and doing justice form the heart of the Christian life and help ordinary churchgoers "withstand the latest fads that are marketed in our culture."

Ken says that when *The Passion* was released, reports of its anti-

Semitism, biblical inaccuracy, and violence troubled him. In those regards, the movie would challenge Providence's commitment to friendship with its Jewish neighbors, its strong devotion to Bible study, and its
practice of Christ's peacemaking. Ken saw the film, and in subsequent
weeks led a teaching session attended by more than two hundred church
members. They delved into difficult questions of the film's theology,
portrayal of the Jews, and use of violence as related to Christian spirituality. At the end, he asked them to reflect on the question "Should I go to
this movie?" Ken advised his congregation against it. Many people chose
not to see the film.

But Ken also realized that helping his congregation say no to being
a mass audience for a religious product means saying yes to something
else. Part of the movie's success could surely be attributed to the fact
that people want to *see* Jesus—they want to be able to connect emotion-
ally with God. Much of American Protestantism has depended on words
alone, not visual or artistic renderings of the tradition. Throughout Lent
that year, Ken sought ways to offer "something more substantive, more
biblical, and more life-giving" to the people of Providence. Members
of the church made commitments to spend three hours (the length of
the film) reading the Passion stories of the Bible; they listened to Mass
and Requiem settings of the Passion by Bach, Beethoven, Mozart, and
Rutter; they reflected on the congregation's practices of justice to the
oppressed; and they paid special attention to the liturgies of Holy Week.
One woman remarked to Ken that the darkened beauty of the Good Fri-
day service was her reason for not seeing *The Passion*. She "didn't want
to see images from a movie when sitting in darkness listening to the last
words of Jesus."[115]

All across the globe, people think they will find meaning through
what they buy or aspire to buy. As one Church of England report
puts it, "Where previous generations found their identity in what
they produced, we now find our identity in what we consume."[116]
Christians have not escaped the pervasive consumerism that defines
religious identities, traditions, and faith practices. Indeed, consumer

culture is so powerful that it absorbs "all other cultures as 'content' to be commodified, distributed, and consumed," in a way that renders faith increasingly unable to reshape our lives.[17] In the process, Christian symbols and practices themselves often become products in service to consumerism, a faith that can be marketed to spiritual nomads. That is, of course, what happened with *The Passion of the Christ:* the primary symbol of Christianity, the cross, was turned into a marketing event.

I encountered people who did not buy the latest Christian products in order to make their lives better; they were not primarily spiritual consumers. Instead, they were Christian practitioners, pilgrims who knew that faith is a craft learned over time in community. From congregations across the country, mainline Protestants commented on their spiritual growth:

- "I have become more intentional in my prayer life and in reading and studying scripture and church history. I am more attuned to my spiritual life."
- "I get to teach and work with children and listen to their insights about God and Jesus. I get to use the artistic and creative talent that God gave me in ways that make more sense than they ever did before."
- "I think material possessions are becoming less important to me; I sense that I'm developing inner tranquillity and peace."
- "I serve gladly (mostly!) and encourage rather than scold."
- "I have become a more disciplined Christian—understanding that faith is action. I commit a lot more time and money to the church than I have ever done in the past."
- "I have become more faithful and prayerful."
- "I am able to see God in others. I am able to feel God within me. I am prayerful throughout the day. I am continually learning to trust God."

- "My choices have changed. I've given up some things I love to help bring the message for a better life to others who need it desperately."
- "I am much more focused on the needs of others and in providing for those who are less fortunate than me. My charitable giving—both to the church and to other organizations—has increased dramatically."

In all these cases, people did not change because of a program that had been marketed to them. Instead, they changed by engaging things like hospitality, prayer, theological reflection, and service. These pilgrims found the church to be a corrective to consumer culture—directing their lives away from what they purchased and toward what they practiced.

Fragmentation: From Individuals to Community

"After 9/11," said Aaron at Redeemer UCC in New Haven, "I must admit that I have retreated into myself while flying. Perhaps responding to everyone else's dour attitudes, I had begun to purposefully separate myself from others on the journey. Is this a positive Christian attitude? The answer is NO!" Aaron's insight expands far beyond his own response to terrorism. In his comment, I heard a larger story—one echoed by many people. If you become a pilgrim, you cannot live in isolation from others; you cannot "purposefully separate from others on the journey." As part of personal transformation, you become a member of community.

Radical autonomy, subjectively driven lives, and consumer choice lead in a predictable direction: toward cultural fragmentation. After all, individuals arrive at separate and distinct meanings, with everyone appealing to a variety of moral, ethical, and spiritual authorities for guidance. Although large numbers of people still choose to assent to certain authorities (such as the U.S. Constitution), the possibility for interpreting even traditional authorities is nearly endless. In a recent book, *The World Is Flat,* Thomas Friedman points out that top-down, centralized, chain-of-command authorities are quickly becoming history as networks of participatory and relational authorities take their place.[118] The shift from established authorities to emerging ones is a process of chaotic cultural reorganization whereby fragmentation is an inevitable part of the journey of change.

In an age of fragmentation, however, many people are tempted to revert to top-down authority as a way of controlling chaos. All the churches I visited are part of denominations in which some interest groups are attempting to centralize doctrine, polity, and praxis as an answer to fractured culture. What if the answer to fragmentation is not centralized authority? What if the answer is authentic community?

Over the course of this three-year study, I observed congregations that had moved away from being hierarchical, top-down communities of authority toward more participatory forms of church, thus flattening their congregations. Instead of reasserting the ministerial or doctrinal voice of authority, they had opened their congregations to more voices, bringing a multiplicity of perspectives to bear on community life. As a result of embracing variety, the worshiping community generated spiritual authority—shifting Christian leadership away from external and distant sources to the inner work of paying attention to the Holy Spirit. By moving more deeply into diversity, they formed the New Testament vision of church as Christ's body in the world. The congregations along my way navigated between the extremes of spiritual individualism and authoritarian religion by emphasizing the power of relationship in community. Flat church.

Aaron's own congregation, Redeemer UCC, exemplifies this. "I think it is a community of transformation. Our church is a place of transformation and I think I'm always being transformed," says Pastor Lillian Daniel. "People push each other, they push me. And I've watched some amazing transformations happen in people's lives that are directly related to their participation in the church." Their strong practice of testimony shifts authority away from the minister toward the people—moral example, religious instruction, done by the community and through the community's experience of God in its midst. Testimony led Redeemer away from the old minister-centered congregation into a new expression of the ancient tradition of New England democratic faith. By sharing the pilgrimage in community, they changed both themselves and the church.

As many people told me, it is difficult to sustain the pilgrimage life alone; they wanted to be part of a practicing community. William in Memphis said that it was important "being part of something bigger than yourself. I don't feel that growth is possible if you are totally on your own." Or as one Seattle woman put it, "I sometimes want to drop out again. But somehow I realize that this is not a do-it-yourself deal. I cannot pull this off by myself. I need fellow travelers to teach me."

Forgetfulness: From Amnesia to Memory

In Yorktown, Virginia, Annie, a member of Saint Mark Lutheran Church, shared her struggle to find a faith community. As a military officer, she had moved her entire life. "In every place we lived," she said, "I searched for a church. Over and over, I would say, Uh-uh, it's not here." She had been to many different churches, and been a member of a number of Protestant congregations. "I feel as though I've just come off safari in a jungle of new-fangled, all-tangled-up religious experiences," she confessed. "It was a trip not taken by choice and at times I felt like the prey rather than the hunter." When she came to Saint Mark, she finally realized what the "it" was that had been missing from both her life and the many churches she had visited—tradition.

The people of Saint Mark work hard to create a lively sense of tradition, the beauty of liturgy, classical disciplines of prayer, and the deep wisdom of Lutheran theology. Annie claims that "tradition made just enough of an impression in my younger life to leave markers on my path through the jungle, so that I might find my way out." She also says that Saint Mark has been strengthened as a congregation by its care for tradition. "It enables us to survive and thrive and is worthy of sharing." She says it grounds her, giving her the fortitude she needs to survive—and hope "for a better future for generations to come." For much of her adult life, Annie had been longing to remember, to connect with a past from which she had been disconnected.

The final quality of contemporary life that feeds nomadic spirituality is forgetfulness. Mobility, technology, education, changes in women's roles, divorce, cohabitation, travel, and urbanization all combine to cut people off from sources of memory—family, neighborhood, and heritage. In a fragmented and decentralized culture, it is easy to forget (and sometimes purposely so) the chain of memory that ties past, present, and future. In a very real way, memory is dependent on relationships; in a culture in which relationships are broken, memory becomes impossible. Thus, forgetfulness has deep consequences for religious communities. French theorist Danièle Hervieu-Léger goes so far as to argue that contemporary societies are less religious because they are "less and less capable of maintaining the memory which lies at the heart of religious existence." They have become "amnesic societies."[119]

In conversation after conversation, I heard stories of lost memory. People shared stories about leaving the traditions of childhood, moving a number of times, going through divorce and remarriage, or, sometimes, purposefully breaking with the past. But such breaks created a counterbalancing longing for finding a past, to discover memory. People wanted to make new relationships, and form new familiar ties through shared Christian practice. As William, at Holy Communion, said about his attraction to Episcopal liturgy, "It is that feeling of continuity, things with a long history, a tradition, a ritual. I find those things comforting, meaningful." Another member of Holy Communion said that he "was looking for a place that had an emphasis on ancient practice." He continued, "There seemed to be a practical modernness living in harmony with a reverence for tradition here." At Iglesia Santa María in Falls Church,

Virginia, linking to history provides a bridge of memory that stabilizes immigrant lives. Roberto told me that he attends because this congregation encourages traditional expressions of prayer practices from his home in Bolivia. Kerry in Seattle appreciated Lutheran tradition "that's been handed down for so long; there's a sense of background supporting the liturgy and all the things that we do." Even at Cornerstone United Methodist in Naples, Florida, founded in 1996, people found deep meaning in "the amalgamation of old and new." There, on a sun-drenched day with the beach beckoning, thirty-something Valerie shared her excitement with me, "It's extremely interesting to learn the history of the church and why we do things; why it is not just ritual; and why it is part of our faith."

In many ways, my research tracked desire for memory. I met many people like Valerie, hungry to remember a past she never knew. I watched congregations reach back to recover lost traditions of the biblical story, worship, prayer, justice, and formation. People testified to finding meaning in the practices of ancient Christianity, Celtic spirituality, medieval mysticism, Catholic devotions, Lutheran and Anglican liturgies, and Wesleyan piety. Mainline Protestants are busily weaving the past into a new kind of spiritual fabric—a kind of cloth of wisdom that can be worn by contemporary pilgrims.

In an age of forgetfulness, I met communities of memory—not of stilted traditions, but living ones that connect people to the past. People were not seeking tradition because they desired answers, authority, social order, or doctrinal purity. They simply wanted to remember. By remembering, spiritual nomads locate themselves in a story, find new-old traditions, discover a heritage that makes sense of their experience, and recreate family. Remembering meant just that—pulling together the fragments of fractured existence and putting them back together again.

In the summer of 2005, an angry post came across on one of my listservs. It was from a conservative Episcopalian who was furious about his denomination's conflict over homosexuality. "The problem with most of the church," he thundered, "is that it doesn't preach a gospel that transforms people's lives!" He continued claiming that only those churches that shared his theological and political perspectives about faith possessed the power to change people. Of his partisans, he announced: "We are the Transformational Christians!"

When I read his post, I could barely believe that someone could claim exclusive rights to the workings of God's spirit on the basis of a religious litmus test. I thought of Bernard, Foster, Diane, Ken, Aaron, William, Valerie, and Annie. I recalled all the stories I had heard—hundreds of stories of lives being changed in mainline congregations. Their stories surprised me with their sparkling spiritual beauty, and often, as I listened to the words people shared, I cried. I thought of their congregations as mostly moderate and liberal in their theology and politics—not even recognizably Christian according to the standards set by my listserv correspondent—and I thought about how powerful they are as *metanoia* communities. I remembered the testimony of Darrell Carpenter at Redeemer UCC, a churchgoer who also happens to be gay, whose words sum up what happens when a person is transformed from tourist to pilgrim: "I took a leap of faith. It was a leap back from the wilderness into a new relationship with God, one based on my true nature. I felt radiant, lighter than air. I felt that I had found home."

SIXTEEN

Transforming Congregations

"The sermon today is the rector's annual report," joked the Reverend Bruce Freeman at Church of the Redeemer (Episcopal) in Cincinnati, "where I wrap my message in a sermon so that you think you are getting a real sermon!" It is March 2005, and this is Bruce's first annual meeting at Redeemer, his first rector's report in his new congregation. For more than twenty years, the people at Redeemer have intentionally engaged Christian practices as the heart of their communal faith. At a time when many mainline congregations still tried to do church as their grandparents had, Redeemer reconfigured itself as a pilgrimage community, a place of personal transformation based in the life of study, prayer, and discerning the work of the Holy Spirit. It has not always been easy. Along the way, they have had some dark times—like the three years' spent searching for their new minister, the search that resulted in Bruce moving from a church near San Francisco to join Redeemer on its journey.

In his first months, Bruce listened carefully to the language of this pilgrim community, trying to understand its distinctive practices and the way the church organizes its communal life. They have many gifts, including a special practice of "the ministry of encouragement" and unique practices of discernment. On the first day of his new ministry, Bruce was given an extraordinary gift—a member who had just passed away left Redeemer more than $12 million to be used at the congregation's discretion. In today's sermon, Bruce reflects upon Redeemer's many gifts. To Bruce, gifts should not occasion self-congratulations. Rather, gifts are an invitation to change. He talks about the call of Jesus' disciples and the relationship between abundance and risk.

The New Testament reading is about the great catch of fish, whose very abundance threatens to sink the apostles' boats. "This is a metaphor for the church in general and Church of the Redeemer in particular," Bruce says. "We have caught onto an abundance of Spirit, an abundance of gifts. But this call involves risk; it is both a challenge and an opportunity." Bruce highlights Redeemer's many successes as a parish—its faithfulness, intelligence, humor, and commitment. Yet he gently reminds them that these gifts are a renewed call to "open itself and share itself with new and wider communities."

Throughout his sermon, Bruce emphasizes Redeemer's amazing capacity for change—Jim Hanisian, the former rector called them *progressive conservatives*—based in their openness to the Holy Spirit. But the Spirit's call is not just something that happened in the past. "God is equally present now," Bruce says, "and we need to pay attention to the Holy Spirit here and now. Redeemer is called to new people, new communities, and new ways of being."

No one gasps. No one looks worried. No one panics as Bruce calls for change. They listen carefully, open and expectant. If they are anxious, they have learned that such feelings are a natural part of paying attention to God and taking risks. After twenty years of being a different sort of church, change is a way of life for them. The young associate minister, Alice Connor, says, "They have a certain trust that things will happen. They are willing to be patient and let them happen." A longtime member agrees: "Redeemer has always been in a state of change and transition. We trust that the Holy Spirit is working through all things. I really feel that." Tim, another longtime member, comments, "I think that we try to be who we are, to be better at who we are and who God wants us to be."

All across the congregation, people do not speak of being. Rather, they speak of becoming, of calling, of listening, of responsive acting. Nothing at Redeemer is a finished product. Instead, it is, as one member said, "open on the end." Alice Connor says that Redeemer is not a "what's the point?" kind of church where people do things because "we've always done it." Instead, Alice attributes Redeemer's lively tradition to the fact that "the Holy Spirit is guiding us." Longtime member Lynne Thornton opines that "tradition needs to be fluid."

Church changes? How can that be? After all, the New Testament teaches that "Jesus Christ is the same, yesterday, today, and forever." Many Christians interpret this to mean that Christianity and the Church never change. Indeed, church is often viewed as a place to escape change, to cling to the old ways. From this perspective, change is somehow secular, an accommodation to worldliness that whittles away at true faith. Yet, at Redeemer change is a spiritual practice, one deeply based in an alternative stream of New Testament theology—the theology of the Holy Spirit.

Both the Hebrew and the Christian scriptures depict the Holy Spirit as the wind or breath of God that blows as it will, ever changing and ever recreating. In Christianity, the Holy Spirit is God's mysterious presence, often pictured in the New Testament as a risk taker and rule breaker, the person of the Trinity who does not play by the book. Throughout my pilgrimage, people talked of the Holy Spirit and change, grounding their experiences of congregational life in the life-giving wind of God. Indeed, they rarely spoke of God as Father; they often talked about Jesus, but they most frequently used the language of Spirit to explain their churches. Presbyterian minister Graham Standish told me that, in recent years, his congregation had experienced "a natural openness to God, more organic than programmatic, back to the way the original church was."

I have heard the writer Phyllis Tickle explain that the early centuries of Christianity were the time of the Father, the Reformation was the time of Son, and these days might well be the time of the Spirit.[120] Certainly, her trinitarian history meshes with what I saw on the road. Everywhere, and rather unexpectedly, people in emerging mainline churches were allowing themselves to be remade by the breath of God. They easily spoke of the Spirit, referring to that often mysterious person of the Trinity, and expectantly anticipated God's movement in their midst. They seek to be, as one person described it, "a telling presence" of God in the world.

Following the Spirit means change. And it means that God has distinctive calls for each congregation, each unique, each responsive to the breath of new life. My pilgrimage taught me that the Spirit is not only about individual transformed churches, but that, when viewed corporately, congregations form a mosaic of regenerative change. Together, they point toward an emerging form of Christian gathering, the pilgrim church. There is no one-size-fits-all kind of pilgrim congregation. One of their few shared qualities is their ability to change, their recognition that pilgrim communities are communities engaged in near-continual spiritual transformation. In their midst, I encountered a variety of new ways of becoming of church—each a living recreation of Christian tradition. Together, they allowed me to see hope.

Every congregation I visited had changed in the last decade. In many ways, congregations are like individuals. People change when they encounter God in meaningful ways. Over the years, Christian pilgrims convert and reconvert as they experience *metanoia* anew, and as they grow toward what Saint Paul called mature faith. Just as this process is true for individuals, so it is for congregations. People need community to change, to sustain a life of pilgrimage, and to go deeper in change. Pilgrims need pilgrim congregations.

In the churches along my way, change was not gimmicky innovation in search of cultural relevance. Too often, churches think that if they add guitars to worship, put DVDs in Sunday school rooms, or open a food court in the foyer, new people will join. This kind of change smacks of market tinkering—adjusting the product to improve sales. In my journey, churches changed at a much deeper level and for different reasons. In many cases, change was made inevitable by numerical decline, financial crisis, or neighborhood transition. Spiritual anxiety gripped the community, pushing the congregation to realize that it needed to be different. Whether threatened by spiritual boredom or facing church closure, each congregation had asked two questions that sparked deep change: Who are we? What is God calling us to do? They discovered a renewed sense of identity and a clear purpose in serving the world. They experienced a change of heart that transformed their communal understanding of who God had made them to be.

Saint Mark: Suburban Village

Saint Mark Lutheran Church has been a solid and successful church since it was founded in the 1960s. In the early 1990s, however, tensions developed around the leadership, especially the former pastor's tendency to, as one person told me, "change things all the time." According to most accounts, change was random and unpredictable. The church, then numbering about 570 members, began to drift, not entirely sure of its future—or, oddly enough, its past. The sense of being unmoored created tension, anxiety, and conflict that resulted in a change of pastors. The current pastor, Gary Erdos, recalls asking early in his ministry at the church, "What are your traditions?" They would say, reports Gary, "Well, we really don't have any." Forty-something Pastor Erdos laughs: "I found it odd that I became a bastion of stability and tradition in a relatively short period of time!"

At Saint Mark, anxiety about change gave way to real spiritual hunger to go deeper into tradition; they felt called to explore Lutheran worship, Christian formation, and ancient prayer practices. Gary changed the liturgy by regularizing it, providing theological vision for the high-church style of Lutheran liturgy (Gary calls it "western Christian liturgical identity"), which the church warmly embraced. He responded to the congregation's sense of spiritual hunger by offering a process of prayer formation following the teachings of Saint Ignatius of Loyola. They developed hands-on Sunday school programs for the children based on Montessori methods of learning, paying close attention to the scriptures and to Lutheran theology, history, and identity.

Because Saint Mark was a mission church founded in the 1960s, its people had never really connected with the larger history and traditions of Christianity. Meeting in a small, industrial building on the edges of suburbia, the congregation had lived in spiritual isolation from tradition, giving it an idiosyncratic air. In the mid-1990s, as the church approached its thirtieth anniversary, it faced a midlife crisis of identity and purpose. When Gary arrived, he introduced them to a past that they barely knew, and helped them restitch their connections to the larger Christian tradition.

Within a few years, the people of Saint Mark decided that they needed to renovate their buildings to match their growing sense of identity. They connected the old sanctuary and the education building with a large, glass-walled gathering space, an indoor courtyard really, complete with a fountain and the "open-air" Café Saint Mark. Sitting in the sanctuary, one can see across the glass-enclosed courtyard into the nursery. The whole thing feels like a village square—church, children, and café—around the water fountain in the middle of suburbia. And yet it is also a Lutheran village, where symbols and words combine to constantly remind the congregation of its identity, beliefs, and language in a way that is not exclusive but welcoming. Saint Mark is not a walled village. Rather, it is an open one.

Holy Communion: Spiritual Center

At Holy Communion, the church's lovely grounds and obvious resources bespeak a history of grace and plenty. Yet, beyond its pristine gentility, Holy Communion is a strong community, one that often breaks new ground and faces hard questions. They know how to change. Their former rectors had navigated difficult times of change in the South, leading the congregation through the choppy waters of the civil rights movement and its aftermath. Holy Communion has long been a congregation that tries hard to do the right thing.

Somewhere along the way, the church created a deep reservoir of prayer and discernment, as a handful of its members embraced practices from the traditions of Benedictine spirituality. By the year 2000, however, the reservoir seemed dammed. Their longtime priest had retired, and the people of Holy Communion wanted a new minister who could help release the waters of the Spirit. Eventually, they found the Reverend Gary Jones, an Episcopal priest who was formed in the Anglican contemplative tradition. Gary's first day at Holy Communion was September 11, 2001. He did not need to argue for change; he did not need to break down walls of resistance. The tragic events of the terrorist attacks did that. The new minister and the old church faced a changed world. And, instead of retreating, they marched right into a future of change.

Drawing from the traditions of prayer that had long been present in the congregation, Holy Communion reenvisioned itself as the "spiritual center" of Memphis, an open-monastic kind of community, based in the ancient Christian triad of learning, prayer, and service. Centered in this contemporary neomonastic vision, Holy Communion practices hospitality in a unique way. Like ancient Christian communities, it opens its doors to any comers with no expectation that visitors will necessarily join the congregation, hoping only to be a "sacred presence" in the midst of the world. Their worship services, book events, and special speakers—one woman referred to this as their "embarrassment of riches"—serve the whole community of Memphis, seeking to ground the city as a "spiritual center" to which all are invited. As part of its new sense of identity, Holy Communion sees its monastic vision as a "regional religious studies resource," a kind of spiritual college for learners of faith, sharing its abundance with others. "We take a lead," said one member, "on issues that are affecting our lives."

But Holy Communion's "spiritual center" is neither ad hoc nor individualistic. Having a sacred *place* where people gather and a distinct *tradition* of worship offers spiritual seekers longed-for connections of community. Several people at Holy Communion described their church as "common ground." One woman explained that at the church "we learn to care for one another and get out of ourselves." Throughout the congregation, people spoke of finding "connection" at Holy Communion to God, to one another, and to their community. Another member said, "It is nice being part of a community, being part of something bigger than yourself; I feel there's growth here that I couldn't do on my own."

By going deep into prayer, the people of Holy Communion remade their church as a circle of spiritual connection. The symbol of the circle is evident, including in the church's signature logo—a cross within a circle. "The circle," states one parish publication, "is a Christian symbol, a round shape with no apparent beginning or end, which symbolizes eternity or God." Perhaps the image of the circle is a native one, echoing an old southern gospel song, "May the Circle Be Unbroken." In seeking to be a spiritual center for Memphis, the people of Holy Communion have found that they are actually spiritually centered—in themselves, in their congregation, and for their community. Rather than a one-dimensional circle, Holy Communion is a community of concentric spiritual centers that ripple from the heart of its people to the world beyond the church. By striving to be a sacred presence, they found the sacred present within.

Calvin: Jazz Church

"This is a jazz church," says Bruce Smith, the music minister at Calvin Presbyterian. "Not just improvisation, but jazz in the sense that jazz pulls on all styles of music. You have to listen to everything. You become a better player. It comes out in your music."

Perhaps not surprisingly, for Bruce his metaphor extends to the whole of the Christian life and the congregation. "If you haven't listened to classical music, to Bach and the Baroque masters, there's going to be something missing. As a single player," he explains, "the more I expose myself to various types of music and collect the history—I have a collective experience, and I'm immersed in collective history. It's like writing, you know; you become better in your vocabulary the more you read. Your ideas become sharper because you read more. The church is that way, I think. It is a collective body, [and] we invite and celebrate this wide range of styles."

Bruce goes on to say that some churches "don't have a lot of range." He worries about the word *tradition,* saying that as a word it "does turn some people off." At Calvin they talk instead about collective historical experience, something that "everyone brings." Calvin comprises former Roman Catholics, New Age practitioners, evangelicals, and mainline Protestants. Bruce laughs: "We began to collect a congregation that came from all these backgrounds!" Very "naturally," he says, their music "came out."

Calvin did not experience any great crisis. Rather, until 1996 the church struggled with the same slow numerical decline that afflicts many small-town Protestant churches. Loss of vision and an increasing sense of hopelessness accompanied the drop. Then, as they opened themselves to spiritual practices of discernment, prayer, healing, and diversity, a new energy began to move through the community. Membership rebounded. One person noted that people do not come to Calvin because of "some great marketing machine." Rather, people respond to "what we're doing," something minister Graham Standish calls "the organic nature of spirituality." Calvin's approach stands in stark contrast to typical Presbyterian ways of doing business. The denomination is noted for its devotion to rules, order, planning, and program. However, by basing their church's whole sense of identity on faith practices, Calvin's people eschew externally derived order in favor of improvisational and internal harmonies of the Holy Spirit's jazz.

"When I said 'organic,' that's important," says Graham. "We always talk about the need to get back to the way the original church was. I've been schooled in all the prayer disciplines, contemplation and things like that. Yet my sense is that in the early church, they did it in a way that was much more organic, more natural, more part of their lives." As a congregation, Graham insists, Calvin moves toward what is "organic" and "natural," learning from collective Christian experience to create open-ended community.

Members testify to the power of becoming a jazz church. "Since Graham's arrival," one says, "Calvin Church has grown deeper spiritually. Our leadership is always asking, 'What is God calling us to do?' rather than what they want for the church themselves." Listening to God's voice, praying, and collecting the wisdom of others makes Calvin "a dynamic place."

Cornerstone: Radical Liturgical

A question strikes most newcomers to Cornerstone United Methodist Church: how did a paschal candle, altar table, font, and crucifix find their way into a praise church? Meeting in an industrial-like building, Cornerstone looks anything but "churchy," especially with its moveable chairs, lighting and sound systems, video screens, and rock-band setup. Yet, sitting in the middle of what is standard equipment for most conservative evangelical churches is a substantial wooden baptismal font, a table for the Lord's Supper, and a pulpit. An abstract Resurrection crucifix hangs above the table. Every Sunday, minister Roy Terry begins by playing his electric guitar with the praise band, then moves to the pulpit to preach, and finally dons a chasuble to celebrate Holy Communion behind that table. The congregation sings praises in a wide range of styles—from contemporary music to Wesleyan hymns to Latin chant.

Methodist bishop Timothy Whitaker dubbed Cornerstone "radical liturgical," a moniker that captures the essence of the congregation. As a new church, Cornerstone set out to be a body that participates in the Christian story "that transcends time and culture," and sought to center its worship on the "core elements" of praise, prayer, teaching, and celebrating the Lord's Supper. "If the church is serious about its full and humble participating in God's story," says Roy, "then the church really does have something to offer! If this is all about God, and not about establishing human social clubs and institutions, then it opens the door." Roy and the leadership team identified practices that created hospitality, making Sunday worship an invitation into a Christian way of life. By doing what was old—even in a contemporary form—Cornerstone found that ancient practices "gave new breath to creative imagination and freedom in worship." People responded and the new church grew.

Having successfully launched itself as a congregation, Cornerstone might have been tempted to rest on its laurels. However, the church understood that the Christian life is a journey of change. Roy recalls that "becoming God's church" was the key lesson they learned in their first years in worship. He says, *"Becoming* indicated that all participants are on the journey of faith, and the practices that form the community have been made available for all throughout the ages." Like Graham Standish at Calvin, Roy emphasizes the organic nature of Christian community. "When the Body of Christ, the church, is about the business of *becoming,*" he states, "it removes the dross that clogs the free-flowing winds of celebration and transformation." At Cornerstone, the radical practice of Christian worship led into a communal life of perpetual pilgrimage. "Becoming" Christian is, in this life at least, a journey that does not end. As Roy quips, "We're more interested in forming disciples than recruiting members."[121]

Epiphany: Downtown Common

Church of the Epiphany's website address, www.epiphanydc.org, contains a clue to the church's dawning sense of identity. "D.C.," says minister Randolph Charles, "as in Washington—and as in 'downtown common'! That's what we are becoming, a spiritual downtown common." In recent decades, being a downtown church had become a struggle for the old congregation. As one person said, "Our members live throughout the city and outlying counties; it is difficult to keep them connected." However, they have begun to see the problem as an opportunity. "Soon after I got here I realized that as far as I could faithfully perceive," says Randolph, "God was calling us to have a ministry with downtown poor, with downtown workers, and with parishioners." Initially, some people thought "church was only for parishioners" and resisted opening the congregation to a wider ministry in the city. Indeed, a small group tried to have Randolph fired. But the majority of the congregation sensed that God wanted the church to move in new directions. Epiphany's location as a city church made the more narrow understanding of church increasingly impossible. Randolph stayed and the congregation began a long, and sometimes hard, process of change.

On any given day, Epiphany is open. There are weekday services at lunchtime, including a concert series, labyrinth walks, book groups, and prayer groups. People who work in offices around the church come in for spiritual refreshment or to eat lunch in the small garden next to the building. There are homeless people, too. The office of *Street Sense,* a newspaper produced by the homeless community, is upstairs at the church. Public school children from across the district come to the church to participate in an arts program. The Reverend Anne-Marie Jeffrey, the congregation's "urban missioner," daily ministers to the neighborhood's needy residents. Epiphany is on the Civil War tour of Washington, D.C., and tourists often come in, looking for the Jefferson Davis pew or imagining the grand building as a hospital for wounded soldiers. As one woman says, "Epiphany reaches out to an unbelievable [number] of people. I think it is just incredible."

Epiphany is a contemporary version of the old town-square church. Sitting on the "common," the busy public space where all manner of humanity does its business, Epiphany is finding renewed life by opening its doors and serving whoever wanders by. Although Epiphany was originally founded as a city mission, and has a long history of serving the city, that sense is changing and deepening today. Increasingly, the church sees itself less as a parish church and more as a lively—and sacred—public space. Like other churches on my journey, Epiphany draws from its past while carefully considering what God is calling it to do in the present. "We don't do things arbitrarily," says one woman. "We adopt them as part of our community when it feeds the spirit. When things don't work, we shed them."

Change energizes Randolph Charles. But, like his congregation, he prizes continuity and tradition as well. He says that a guiding question of his ministry is "How can we see and honor the values of the early church and apply them, and maybe reshape them, and learn from those principles today?" His view of living tradition "is the way I see what the church is." He calls ancient practice "the central cord" and the "river that runs through my understanding of church." At Epiphany, serving the city means being connected by the cords of tradition—the church does not see itself as just any public space, a social service agency, or a Washington tourist attraction. Rather, Epiphany's downtown common is a community of practice, grounded in the Eucharist that invites urban wayfarers into a Christian way of life.

Suburban village, spiritual center, jazz church, radical liturgical, and downtown common were not the only imaginative congregational transformations. Along the way, I encountered a church that called itself an urban abbey, a cathedral that understood itself as a Christian piazza, a couple of inclusive communities, an artist colony, a congregation walking an ancient way, a church for "everybody else," and a "church of the misfits." In none of these cases did they come to their communal self-understanding through a program or marketing scheme. Rather, each congregation searched out questions of identity and purpose before arriving at a new sense of who they were and what God was calling them to do. The metaphors they imagined for their congregations were all dynamic, indicating in every case that church is the body of Jesus Christ, a living organism that grows and changes over time. For them, church was an adventure into creating authentic spiritual community.

What a contrast to the church of my childhood! At Saint John's United Methodist, church was primarily a building where we worshiped and a set of traditions we inherited but could never change. We were white-glove Methodists, all dressed up each Sunday, and all sitting politely in our pews. I do not recall that anyone in church ever looked particularly happy. Church was a matter of duty. We certainly never thought of church as an organic being, or as a place of authentic community. Even then, however, some people may have been hoping for more. Every Sunday, when my mother packed us off to church, my grandfather would thunder, "Why are you taking those children to that place full of hypocrites?" Mother would just shrug as she bundled us into the car.

Unlike my agnostic grandfather, I have remained a Christian, but I can sympathize with his point of view. Too many congregations are phony; too many attempt to present to the world what author Susan Howatch calls "glittering images." Many of the people I met on my journey had spent years searching for an authentic spiritual community because they knew that authenticity in a church is a sadly rare thing. For whatever reason, the churches I found have taken a different path—one of transparent community. They do not, however, elevate authenticity to a point of pride. Rather, they interpret their uniqueness with humility and humor—regularly referring to their congregations as "quirky," "real," "sincere," "authentic," "accepting," "rough around the edges," and even "eccentric."

Because of their unique sense of identity, almost all the congregations expressed reservations about their larger denominational identity. Throughout my journey, many people told me that they were uncomfortable with the structures, institutions, politics, and formal organization of their denominations. They often portrayed denominations in the same way they talked about political parties, "out of touch," "irrelevant," and "burdensome." Because of this discomfort, they resisted denominational labels, instead favoring the generic "Christian" to describe themselves—and reflecting the larger cultural trend toward "postdenominational" faith.[122] When this resistance to denominational labels is added to their creative images for church, they almost appear to be religious independents—rather loosely attached to the formal structures of established religion. In most cases, these people were largely uninterested in institutional religion.

It fascinated me that, despite their postdenominational leanings, in every case they loved their congregations—congregations that were still identifiably Presbyterian, Lutheran, Methodist, Congregational, or Episcopal. In grassroots fashion, the people on my journey had appropriated what Randolph Charles called "the central cord" of each denominational tradition. They extolled the practices of "Anglicanism" instead of the Episcopal Church; "Wesleyan Methodism" rather than the United Methodist Church; "New England Congregationalism" instead of the United Church of Christ; "Lutheranism" instead of the Evangelical Lutheran Church of America. Their connection to the larger Christian tradition was not that of formal structures; their connection was through the lived tradition of practice. They approached tradition in the same organic way that they explored identity, typically intertwining new congregational vibrancy with living practice. Because tradition was a living thing, it, too, like their congregations, would grow and change. They experienced authentic church not as a matter of organized structures but as a matter of transformative traditions.

Much to my surprise, the congregations on my journey were post-"postdenominational," remixing elements of tradition, practice, and wisdom—the collective histories—that seem to resonate with contemporary pilgrims. Largely ignoring the old ways of structuring religion, they have embarked on a journey of change that is taking them beyond the walls of their individual congregations to the possibility of changing the wider practices of Christian community. Although they exist in complete isolation from one another, these churches have all stumbled into the same realization: authentic spiritual community is a journey of becoming God's church—a church called to, as Bruce Freeman said, "new people, new communities, and new ways of being." And this is not a dream, transformation beyond possibility, or the wild imaginings of a few spiritual visionaries. It is happening in old mainline Protestant churches—regular congregations that decided to become a more authentic kind of church.

SEVENTEEN

Transforming the World

The Episcopal Church of the Epiphany in Washington, D.C., just three blocks from the White House, sits in the shadow of worldly power. Its closest sister parish is Saint John's Episcopal Church, Lafayette Square, "the church of the presidents." When President Bush is in Washington, he attends Saint John's, as did his father before him. It is a powerful pulpit in a powerful church, the kind of place where trappings of church and state intermix, and where the cultural remnants of old-fashioned Protestantism still hold sway.

If not for the fact that Saint John's is a short walk from the back door of the White House, Epiphany might well have become the church of the presidents. But it did not. Through its long history, Epiphany has had plenty of distinguished members—politicians who served in presidents' cabinets, Supreme Court justices, military officers, congressmen. But an odd thread weaves through the parish's history: despite its close association with political power, Epiphany has always been able to see that God's reign and Washington's worldly kingdom are two different things. Since Epiphany's founding in 1842 as a "city mission," at every important turn in its life the church has chosen to stand with the poor instead of the rich, with those in need of healing instead of the healthy, with the eccentric instead of the polished.

Not too many famous people attend Epiphany these days. Despite its glorious classical music and elegant liturgy, Epiphany walks to a distinctly alternative beat. The church comprises a remarkable mix of homeless people (nearly two hundred of them attend the 8:00 A.M. Sunday service), urban singles, middle-class African-Americans, gay and lesbian couples, and Washington do-gooders (mostly those who work for nonprofit agencies in the city). And, somewhat surprisingly, the congregation also has Democrats and Republicans, antiwar activists and military families. It is a demographically untidy place. As one member told me, "At Epiphany, every person is his or her own ethnic group!" Yet this mishmash of humanity forms a congregation marked by its practices of hospitality and healing, a church that breaks down the barriers between people and reforms patterns of human community. There is power at Epiphany, but not the worldly power of the White House. As one man put it, "The first time I walked into Church of the Epiphany, I actually *saw* the kingdom of God."

The kingdom of God is one of the most enduring themes of American theology. Since the days of the Puritans, American Protestants have seen their work for God somehow related to the coming of the kingdom, believing that the activity of American politics will, to use their language, "hasten the day" of Jesus' second coming. Throughout American history, this has manifested itself in various ways. The Puritans, along with hosts of other Protestant colonists, believed that fleeing England and forming a pure church *and* a pure society would reform the body politic and bring about God's reign. In the nineteenth century, American Protestants linked kingdom theology to great political crusades, including the antislavery and women's suffrage campaigns. And, at the beginning of the twentieth century, visions of God's kingdom fueled the social gospel movement and progressive politics.

Today, millions of evangelical Protestants read books like *Left Behind,* eagerly anticipating the end of the world and the arrival of God's kingdom. Although many Americans do not recognize it, such apocalyptic visions are actually linked with the politics of the religious right. To cite just one example: on the campus of Regent University, at the center of Pat Robertson's vast political empire, stands a massive statue—on the scale of monuments in cities like Washington, New York, London, and Paris—of the Four Horsemen of the Apocalypse riding forth at God's command to destroy the earth. In American Protestantism, whether left or right, kingdom theology is always political theology.

Just a few weeks before he died, Jack Harrison, a longtime member of Epiphany, preached (by proxy) a farewell sermon to his beloved community. The text that day, from the Gospel of Mark, was the one in which Jesus sends his disciples into the world on a mission in God's name. Although much of the sermon underscored the practice of healing, Jack pushed the congregation beyond personal healing to the larger hope of healing, God's *shalom* for the world:

> *We learn from Mark that Jesus sends the twelve disciples out into the world of daily work and human relationship lightly equipped, but with some newly learned skills that they gained as companions of Jesus. A few may have preached on street corners, but most of them probably went to familiar places of work and kith and kin, making their own livings as needs be, carrying out their missions of relieving the disturbed from unclean spirits, treating illnesses physical and mental, and conveying the bedrock truth that Jesus was imparting to them that the kingdom of God was at hand.*

"God's reality is here with us, folks," Jack continued. "Believe it! You don't have to do anything more to make it happen. It's here already. This is why we're doing all this for-the-church activity. We are always, always, working for God's world."

To some, Jack's sermon might sound escapist, emphasizing healing and evangelism, the divine mission of the disciples, and seemingly eschewing worldly concerns. But set as it was in the frame of Epiphany, with its radical practices of the kingdom, I heard something else. I heard politics. After all, he was extolling his friends to go about their daily work *in Washington, D.C.* as if "always, always working for God's world." In his final sermon, Jack chose not to dwell on the sadness of impending death or to play on the congregation's grief. Rather, he preached about kingdom politics, pushing toward the "external part of our mission and purpose, which I think we are always in danger of losing." Although Jack was walking through his own shadows, he intentionally shone the light on Epiphany's vocation—to be a new kind of Christian community where the gospel of the kingdom will have new kinds of consequences for the body politic.

Not long ago, I spoke in Baltimore, only a few miles from Saint John's United Methodist Church, my childhood parish. I learned a lot about church and politics back in those days. Mostly I learned that mainline Protestants had huge political power and that we had essentially reduced all political engagement to two issues, the civil rights movement and the Vietnam War. I had also seen the power that politics had to fracture denominations and churches, as the gospel preached from the pulpit seemed increasingly removed from the lives of the people on pilgrimage. That distance, and the sense of spiritual alienation it created, caused many departures from old mainline congregations—including my parents' exit from Saint John's. From firsthand experience, I understand why so many mainline pastors shy away from politics in the pulpit. It is tough to preach a political faith and maintain Christian community. Whenever I return to Baltimore, I remember those heady yet painful days.

In the Baltimore workshop, I shared my research about Christian practices and pilgrim congregations with a thoughtful group of Episcopal clergy. After the presentation, a clergywoman in her thirties, asked:

"What are the implications for us of all this? It isn't just about church. It is about politics. What does this mean about politics? What does this mean for our larger life, the issues and divisions we face?"

Her question is a good one. For more than two centuries, mainline Protestant churches have stood near the center of national life, affecting political and social changes of all sorts. I wonder about the same question. Whenever people gather, especially in American churches, there are bound to be political consequences.

I told the young priest what I had observed: in these particular mainline churches, people had rejected business-as-usual politics, were fed up with division, and resented the fact that Christian faith was being used as a tool to advance a single political agenda. Instead of being involved in politics as they were in the 1960s—primarily the politics of policy and protest—they engaged in hands-on personal politics, things like setting up homeless shelters and local environmental projects.

An older member of the audience, clearly a veteran of the 1960s' social movements, complained, "That's all very good, but that is not politics. That's compassionate service. The church needs to change social systems, address policy, and seek structural change!"

Although she expressed sentiments common to the mainline of the 1960s and 1970s, I had seen an almost entirely different political vision in the study congregations—a nearly wholesale rejection of the definition of politics as systemic change and policy platforms. In the congregations I visited, politics was being redefined as communal practices of service, grassroots social transformation that works "up" toward larger change. Unlike old-style mainline Protestantism with its more secular politics, these churches started with a theological vision of God's reign, found their strength in spiritual disciplines of prayer and worship, and embarked on public involvement from a distinctly Christian sense of identity. Although they vote in very high numbers, they eschew partisan politics in favor of forming a new sense of the body politic, seeing American communal life in the same organic, dynamic, and transformative ways that they see their own lives and congregations.[123] "We feed the hungry and provide for the homeless. We bear witness to the sort of people God calls us to be in our jobs and at school," explained Lutheran pastor Gary Erdos. "We invite our neighbors and friends to come and see the community that shapes who we are with the message of Jesus. We have been transformed by the message of Jesus and we hope to, in many small and great ways, transform the world around us by the message of Jesus we bear."

As American Protestants have always done, the people and churches on my journey linked God's reign with the body politic. Yet, they understand that kingdom differently than both their own mainline ancestors and their modern-day evangelical cousins. Unlike conservative evangelicals who seek to redeem America by remaking it in their moral image, many of the mainline pilgrims I met hope to, as Gary Erdos said, "transform" the world through the teachings of Jesus—by following the signposts of the Christian way. Redeeming America assumes that the nation needs to be saved (primarily from sexual immorality); transforming America assumes that the nation can achieve its best self.[124] It is a subtle but important political distinction. Mainline Protestants hold a distinctly Christian political outlook, too, but theirs is a view based in generosity and gratitude (as one person explained, "Everything is a gift") that is open-ended, fluid, and inclusive.

As congregations like these gain voice and confidence, their politics will have, as my young priest friend noted, different consequences than mainline politics of the past. Where all this might lead is anyone's guess. But, as I traveled with them, I sensed that I was witnessing the birth of a new sort of kingdom politics as mainline Protestants tried to reclaim a positive Christian message by rejecting both theocracy and secularism and forming a new radical religious center.

Purple America

Yorktown, Virginia, renown for its military history, is today home to several military bases. Not far from the Air Force base, Saint Mark Lutheran Church serves as a spiritual home to many military families. Saint Mark is a relatively conservative congregation, theologically moderate, and politically more Republican than Democrat. And very military—service to God and country is important to them. They pray for soldiers, mourn with widows, and care for military families. One of the church's ministry groups organizes gift boxes for service members overseas. During one of my early visits, I was surprised to see one young man at church in fatigues. On the face of it, Saint Mark appears to be a "red" church in a "red" county in a "red" state. Conservative Christians at prayer.

In the days following September 11, 2001, the people of Saint Mark gathered to worship, pray, and hear the word of God amid their personal fears and their certainty that war loomed near. At their very first service in the new age of terrorism, Pastor Gary Erdos led them in prayer. His prayer was not for glorious victory or God's vengeance on the terrorists. Rather, he prayed for Osama Bin Laden—for the people of Saint Mark to forgive their enemy. Nobody got mad; no one stormed out of the congregation. In this most military of places, they prayed for forgiveness.

"We say by the command of our Lord Jesus Christ we pray for our enemies," says Gary. "Not because we want to, not because we like it, but because we are saying that's who we are when we gather in this place. Forgiveness is a practice of faith. We do that as a people worshiping God."

Looking around Saint Mark, I notice that there are no American flags in the sanctuary, an unusual omission in Virginia. "About twenty-two years ago, the flags were taken out of the worship space," Gary reports. "We lost a few members at the time when they did that. But the flags never came back in. You know, that's never even been a question in this place. There is a sense that when we come and we worship, we are a different people."

Saint Mark has a Fourth of July picnic; they pray for those who have served or died in wars on Memorial Day and Veterans Day. But the dominant identity of the congregation is not the military, or being politically conservative, or being Americans. Indeed, I often heard people at Saint

Mark express theological reservations about Pat Robertson's headquarters in nearby Virginia Beach and his fundamentalist politics. Retired military officers leveled trenchant theological, policy, and strategic critiques of the Iraq War against both the Pentagon and the administration. Contrary to my initial impressions, Saint Mark was no slam dunk for the Christian right.

Instead, Saint Mark's dominant identity is that of being God's people, a line of faith and practice that reaches back to the ancient church. "I think that is palpable for many people here," says Gary. "We come with our own national identity. And that's okay. But as we gather as God's people, we need to say that we are something else at least an hour out of the week. We are a liturgical people worshiping God more than a bunch of Americans."

Gary's comment clarified something I had noticed in most of the congregations on my journey—something I now call liturgical politics. Throughout my travels, people told me that they learned to be a "body" around the communion table—that the kingdom vision of the Lord's Supper, sharing the meal of forgiveness, healing, and peace, broke down old political boundaries and led congregations in a search for something else, a different way to organize community, communal action, service, and doing justice. As a member of Epiphany said, "What attracts me to Epiphany is not only the outreach, not only the diversity, not only the liturgy, but how all those things work together. There's lots of churches that offer pieces of this, but this one brought it all together for me."

At Epiphany, the metaphor of the body of Christ, the broken healer, proved a powerful spiritual insight for the American body politic. There, the Welcome Table—the Sunday morning worship and breakfast for the homeless people in the neighborhood—has led to a profound transformation of the congregants' attitudes toward and commitments to the poor. As Epiphany's minister, Randolph Charles, noted, "We've changed our behavior with the homeless to make sure that we're not looking down, but we are instead beside, on equal standing." No longer an abstract issue, "the poor" are members of the church, friends in ministry, and fellow worshipers. This hands-on encounter, the sharing of the Lord's Supper, generates Epiphany's lively political and community involvement.

Like Saint Mark and Epiphany, Church of the Redeemer in Cincinnati focuses on creating community across political and theological boundaries. There one woman remarked, "We're not really red, and we're not really blue. We're sort of purple." Her comment rang true. Some congregations along my way leaned toward being blue-purples (especially in urban areas and in the west); others, red-purples (especially in suburbs and in the south). None matched the media stereotype of Christian politics; none was a pure form of any political party. Like their Roman Catholic brothers and sisters, they are somewhat politically unpredictable and do not form a reliably unified voting block.[125] In the 2004 elections, I estimated, slightly more than half of the people in the congregations voted for John Kerry, while slightly less than half voted for George Bush.[126] Purple churches.

Purple is more than a blend of red and blue, a kind of right-left political hybrid. Purple is an ancient Christian symbol. Early Christians borrowed purple, the color of imperial power, from their Roman persecutors and inverted its symbolism. For Christians, purple symbolized God as ruler and God's reign. Yet, that kingdom was not one of imperial power—it was birthed from the martyred church, unified around a crucified savior, and formed by the spiritual authority of the baptized in a community of humility and forgiveness. For Christians, purple is more than a blending of political extremes. Purple is about power that comes through loving service, laying down one's life for others, and following Jesus' path. Like forming a congregation of two hundred homeless people or praying for Osama Bin Laden.

Episcopalians refer to their church as the *via media*, the middle way. The term is drawn from their liturgy, developed in the seventeenth century—an age of religious and political extremism—from both Protestant and Roman Catholic sources. They have long understood their liturgy as political, the moderating spiritual glue of a diverse people in prayer. On my journey, I could see the outlines of this liturgical political impulse playing out across the old Protestant mainline. In an age of political division, being churches of the *via media* is no easy thing. Standing against extremism, in a positive and hopeful way, requires knowing what you believe and putting it in practice.

Reclaiming the Message

In Seattle, Judith shared her feelings about being a member of Plymouth United Church of Christ. "Being part of a liberal church you really feel like you have to explain yourself." Her secular friends do not attend church and think that all Christians are fundamentalists. "I feel like I need a big disclaimer," she confessed. Recently, she read Jim Wallis's *God's Politics* and found the book helpful. "He talks about faith not being private." Judith does not believe that religion is private. Rather, Christianity has public consequences, and she sees her church as "different" because by virtue of its being "liberal Christian, that does great things in community." But, she equally confesses, "it is only kind of liberal," because of the church's intense commitment to Christian practices of hospitality, prayer, and theological reflection. Despite its liberal pedigree, Plymouth has become a different sort of church. She finds the church's stance on serious—but not fundamentalist—Christianity "hard to explain" to friends.

Others felt the same way. In a recent conversation, Howard Anderson, an Episcopal priest at the Washington National Cathedral, told me, "I don't know what people are talking about when they talk about liberalism in the church. Things have changed so much. There aren't many liberals left in the Episcopal church!" I have heard biblical scholar Marcus Borg struggle with what to call the new spiritual impulse in mainline congregations. "It isn't really liberal. And, although many people refer to it as progressive, it isn't really that, either." He has sometimes called it neotraditional Christianity but more recently has settled on "transfor- mational Christianity" as an apt moniker for the emerging mainline.[127]

Struggling with how to name themselves, many people I met felt bereft of a public vocabulary with which to share their faith—everything about Christianity in the press, the larger media, and politics is about conservative Christians. "I am tired," a Virginia woman said, "of only one theological or political view being considered moral." Another Virginia Episcopalian stated, "Many of us are closet Christians. We have such a fear of offending others that we keep a big part of our lives quiet. We need to come out of the closet and let the world know us better." A Lutheran in Washington state opined, "The rest of us, Christians as well, don't really receive any attention at all. But the rest of us are Christians with moral issues." Or, as a Tennessee Presbyterian explained bluntly, "We are in a struggle for the soul of Christianity." Numerous people shared their concern that mainline Protestants need to reclaim the Christian message from fundamentalists.

In Arizona, the people of Scottsdale Congregational UCC, long an activist liberal congregation, take the challenge of reclaiming the message seriously. A section of the Phoenix Affirmations they helped write reads:

> *The public face of Christianity in America today bears little connection to the historic faith of our ancestors. It represents even less our own faith as Christians who continue to celebrate the gifts of our Creator, revealed and embodied in the life, death, and resurrection of Jesus Christ. Heartened by our experience of the transforming presence of Christ's Holy Spirit in our world, we find ourselves in a time and place where we will be no longer silent.*

The Phoenix Affirmations are a holistic faith statement that links spirituality with politics—a call, really, to liturgical politics. In many ways, the final affirmation sums up the politics of the entire document: "Acting on the faith that we are born with a meaning and purpose; a vocation and ministry that serves to strengthen and extend God's realm of love."[128]

At Scottsdale, they talk about "the path of Jesus" as "our path," as the basis of their political involvement. Jesus' path is one of loving God, neighbor, and self "practiced together." Understanding the theology of political action has energized the congregation. As Anna said, "I think the Phoenix Affirmations are the foundation of being able to state in a concrete way why we are Christians and why we do what we do as Christians." Anna also noted that their pastor, Eric Elnes, a Princeton-trained biblical scholar, helps the congregation understand the clear connections between the scriptures and "today's politics and culture."

Unlike many mainline pastors who worry about preaching politics, Eric has no such fear. He regularly builds entire worship services around political themes. Yet, Eric's political preaching differs from mainline sermons of a generation ago. Instead of preaching authoritatively and directing people how to think, Eric's political preaching invites the congregation to participate in constructing a biblical response to contemporary issues. His distinctly casual style invites comments and questions from the congregation. In addition to hearing word-oriented preaching, members of the church perform dramas, play music, or create works of art illustrating Jesus' message. Thus, political preaching at Scottsdale has shifted from clerical directive to a communal spiritual performance piece. Instead of telling people what to do or how to vote, preaching draws the congregants into Jesus' story and teaches them to reflect on their personal roles in the biblical narrative.

As a result of study and prayer, members of the church walked three thousand miles across America in the summer of 2006. On the way, they encouraged "progressive Christians" to stand up and speak for their faith concerns. "There's a real ground flow taking place," says Scottsdale member Ron with great optimism, "in reclaiming the message of Christianity."

Rejecting Theocracy; Rejecting Secularism

The message is framed, at least in part, by standing against two extremes, both of which mainline Protestants find unsettling: fundamentalism and secularism. This is the essence of their via media: In the midst of the cultural divide, the pilgrims on my journey struggled to create a public theology that is open, inclusive, and tolerant, a vision that persuades by goodness, service, and beauty, not by condemnation, force, or violence. Seeing religious intolerance as dangerous, they have no interest in creating a Christian commonwealth or any sort of theocracy. Unlike Christian fundamentalists, they strongly support the legal separation of church and state. However, they equally define themselves against secular liberals and praise the informal influences of faith on politics.

On a February day in 2004, at a prayer workshop in a southern mainline congregation, a woman told a story about visiting her mother's conservative church in Florida: "It was awful! After the offertory, they sang three verses of 'My Country 'Tis of Thee.' Then, the priest talked about the need to eliminate the separation of church and state!" Others at the workshop concurred, "How terrible!" And they joked, "What's next? The national anthem? Imposing ashes that say Bush/Cheney 04?" Behind the humor, however, this conversation is more than an anti-Bush tirade. It reveals *why* many people in mainline churches worry about the current political climate—they are deeply distressed about the mixture of church and state and its implications on a variety of issues. They are concerned that the religious right is working against religious freedom and toward some kind of Christian theocracy.

Many people shared their distaste for the way the political right has manipulated religion. As one person put it, "I think that George Bush's fundamental approach to his faith is dangerous." Or as a sixtyish woman complained, "The Republicans insinuate that if you have different beliefs than theirs, you are not a Christian. In fact, a Christian friend of my daughter-in-law told her that if you were a Democrat, you couldn't be a Christian since Democrats are baby killers. This black-and-white approach is part of the Republican message. If you are a Democrat and support gay people and laws that give individual choices, you aren't a Christian." A New England Congregationalist, a man who grew up in a conservative Christian home, referred to this as the "facilely Christian veneer of the current administration." He worried about people being "tarred as immoral" on the basis of their political opinions. "The term *moral issues* has been hijacked to refer to only a subset of issues without looking at the larger picture."

Perhaps nowhere did anxiety about the religious right run higher than in churches situated in areas dominated by conservative Christian politics. Saint Andrew Christian Church is located near Overland Park, Kansas, a center of both antievolution and antigay movements. Saint Andrew does not reflect neighborhood politics. Instead, the congregation practices justice through valuing diversity, accepting gay and lesbian members, partnering with a church in El Salvador, and working for the environment. "Our congregation is a total anomaly," Rev. Holly McKissick explains. "We are a very progressive congregation in one of the most conservative neighborhoods in the country." She admits that the church has "some conservative members," but says that most of those at Saint Andrew are political progressives. "This church is the *one* place where they are 'safe' and can express their frustration over the current system." In 2005, eighty-eight new members joined the church and Sunday attendance jumped from 320 to 440. Holly speculates that "the growth is tied to the devastation progressive folks felt after the last presidential election." Indeed, at Saint Andrew, people seem to be voting with their feet—liberals joining a church as a way of protesting the politics of the religious right.

The people I met may be worried about theocracy, but they are equally concerned that liberals, especially secular ones, do not respect or value religious perspectives on politics. So, unlike secularists, they do not separate faith from ethics and political conscience. At "blue" Saint Andrew, for example, Holly McKissick attributes the congregational commitment of social justice to joyful worship and serious Christian practices. All the study congregations, whether moderate or progressive, linked political passions to Christian spirituality. I heard many people criticize the Democratic party for being "irreligious," "too secular," "having no room for people of faith," and stating flatly, "They just don't get it."

"Getting it" means that church and state must stay separate but that politics may be a soul-making enterprise, because the nation needs moral grounding in broad faith principles (Christian, Jewish, and others). As such, these congregations carve out a distinctive space, drawing from both justice-oriented politics and traditional Christian practices. They believe that following the teachings of Jesus has important social consequences—such as peacemaking, care for the poor, healing, and hospitality. As one Nashville woman said, "When I think of what Jesus taught, I am convinced that he would not want this country to attack another and kill at least fourteen thousand Iraqi citizens. Jesus is the prince of peace, not war. Jesus ministered to the poor and needy, but these people are rarely mentioned by this administration."

One Virginia woman said that her Episcopal church "helped me to think theologically about the issues." Another person said that serving as a leader in his congregation had strongly shaped his spiritual life: "My experiences at church have taught me that the world is not black and white. We live in a complex world with many differing and honorable views on many issues. Opening yourself up to the views of someone who disagrees with you makes you a better leader." Many people remarked that mainline religion had taught them that "all people are God's children," and learning to "honor people as unique" was an important political principle.

Admittedly, the theological convictions of mainline pilgrims in my study leaned toward the Democrats. Their views broadly reflected those found in national surveys: although mainline Protestants were split nearly equally between Bush and Kerry, mainline Protestants who attend church regularly showed a slight preference for Democrats.[129] The active mainliners I met largely matched this profile. Indeed, one Lutheran confessed, "I was a Republican until I started attending church." A Virginia

Episcopalian reported that more conservatives left her church in the wake of the 2004 elections—feeling like a distinct minority—than when the denomination consecrated a gay bishop. One Presbyterian, a Tennessee Democrat, shared his conviction that "There is a continuity between my spiritual life and the positions I take on politics. The ethics that express themselves in positions are inextricably based on a worldview that is determined by God's word and the teachings of our church through the ages."

But I heard from Republicans, too. As an Episcopalian, a Tennessee Republican said, "I believe that my spiritual life and church experiences informed me and formed my opinions in ways that led me to vote for Bush." He added that Senator Kerry was "very ambiguous on issues." However, the mainline Republicans typically said that they voted for Bush on national security or tax issues—not the 'moral values' issues that swayed their evangelical cousins. Whether they voted Democratic or Republican, several people confessed that they made their choice reluctantly, feeling like neither candidate spoke directly to their understanding of faith, practice, and ethics.

I witnessed mainline pilgrims standing on this razor edge of politics—not promoting a Christian nation (even outright rejecting the idea), but holding out the promise of a transformative Christian political conscience. Again, left with no public vocabulary, they tried to explain their views. We're not this, they said, but we're really not that, either. In the days following the 2004 election, Nora Gallagher, a member of one of the study churches, a woman who considers herself a "religious liberal," wrote that she admired people who can speak "clearly and comfortably about justice, the defense of the poor, and the deeply countercultural message of the Hebrew Scriptures and the Christian gospels." She added, "I think it would be good for secular persons to be less contemptuous of those who are religious, and to understand that many people who are religious are neither ignorant nor fundamentalist." She saw many of her fellow liberals as guilty of a kind of "bigotry of the left."

"But I fear," she went on, "that all this talk will simply turn into pandering to the Christian right, or wrapping faith in a new package in order to win elections." Nora fears that the left will make a "Faustian bargain" like that of the religious right in order to gain political power. Whenever such bargains are struck, she insists, the inevitable results are empire, war, and crusades. "I am glad that my church is now marginalized in the secular culture," she confided, "so that it might explore what it means to not be twinned with power."

Faith, Nora reminds her readers, "is what is mysterious, potent, and finally unknowable," not a "collection of campaign slogans and sentimental sound bites." Expressing an opinion echoed by others on my way, Nora concludes, "My hope is that we ... will feel free to speak openly of our hopes and our doubts not as a cudgel to hammer everyone into line with us, but to describe what gives us meaning and what inspires us to act on behalf of others."[130]

Radical Center

"We are a deeply Wesleyan, center-field congregation," explained Jim Harnish, pastor of Hyde Park United Methodist Church in Tampa, Florida. "We have folks on both ends of the liberal-conservative continuum who are bound together here by a central commitment to our mission and the core of orthodox Christian faith." When asked if his church was red or blue, Jim replied, "Our congregation has lots of both red and blue people within it. Maybe we are purple."

To outsiders, Florida may not seem purple. As a politically cantankerous and conflicted area where people often do not get along, it may seem an odd place to find a new via media practiced through liturgical politics. But Hyde Park serves as an interesting example of churchgoers striving to create community beyond political division. In the months leading up to the 2004 elections, the pastoral team spoke out against the war in Iraq. "We have a large number of people who were deeply committed to doing anything they could to defeat President Bush," says Jim

Harnish. "At the same time, we had a large number of Bush supporters." Indeed, Hyde Park parishioners appear to run the gamut from those who read the progressive Christian magazine *Sojourners* to those who listen to conservative radio host James Dobson. Knowing that such a combination could prove combustible, the pastors steered their way through the difficult preelection months "with respect for the differences of conviction in the congregation." As Jim relates, they worked hard to ground political values to the Bible and spiritual practices while trying to avoid direct endorsements of candidates and political parties.

In the eight months before the elections, the people of Hyde Park also spent a great deal of time in spiritual discernment, seeking God's direction for their congregation's future. Basing their process in the New Testament verses of Acts 2:43–47, a description of early Christian communities, the congregation developed a new vision statement. On the Monday before the national election, Hyde Park members unanimously approved their vision statement and its mission imperatives, a document committing the church to being a "biblically rooted, warmhearted, open-minded" community. On Tuesday, they went to vote for president (the pastor estimated that they voted 60 percent for President Bush and 40 percent for Senator Kerry) with a genuine sense of being part of a unified spiritual community, a church not being manipulated for someone else's political agenda.

In the days following the national election, many mainline pastors reflected on the role that religion had played in the political process. Jim Harnish was no exception. "Most of it has been pretty shallow stuff," he wrote. "I'd say that both candidates tried to use religion to garner votes but neither touched on some of the deepest and most consistent 'moral values' in scripture. Neither candidate took seriously the biblical challenge to our nation's wealth in contrast to the world's poverty. Neither side wrestled with the biblical call for us to be faithful stewards of the environment. Neither side acknowledged that both abortion and war are moral issues. Neither candidate questioned whether there might be some way to deal with terrorism other than the use of force." Jim quotes with approval Martin Luther King, Jr.'s hope that "the religious community could help a divided nation find common ground by moving to higher ground."[131]

People often define politics as winning elections, but the origin of the word *politics*—from the Greek word *polis*, "city"—suggests otherwise. Christians refer to the way they organize their churches as "polity," meaning governance. In much of the Christian tradition, however, politics has been about more than parties and platforms. From that larger perspective, politics is the life of the city, organized in keeping with biblical practices of justice and mercy.

In recent years, the definition of politics has become a point of argument among Christians. Those who associate with the Christian right tend toward understanding politics as partisan activity that Jesus appears to approve. They believe that the world is in a cosmic battle of good versus evil, and that they are God's soldiers in this divine war. Disagreement, debate, and compromise are impossible because God has determined the rules, laws, and commands of civic life. They treat the Republican platform as if it were an interpretation of Holy Scripture. Politics necessarily entails converting others to their views—or at least forcing social conformity to their version of Christianity. By defining politics as winning, often in terms like "destroying the enemy" and "defeating Satan," they—rightfully—frighten people away from any talk of Christians in politics.

Yet, mainline Christians, like those at Hyde Park, reject the combative definition of religiously motivated politics. By voting for different candidates, while holding together in a community with larger values and positive goals, they demonstrate that politics can be a respectful activity of building a city based in the common good. Because congregations are located in the *polis*, they serve as a kind of spiritual leaven for the whole city, working for "higher ground" for all its citizens. As Jim Harnish urged his congregation, the life of the *polis* needs to be based in "healing of the heart," a kind of conversion of the city that involves "listening to the needs and concerns of the global community," and a "change in lifestyle." For Christians, this entails "people of faith reflect[ing] on the life of our nation from a larger and deeper biblical perspective" where congregations can be "the place for that kind of listening to begin." One of the most significant things I observed on my journey is that these churchgoers believe that conversion is not something Christians do to other people—conversion is a continual process of discipleship of the individual and the Christian community. That self-reflective *metanoia* is the genesis of political activity. Christian politics is a conversion toward God's reign of peace that starts with the self and naturally moves, in concentric circles, outward to the congregation and the world. Much of what I witnessed reminded me of words by Jim Wallis that I first read when I was a college senior, in the early 1980s, "The times in which we live cry out for *our* conversion."[132]

This kind of Christian political vision gets little play in the media or at political conventions. It is not the vision of James Dobson, Pat Robertson, or D. James Kennedy; rather, it is the Christian vision of thinkers like Dietrich Bonhoeffer, Martin Luther King, Jr., and William Sloan Coffin. It is evident at places like Hyde Park—and other congregations on my pilgrimage. Across the country, people shared with me their hopes for a positive Christian social witness based on a meaningful way of life—the faith practices of discernment, hospitality, theological reflection, and doing justice. And they were not just *talking* about this vision; they were busily enacting it in a myriad of ways within their congregations and in the towns and cities in which they live.

A couple of hours south of Tampa, in Naples, Cornerstone United Methodist Church has started something called the Amos Center, "a Christian, ecumenical and prophetic institute putting faith into action as a positive force for reconciliation, peace and justice." Steve Hart, a member of Cornerstone and an active Republican (he has worked for Republican legislators), founded the Amos Center as a corrective to the "dangerous political and theological movement" associated with the religious right. Steve confesses that for a long time, "I continued to see this as a movement of the fanatic fringe." Through more recent events, however, Steve came to believe that the religious right threatened both the larger body politic and Christian churches.

Although the Amos Center began at Cornerstone with Steve's vision and the support of Roy Terry, the church's minister, the board comprises Methodists, Episcopalians, Presbyterians, Disciples of Christ, and Roman Catholics. Taking their cue from Jim Wallis's *God's Politics*, they decided that Christians could unite around the issue of poverty. Thus, they set their first goal: to conduct an ambitious study of poverty in southwest Florida that would enable them to create an interfaith "work plan" to reduce poverty in their region.

Steve explains the Amos Center by claiming that "as Christians and other people of faith we cannot—nor should not—set ourselves apart from this troubled world." He, like Jim Harnish at Hyde Park, begins his political vision with human limitation: "We are broken individuals maintaining a broken society made in our own image." Fretting that religion in politics has "created a polarized society" comprised of "extreme ideologies," Steve hopes that people of faith will repent of "civic arrogance." The goal, he believes, is the one Abraham Lincoln proclaimed near the end of Civil War: it is a "tragic error when we claim God is on our side. Rather, we should strive to make sure we are on God's side."

Calling the new organization the Amos Center was done with a nod to its double meaning. Certainly, "center" implies a gathering place, a physical location for conversation and work. But also implied is that, in some way, it represents a "center" in American politics. "The Amos Center will not concern itself with Republican or Democratic politics, nor with liberal or conservative politics. It will not resort to polemics and polarization." Rather, Steve hopes "it will promote God's call for justice and social responsibility . . . and seek the reconciliation of our society."

Whether they were members of "center-field" congregations or were establishing a center for reconciliation, Florida Methodists appeared to be busy trying to overcome division, mitigating the excesses of extremism, and seeking a better way of community.

*   *   *

Across the country, people in mainline churches consistently expressed hopes like Jim's and Steve's. Even though most were not pastors and few had plans as ambitious as the Amos Center, they certainly represented a "center" in American politics, a religious center, as described by the biblical prophet Amos, where "justice will flow like water and righteousness like a mighty stream." Even in the midst of a divisive political season, no matter how they voted and how strong their own opinions, these mainline Protestants still hewed toward the great American middle, a religious/political via media.

"Centrism is not an abstract or academic concept," wrote political columnist John Avalon in 2004. "It is a commonsense balance between idealism and realism intuitively understood by most Americans." In *Independent Nation*, a sadly ignored work during the polarizing presidential campaign, Avalon reports that 50 percent of the electorate defines itself as moderate. He claims that "the old left-right paradigm is not working anymore" and that there exists a "vital center" of American politics.[133]

Avalon's book was about politics, but he only mentions politics and religion when referring to the religious right—seeming unaware that there are faith dimensions of centrism. Early in my pilgrimage, I realized that I was traveling with the center at prayer. Centrism is more than pragmatism, more than blending, more than common sense. It can be, as I witnessed, a deeply religious worldview, one based in humility, hospitality, and hope. As Scott, a member of Calvin Presbyterian in Pennsylvania, explained:

> We have a strong belief in God, but we don't let ideology drive us to the point where one issue becomes paramount. On the conservative side, we have people who feel very strongly about abortion, but they're not going to let that define them as a human being and wedge out everyone who feels differently. On the liberal side, you have people who are very accepting and open but they're not going to let political correctness run everybody away. We're pretty centrist—as far as we have people who realize that

there's a stronger purpose in life than ideologies and agendas. We're a happy, positive people, who have a strong faith.

Scott's comments are instructive. Politic theorists argue that centers cannot ultimately hold because they lack constructive vision and organizing principles. However, Scott points out that his congregation does, indeed, possess an organizing principle: "strong faith." Indeed, Scott talked about "being together" as a congregation as a higher value than political opinions, a view I heard expressed with great regularity. As a member of blue-leaning Church of the Epiphany said, "I don't know if it would be as interesting without our Republican friends!" One of her fellow members summed up the congregation's viewpoint: "We have an appreciation of difference, you know, different people and wanting to be open to other ideas and other people's way of doing things." Their minister, Randolph Charles, says, "We're just not a one-issue church; and I'm not a one-issue priest." A California Presbyterian would explain it as "holding the tension of great opposites; an opportunity, a challenge to elucidate issues and really communicate instead of just getting together talking about how wonderful we are and that the people over *there* don't get it."

Ultimately, all these people taught me that their practices compose a kind of third way in politics, a way based on the faithful self in community. They support a sensible middle, the via media of liturgical politics, instead of ideological extremes, single-issue polemics, and divisive agendas. They believe that transforming the world cannot happen unless religious communities model the practices of God's reign. Therefore, they emphasize the need for healthy, diverse community as a sign of God's transforming love—the church (or synagogue, temple, or mosque) symbolizes all they hope the world will become, a new people bound together by mercy and justice.

"We strive for unity in the midst of diversity," says Roy Terry, pastor at Cornerstone United Methodist. "This is the call of the gospel, and it can be scary." He laughs. "This is God's table. A table that breaks down walls. It calls us to put aside pride and prejudice." The message appears to be getting through. As Valerie, a member of Cornerstone, says, "Who cares what color your skin is? Who cares what your background is? Who cares if you're rich, who cares if you're poor? You're a brother or sister. Everybody's a brother or sister in Christ." Although she grew up in a serious Southern Baptist household, she admits that her new church has changed her. "It's a unique situation," she says excitedly. "It's something that I've never participated in before. I've never been around it, never experienced it, it's never been a force in my life until I came to Cornerstone. And it's so natural and normal. It's not an issue." Valerie smiles. It is clear that she wants the whole world to be the same way. No exclusion, no intolerance, no coercion, no fear mongering, no division. A vision of God's kingdom where the only extreme is love.

Home Again

March 1, 2006, is a beautiful late winter evening in Santa Barbara, California, as I arrive at Trinity Episcopal Church for the Ash Wednesday service. It is that odd time—neither day nor night—when the world seems suspended between what was and what will be. As the sun sets, the neo-Gothic building, constructed of California sandstone, glows golden pink in the dusky light. In the courtyard, some members of the congregation are placing candles around the outdoor labyrinth so it may be walked after dark. From inside I hear the strains of an organ prelude, "Aus tiefer Not," the tune name of the hymn "From Deepest Woe I Cry to Thee." The music is calling the congregation to prayer—and not just any prayer, but the prayer of Lent. This sunset takes us into the most serious part of the Christian year, the forty days of self-examination before Easter.

Ash Wednesday's somber tones underscore my bittersweet spirituality tonight. Although my current home is near Washington, D.C., I lived in Santa Barbara for a number of years and feel I am home again.

In the 1990s I was a member of Trinity and I am glad to be back to see friends and worship with this community. As I walk toward the building, however, I also feel sad. Trinity is the final church visit of my study, the last stop on my three-year journey of exploring Christianity for the rest of us. I am surprised by grief now that my pilgrimage is at an end. I never knew that pilgrimages could end in pain. This year, Ash Wednesday mirrors what I feel.

Although I did not plan it this way (the trip to Santa Barbara was an unexpected addition to my schedule), I am ending where I began. Trinity, the last church on the journey, was also the first. In 1994 Trinity's spiritual rebirth opened my imagination to the possibilities of what Christianity could be—a vibrant community of faith, traditional and innovative at the same time, based in Christian practice, and seeking a deeper way of wisdom. As I walk into the building on Ash Wednesday, I realize that I have not visited Trinity for more than three years. I wonder where their journey has taken them.

As the prelude continues, I sit in the pew and start reading the bulletin. A short notice explains Lent to the congregation:

> *Lent is the season that invites us to ponder those things that keep us feeling separate from God. Inwardly, we may suffer from fear and guilt; outwardly we may remain silent in the face of injustice against our neighbors. The Lenten journey of six weeks gives us time to take these things to God, trusting in God's wide mercy. At Trinity this year, we are focusing on spiritual practices that bring us closer to God, our neighbors, and our deepest selves.*

A bell rings, interrupting my reading and calling us to worship. A procession of clergy and choir silently enters the church.

The service is quite traditional, right out of the Episcopal prayer book, and it includes the imposition of ashes on the forehead and the Lord's Supper. The priest bids us to a Holy Lent. Together, as millions of Christians have done for centuries, we read Psalm 51 as a prayer:

"Have mercy on me, O God, according to your loving-kindness; in your great compassion blot out my offenses."

The Reverend Anne Howard preaches tonight's sermon. I have known Anne for many years, and she possesses a deep passion for spiritual practice and social justice. She is helping to start a national organization for college and seminary students in "prophetic ministry." I look around the congregation and see that her interest in students is having an impact: the pews are packed with young adults, mostly in their early twenties. Later, someone told me that they are students from both the University of California at Santa Barbara and Westmont College, the local evangelical Christian college, an unusual combination in any circumstance—most especially at church.

In her sermon Anne explains that Lent is not about being sad, not some sort of spiritual penance. Rather, she insists, Lent is about change—the change that God can make in our selves, our faith communities, and the larger world. Lent is a time that opens our hearts to transformation, to becoming God's people and doing that which God calls us to do. She concludes by proclaiming that change is the whole point of faith: "Transformation is the promise at the heart of the Christian life."

Transformation is the promise at the heart of the Christian life. In a single sentence, Anne summed up what I had heard from hundreds of other churchgoers. Christianity for the rest of us is not about personal salvation, not about getting everybody else saved, or about the politics of exclusion and moral purity. Christianity for the rest of us is the promise of transformation—that, by God's mercy, we can be different, our congregations can be different, and our world can be different.

Change is never easy—especially spiritual change. After the service, the Reverend Mark Asman, Trinity's senior minister, and I go out for dinner. As we sit down at our favorite Italian restaurant, I notice that he is carrying a book about the great twentieth-century theologians Dietrich Bonhoeffer and Martin Luther King, Jr.[138] It appears well read and is full of sticky notes. I wonder why he brought the book along, but instead of launching into a theological discussion, I ask Mark how Trinity is changing.

"After the energy of the 1990s," he says, "we had a couple of stagnant years. But since 2004 we've begun to grow again." He attributes the growth to a new practice of evangelism but quickly adds, "We don't call it evangelism. We call it Sharing Our Light." Mark explains, "Many people have light; many traditions have light. We don't think those are wrong. But we here at Trinity have light, too. We invite people who are interested in our light to come along on the journey." Trinity now hosts a dinner and conversation series for "inquirers," people curious about the Christian faith. Rather than providing certain answers about God, Trinity's program explores Christianity as a transformative way of life based on "living the questions."[139] He says, "The combination of traditional liturgy and creating open community for questions seems to resonate with young adults. We're attracting more than ever. Did you notice all the students at the service tonight?" I tell him they were hard to miss.

"But it isn't just about church," he adds. He points to the book with Bonhoeffer and King, both martyr-theologians, on the cover. "It is more important than ever for the church to stand for justice, to address pressing political issues." We talk about religion and politics. Mark continues, "We're clearer than ever about 'sharing our light,' but we're also clear about the fact that 'our light,' that is, God's light, is not what is happening politically right now. There's a lot of darkness." I agree.

Listening to him, I realize that although he sounds a little like mainline preachers of the 1960s, things are very different now. The old Protestant mainline is no longer mainline. It no longer speaks from a pinnacle of cultural privilege and power. In some quarters, especially in those congregations along my journey, it has become a pilgrimage church, a community of exiles who practice Christianity. Other Christian voices, notably those of politically conservative evangelicals, seem more "mainline" now. I can remember, back in the 1960s, when mainline Protestants held the kind of political power evangelical Christians now do. "Being at the top was," as a friend of mine says, "the beginning of our long slide into irrelevance." When I read stories about the influence of the religious right, I always wonder if they will share the same fate as the old mainline.

Although it took some time for mainline Protestants to recognize what was happening, we have learned quite a bit in the last forty years as our churches and our world have changed. Mostly we have learned, as Jesus once taught, that we belong to God and not Caesar. Mark's comments about justice and "pressing political issues" come from a different place, from the margins of American religious culture. There are no prominent churches in Santa Barbara. No single religious world view. No dominant race, ethnicity, or language. Mark ministers in a fragmented world, a culture far removed from that of Trinity's earlier clergy, a new kind of postmodern neighborhood. And Mark's political concerns are grounded in spirituality, arising more from theology and prayer than from the secular concerns of a political party. At their best, mainline congregations like Trinity are neither secularized nor escapist. Many of the old neighborhood churches are trying to be communities of faithful practice in this new neighborhood—embodying God's transforming power. Chastened by our former hubris, now seeking a different way of being in God's world, congregations like Trinity are the "other" Christians now.

Mark sounds increasingly urgent as he talks about Bonhoeffer. "We're thinking about what it means to be a 'confessing church,' a community of spiritual practice that witnesses to God's dream of a just and peaceful society." To that end, Trinity is hosting a conference later in March that will address "the issue of America's growing empire and the prophetic voice of the Christian community." I have known Mark for a long time, and I have never heard him talk in quite this way. I am struck by his theological clarity, his spiritual maturity, and his sure sense of call as a minister of the gospel. I look at my old friend, now with gray hair and glasses: he is growing wise, I think to myself.

As Mark speaks about Trinity, I remember what I have seen in all the churches in my study. In each place, and in the many stories of churchgoers I interviewed, I witnessed the same spiritual triad: connection to tradition, commitment to Christian practices, and concern to live God's dream. Together, tradition, practice, and wisdom embody the Christian life. These things offer the possibility of change, of communities that live change, and the transformation that is the promise of the Christian life. At the end of my pilgrimage, Trinity reminds me of what the journey has been about: Christianity for the rest of us is transformative Christianity. And it is transforming Christianity, too.

Mark and I finish dinner and walk back to the church. The night is velvet, in a particular Santa Barbara way, the sky streaked with stars. Winter jasmine scents the air. We are well fed—with the spiritual food of worship, with good pasta, and with the company of friendship. As we approach the church, I see the labyrinth glowing in the light of the still-burning candles. My journey may be over, but its path reminds me that pilgrimages never really end. Ends are only new beginnings. And on this Ash Wednesday, I sense hope. Even if just for a short time, I am glad to be home again.

ACKNOWLEDGMENTS

This book would have been impossible if not for the trust and assistance of the dozens of clergy and hundreds of churchgoers who opened their hearts to me in the course of research, and my thanks go to all their congregations as listed in the research section of this book. They participated in this project because they believed in it and they wanted this story to be told. They entrusted me with their faith stories—an act that continues to humble me and call forth deep gratitude. In the three years we spent together, many, many of these people became my friends, and I have no words to express how much they mean to me.

In particular, I thank the core group of study churches for their guidance, honesty, vision, hospitality, and prayers. I especially thank their pastors and lay leaders, especially Graham Standish, Diane McClusky, Gary Erdos, Lillian Daniel, Randolph Charles, Jesus Reyes, Steve Jacobson, Paul Hoffman, Bev Piro, Eric Elnes, Roy Terry, Gary Jones, Katherine Bush, Robbie McQuiston, and Bruce Freeman. I also thank the countless pastors and churchgoers who read earlier books of mine, heard me speak about the research in workshops and lectures, or invited me to their congregations. Your insights, stories, and questions sharpened my interpretation of the data and added to this book. (No doubt some of you will recognize yourselves!) In addition, I thank Marcus Borg, Phyllis Tickle, Wade Clark Roof, and Brian McLaren for their friendship and support of my work. I hope this book honors all the faithful pilgrims who contributed to it.

The project would have also been impossible without the generous financial support of Lilly Endowment Inc., which funded the entire three-year endeavor. I especially appreciate the help and insights of my program officer, Christopher Coble. In addition, the Louisville Institute provided much-appreciated funds for a meeting of the project pastors in March 2006. Along the way, the Alban Institute in Herndon, Virginia, supported publication of project findings and helped disseminate word of the study among mainline Protestant clergy. The senior staff at Alban, especially Alban president James Wind, have served as excellent conversation partners throughout the project. Virginia Theological Seminary in Alexandria, Virginia, provided an office in which we could work. Thank you to all these institutions for the assistance given to this research. I hope that the results confirm the trust you placed in me.

Many thanks go to the people of HarperSanFrancisco whose professionalism and personal encouragement made this a better book than it otherwise would have been. My editor, Roger Freet, deserves credit for good editing, a strong narrative sense, and an excellent sense of humor. In addition to Roger, special thanks go to Mark Tauber, Michael Maudlin, Kris Ashley, Helena Brantley, and Carolyn Allison-Holland. I am so pleased to be working with all of you.

My deepest thanks, however, go to Joseph Stewart-Sicking, my research associate and friend, who spent countless hours conducting interviews, traveling, coding data, interpreting theological, philosophical, and sociological trends, and helping me work better with technology! His patience, persistence, diligence, and intelligence shape this entire narrative. I hope his new employer, Loyola University in Baltimore, will appreciate the many gifts of their junior faculty member. I also thank the Reverend Megan Stewart-Sicking, and baby Samuel Stewart-Sicking, for allowing our work to intrude on their family life during the last three years.

My husband, Richard Bass, is my dearest friend, closest companion, brother pilgrim, and co-conspirator in the practice of Christianity for the rest of us. When I feared this project might actually sink, he rescued both it and me. He and our daughter, Emma, attended many of the churches in the research study. I thank eight-year-old Emma for her infinite patience in visiting so many new Sunday schools, meeting so many pastors, and sitting through so many grown-up discussions about theology. She is probably the toughest church critic I know. That these churches passed the unflinching "Emma-test" testifies to their creativity and energy. I also thank my teenage stepson, Jonah, for two things: his surprisingly mature assessment of mainline religion (as well as his increasing interest in theology and ethics) and his happy acceptance of summer baby-sitting chores. As a family, we have had quite a journey.

Finally, this book is dedicated to two of the most faithful mainline churchgoers I know: my in-laws, Bill and Courtenay Bass, members of First Presbyterian Church in Annapolis, Maryland. For more than eighty years, they have sat in mainline pews, learned from mainline clergy, and given of themselves and their resources to ensure that Christianity for the rest of us remains a vital alternative to narrow religion. To you, and to all those of your generation who have opened the way for creativity, innovation, and vision in the old mainline: we, your children and grandchildren, are immensely grateful.

Diana Butler Bass
Alexandria, Virginia
Easter 2006

Reflection Questions for Reading Groups

PART I
CHAPTER ONE: THE VANISHED VILLAGE

1. Where did you grow up? What was the world like then? How have things changed since your childhood?
2. How do you think your childhood experience has shaped your spiritual longings?
3. Do you relate to the idea of being a "spiritual nomad?" Why or why not?

CHAPTER TWO: REMEMBERING CHRISTIANITY

1. When you think of America's religious past, what images come to mind?
2. Do you, or people you know, suffer from "historical amnesia"?
3. Which image for church presented in this chapter best describes your current faith community?

CHAPTER THREE: THE NEW VILLAGE CHURCH

1. How do you describe yourself: a) spiritual, but not religious; b) religious, but not spiritual; or c) religious and spiritual?
2. What do you think of when you hear the word "*tradition*"?
3. How would a congregation that emphasizes *practice* differ from one that emphasizes *purity*?
4. Do you think that faith is about asking questions or finding answers?

CHAPTER FOUR: FINDING HOME

1. With which image do you most strongly identify: *returnee, exile, immigrant, convert*, or *villager*? Does another image better describe your faith journey?
2. Does your congregation have an impact on your spiritual journey—or do you grow and change primarily outside the context of church?

PART II
CHAPTER FIVE: HOSPITALITY

1. When have you been offered hospitality in a way that was spiritually meaningful to you? When have you offered hospitality in a way that challenged you spiritually?
2. Who are the strangers in, around, or near you? Your congregation? What would it mean to welcome these people into your life? Your church?

CHAPTER SIX: DISCERNMENT

1. What do you think of when you hear the phrase "listening for God?"
2. Do you believe that God has some intentions for our lives and our communities?
3. What is the difference between *preference* and practicing discernment?

Chapter Seven: Healing

1. What do you think about the relationship between the words *healing* and *harmony*?
2. What is *shalom?* Why is it important in the context of healing?
3. How do you feel when you read Jack Harrison's story? How might you have responded to his sermon had you been at Epiphany that morning?

Chapter Eight: Contemplation

1. Have you ever experienced contemplative silence in the context of worship? How did it affect you?
2. What do you think about the culture of sound in which we live?
3. Do you fear silence? Avoid it? Welcome it? Long for it? Resist it? Why?
4. What do you think is the role of silence in the spiritual life?

Chapter Nine: Testimony

1. Which testimony shared in this chapter had the strongest impact on you? Why?
2. How would you feel if you were asked to share your faith story in public?
3. If your group feels comfortable, take turns and share where you are on your journey right now. Try to limit your testimony to two minutes, giving a chance for everyone in the group to participate.

Chapter Ten: Diversity

1. What do you think of the idea of diversity as a spiritual practice? Can you come up with biblical stories and texts that speak to a Christian practice of diversity?
2. Which of the churches presented in this chapter are most like yours? Which would you most like to resemble? What kinds of diversities are present in your congregation? Try to identify as many different kinds of diversity in your congregation as possible.

3. What do you think of Archbishop Desmond Tutu's *ubuntu* theology? Does it reflect your hopes for human community?

CHAPTER ELEVEN: JUSTICE

1. Do you think Pastor Roy Terry is right? Are acts of justice "hardest" for Christians? Why or why not? Can you give an example from your own life of a hard act of justice?
2. Leaders of the religious right often quote John Winthrop's sermon, "A Model of Christian Charity," to prove that America is a Christian nation. Do you think this is an appropriate use of Winthrop's words? What do you make of the idea of a "city set upon a hill?" Can congregations emulate Winthrop's ideal of Christian faithfulness? Can the nation?
3. Is *justice* a noun or a verb? Is justice spiritual?

CHAPTER TWELVE: WORSHIP

1. Share frankly your opinion about worship in your current congregation.
2. Share with the group an experience where you felt the "quarter-second of awe and wonder" as described by Pastor Eric Elnes.
3. Of the worship experiences described in this chapter, which one most intrigues you? Why?

CHAPTER THIRTEEN: REFLECTION

1. How do you understand the Christian life of the mind? Have you ever thought of intellectual curiosity as a spiritual practice? Does your church encourage or discourage theological reflection as an important part of the faith journey? Have you ever considered theological reflection a "way of life"?
2. What do you think about the difference between *liberality* and *liberalism*?
3. What do you make of the last two paragraphs of this chapter? Do they reflect your longings? Your congregation?

CHAPTER FOURTEEN: BEAUTY

1. What is the role of music and art in your spiritual life? In your congregation?

2. How do you respond to the interview with the Reverend Alice Connor? To Phyllis Tickle's story about the teenage boy? Do Alice's and the boy's comments make sense to you? Do they help you better understand the Trinity or the Virgin Birth? What do you think about beauty as a pathway of theological knowledge?

PART III

CHAPTER FIFTEEN: TRANSFORMING LIVES

1. What do you think about Bernard's story? How might your church respond if Bernard and Catherine had walked in the front door?

2. What do you think about the word *conversion*?

3. Which of the *metanoia* stories presented in this chapter speaks most strongly to you? Why?

CHAPTER SIXTEEN: TRANSFORMING CONGREGATIONS

1. How might your congregation respond if your minister preached a sermon like Bruce Freeman's? As a community, do you welcome change? Fear it? Avoid it?

2. What do you think about the possibility of your congregation experiencing *metanoia?*

3. Of the churches described in this chapter, which would you most like to join? Why?

4. If your church was not called by its current name (for example, "First Presbyterian," "Our Savior," or "St. Mary's"), what might it be called? Pick a name that fits with its identity and share with the group the reasons for choosing it.

Chapter Seventeen: Transforming the World

1. Why do we engage, to use Jack Harrison's phrase, in "all this for-the-church activity"? What do you think is the point, the larger goal, of being part of a church or even being a Christian?
2. What do you think of St. Mark's response to 9/11? What most surprises you about St. Mark's attitude toward political questions?
3. What color is your congregation?
4. What does it mean to "reclaim" the message of Christianity?
5. Reflect on the political concerns of the two Methodist churches in Florida. What do the Florida congregations suggest about the role of religion in public life?
6. Do you think the "left-right" paradigm works for American religion? Why or why not?

Epilogue: Home Again

1. Is the Reverend Anne Howard right? Is "transformation the promise at the heart of the Christian life?"
2. What are the implications of transformative Christianity in your own life, for the life of your congregation, and for the larger community of which you are part?

APPENDIX

Research Methodology and Findings

Diana Butler Bass
Joseph Stewart-Sicking

Christianity for the Rest of Us is based on a three-year research project, the Project on Congregations of Intentional Practice (PCIP), funded by Lilly Endowment, Inc., housed at Virginia Theological Seminary, and conducted between 2002 and 2005. The project was designed as an in-depth ethnographic investigation of vital, healthy, viable, and growing mainline Protestant congregations through field research across the United States.

Defining the Phenomenon and Forming Research Questions

In the summer of 2002, the project was conceived in consultation with Craig Dykstra, Chris Coble, and John Wimmer, all of the Lilly Endowment's Religion Division, as a follow-up to an earlier book written by Diana Butler Bass, *Strength for the Journey: A Pilgrimage of Faith in Community* (San Francisco: Jossey-Bass, 2004). At the conclusion of that book, she suggested that a new kind of Protestant congregation was emerging, an "intentional" or "practicing congregation." That possibility seemed a promising addition to Lilly's large library of research on mainline Protestantism. But *Strength* was largely a memoir, with the congregations drawn from her own experience. The question that intrigued the Lilly team was whether more mainline congregations, beyond the scope of Bass's personal spiritual journey, matched the pattern tentatively identified in *Strength*.

In the months that followed, Joseph Stewart-Sicking, a social scientist, joined the planning team for the project. For the purposes of our research, we defined "practicing congregation" as "a congregation which has experienced renewed vitality through intentionally and creatively embracing one or more traditional Christian practices." We then spelled out each element of this definition to identify our research pool and shape our research questions.

We considered a wide range of congregational practices as potential foci for a practicing congregation, including classical spiritual disciplines (such as centering prayer, spiritual direction, or following a monastic rule), congregational leadership practices (such as preaching, stewardship, forming children in faith, worship, and shared ministry), and moral, theological, and ethical practices (such as forgiveness, hospitality, dying well, discernment, peacemaking, and healing). Most important for the study was that each congregation have some identifiable traditional Christian practice or set of practices around which it shaped its life. The theory of the project, along with the definitions of practices that shape its questions, is outlined in an early book published by the project, Diana Butler Bass's *The Practicing Congregation: Imagining a New Old Church* (Herndon, VA: Alban, 2004).

We also were concerned that the congregations studied not only replicated received practices of churchgoing and piety but had become—or were becoming—more intentional, or purposeful, about their practices in community. We were interested in congregations that think about what they do and why they do it in relation to their cultural context, the larger Christian story in scripture and liturgy, and in line with longer traditions of Christian faith. This intentionality should percolate through all aspects of a congregation's life and be evident not only in its leadership but also in the worship and ministries of the church.

Finally, we wanted to define vitality in a way that transcended mere numerical growth. Therefore, we assessed congregational vitality through a set of three markers: coherence of practice, authenticity of practices, and transformation through practice. We identified "coherence" through repetition (when evidence of the practice appeared across the congregation in multiple ways, i.e., language, symbol, and action), "authenticity" through the level of attachment to the practice in the congregation (when evidence indicated that the practice was embraced in ways that shaped overall congregational culture, identity, and vocation, i.e., that a practice was not simply programmatic), and "transformation" through evidence of change in the lives of individuals (testimony, stewardship, participation) and in the congregation (attendance, giving rates, cultural change). These three markers ensured a strong link between a practice or set of practices and concrete changes in the life of the congregation.

Using this outline of the practicing congregation, we formulated initial research questions, which were then refined and expanded by the project's advisory board. These questions guided us in structuring data collection and sampling, and they were refined and focused as the data deepened and changed our understanding of practicing congregations (e.g., that they were able to transcend political and theological divisions).

Forming the Research Pool

Since PCIP is primarily a qualitative study, we formed the research pool by searching for "interesting and instructive examples" in which we could explore the relationship between intentional practice and congregational vitality. To ensure validity to our findings, we formed both a core group of in-depth ethnographic field sites and a validation group of congregations who would add us to their mailing lists and provide participants for completing online questionnaires.

To assemble the research pool, we gathered a group of informed experts (pastoral theologians, writers, speakers, consultants, clergy) in the field of Christian practices and asked them for the names of congregations that met the description we offered in our proposal. Approximately two-thirds of the participating congregations were found through our own contacts and this network. However, several key congregations, including three of the in-depth sites, were found through a combination of detective work and serendipity. For example, we found Calvin Presbyterian Church through a brochure on the Internet from Glenshaw Presbyterian Church. Calvin's pastor was speaking at Glenshaw about his intentional use of contemplative prayer to structure his session and liturgy. Eventually, Glenshaw participated as a validation site, and Calvin served as a key research congregation.

As a church was recommended to us, we gathered as much information about it as we could using informants, mail, and the Internet and then contacted its pastor to discuss the project and assess the congregation's fit to the project purposes. We included the congregation in the study if these materials and conversations indicated that the congregation pursued a discernible set of practices that were coherent, authentic, and transformative. Occasionally, we would exclude a potential participant based on these criteria—for example, a congregation in which the pastor was clearly committed to the practice but the rest of the congregation was not on board, or a congregation in which the practice was more window dressing than transformative. We also occasionally had pastors decline to participate in the study after talking with us, often citing their interest in the project but believing that their congregations were only beginning to explore the idea of embracing a practice intentionally.

While we sought to include as many examples of practicing congregations in the project as we could identify, we assembled the core group so that it would be an instructive sample, with a diversity of denominations, demographic characteristics (including racial, ethnic, and social class diversity; also including male and female clergy, ethnic clergy, and gay and straight clergy), practices engaged in, and length of pursuing these practices. This was done in consultation with the project advisory board. We also composed the core group of congregations so that they would represent different theological and social networks; in fact, only two of the in-depth congregational participants came from the same referral source, and none of the in-depth groups shared a common social network or theological training.

Every participating congregation added us to their mailing list, sent us a packet of their brochures and newcomer materials along with congregational histories when available, and provided us with the names of five informed insiders who would complete online questionnaires. The core group also hosted us for at least three field visits. As the project progressed, we adapted our data collection to include more detailed information from the more active among our validation group, including sermons, interviews, and brief visits when possible. As a result, we ended up with three de facto levels of participation, which allowed us to collect a broader and richer set of data and to have stronger evidence of the validity of our conclusions among the core sites.

The Churches

The final research pool consisted of fifty congregations from six denominations—United Church of Christ (UCC), Evangelical Lutheran Church of America (ELCA), Episcopal Church (ECUSA), United Methodist Church (UMC), Presbyterian Church (PCUSA), and Disciples of Christ (DoC). The oldest congregation in the study was founded in 1636; the most recent in 2004.

CORE RESEARCH SITES (10):

Redeemer UCC, New Haven, CT

Goleta Presbyterian Church PCUSA, Goleta, CA

Calvin Presbyterian Church PCUSA, Zelienople, PA
Cornerstone UMC, Naples, FL
Saint Mark ELCA, Yorktown, VA
Phinney Ridge ELCA, Seattle, WA
Holy Communion ECUSA, Memphis, TN
Redeemer ECUSA, Cincinnati, OH
Epiphany ECUSA, Washington, DC (high diversity congregation)
Iglesia Santa María ECUSA, Falls Church, VA (Latino congregation)

VALIDATION GROUP (40):

Churches Visited and/or Onsite Interviews:
Saint Martin-in-the-Fields ECUSA, Philadelphia, PA
All Saints ECUSA, Chicago, IL
Saint Philip's ECUSA, Durham, NC
Saint George ECUSA, Arlington, VA
Saint Columba's ECUSA Church, Washington, DC
Memorial Episcopal Church, Baltimore, MD
Church of the Holy Comforter ECUSA, Vienna, VA
Trinity Church ECUSA, Santa Barbara, CA
Saint James's ECUSA, Richmond, VA
Saint Gregory of Nyssa ECUSA, San Francisco, CA
St Mark's Cathedral ECUSA, Seattle, WA
Iglesia San José ECUSA, Arlington, VA
First UMC at the Chicago Temple, Chicago, IL
Centreville UMC, Centreville, VA
First Presbyterian Church PCUSA, Lancaster, PA
Westminster Presbyterian Church PCUSA, Minneapolis, MN
Downtown Presbyterian Church PCUSA, Nashville, TN
Scottsdale Congregational UCC, Scottsdale, AZ
Plymouth Congregational UCC, Seattle, WA

Churches Participating Online, by Phone, and in Surveys:
Central Christian Church (DoC), Lexington, KY

Saint Andrew's Christian Church (DoC), Olathe, KS

First Christian Church (DoC), Lynchburg, VA

Saint Brendan's ECUSA, Franklin Park, PA

—All Saints ECUSA, Austin, TX

Trinity Cathedral ECUSA, Cleveland, OH

Saint Francis of the Tetons ECUSA, Alta, WY

The Cathedral of All Souls ECUSA, Asheville, NC

Saint Stephen's ECUSA, Richmond, VA

Trinity Lutheran Church ELCA, Pullman, WA

Abiding Hope ELCA, Littleton, CO

Saint Paul ELCA, Davenport, IA

Providence UMC, Charlotte, NC

Hyde Park UMC, Tampa, FL

Mount Tabor UMC, Winston-Salem, NC

First Presbyterian Church (PCUSA), Cranford, NJ

Glenshaw Presbyterian Church (PCUSA), Glenshaw, PA

Granville Presbyterian Church (PCUSA), Granville, OH

Westminster Presbyterian Church (PCUSA), Xenia, OH

First Congregational Church UCC, Glen Ellyn, IL

First Church Cambridge UCC, Cambridge, MA

CHURCHES DISTRIBUTED ACROSS DENOMINATIONS

Denomination:	Core	Validation
Disciples	0	3
ECUSA	4*	18
ELCA	2	3
PCUSA	2	7
UMC	1	5
UCC	1	4

1 Latino; 1 high black/white diversity

CHURCHES DISTRIBUTED BY REGION:

Region:	Core	Validation
Mid-Atlantic	2	7
Mountain West	0	3
Midwest	1	9
Northeast	1	1
South (includes VA)	4	14
Southwest	0	2
West Coast	2	4

Most of the congregations are listed with links on the project website, www.practicingcongregations.org.

Sampling and Data Collection

For the core group of congregations, we scheduled at least three trips of approximately five days (always including a Sunday) to each site at which we could conduct fieldwork through participant observation and interviews. When possible, these trips were scheduled to coincide with critical events in the church's life. These events were chosen through familiarity with the congregation and consultation with the pastors. Occasionally, when geography allowed for it, researchers would drop in unannounced and attend events without advance notice. On each trip, we would engage in participant observation at any church events (worship, small groups, formation, board meetings, etc.) and write them up as field notes.

After getting a sense of the culture of the church during the first visit, we would engage in additional participant observation and conduct interviews and focus groups on subsequent visits. Participants in these interviews and groups were for the most part selected by the pastors as being individuals with an insider's understanding of the church and with honest and insightful observations and stories to share.

In addition to field notes and transcripts collected at the core sites, we collected data from all participants in the form of questionnaires (a series of three to churchgoers, one to clergy) and cultural artifacts (parish bulletins, documents, brochures, newsletters, videos, etc.). A good deal of secondary data was also assembled in the form of pastors' books and theses and in articles about the congregations. As we collected qualitative data, we assumed a stance of appreciative inquiry, looking for language of success—especially stories—that could be analyzed and shared with others.[135] Consequently, we chose not to focus our data collection on diagnosing dysfunction or conflict, although we remained open to identifying challenges in our conversations and observations.

By the conclusion of the study, approximately 300 people in fifty congregations had participated through interviews, questionnaires, and focus groups, generating thousands of pages of data together with audio and video, newsletters, bulletins, photographs, and other cultural artifacts.

Data Analysis

We analyzed the qualitative data we collected using ethnographic techniques (identifying characteristic language to arrive at a thick description of the congregation and the phenomenon of intentional practice). To assist us in this analysis, we entered the data into (NVIVO) software that allowed us to code it—electronically highlighting documents, transcripts, or pictures to assign them one or multiple codes—grouping themes, variables, concepts, and language into a database of passages reflecting each coding. Beginning with a very fine coding of the data, we increasingly combined passages to arrive at a set of characteristic language and themes that appeared across the entire data set. These themes became the "signposts" covered in the body of the book, illustrated by characteristic language and stories. Not every concept is translated into a book chapter, however. The ten signposts emerged from the most dominant themes in the data.

Assessing Validity

Validity for a qualitative study such as PCIP can be considered from two angles: internal (were the conclusions correct for the participants?) and external (can the conclusions be generalized to others?).

We assessed internal validity in multiple ways. First, for each theme or bit of characteristic language we uncovered, we judged the validity of our observations through the "content saturation" it developed across the entire data set (i.e., whether additional coding revealed new information or repeated language already seen). Concepts with a high degree of content saturation formed the basis for reporting our findings as "signposts." Second, we compared our conclusions derived from the core group with the broader group's coding and made certain that the concepts and models we found held for both groups, often including examples from the validation group in fleshing out our findings. Finally, we provided our analysis to our participants for feedback at all levels to verify that it reflected their understanding of themselves.

There are some limits to the methodology we have chosen. Specifically, the appreciative inquiry stance we took can limit validity because it looks primarily for stories of success at the expense of finding stories of conflict and failure. However, since PCIP's purpose has been to find interesting and instructive stories from practicing congregations, this methodology is well worth its drawbacks.

For a qualitative study such as PCIP, questions of external validity and how far we can generalize the study's conclusions are more complex. Because the phenomenon of the practicing congregation had not been studied in detail before, we looked for instructive examples of practicing congregations from which we could identify concepts, themes, and models that will spark further research into this phenomenon. We were not primarily interested in producing a representative sample of all practicing congregations. In some senses, many of our congregations are purer forms of the practicing congregation than we believe might be seen in the mainline in general. However, this suits our most important purpose, generating a web of detailed and intriguing stories that can generate more awareness of a phenomenon that has gone relatively unnoticed until recently. We do believe that we have identified an important, and surprisingly widespread, subset of mainline congregations. More work remains to be done to explore practicing congregations on a larger scale and to determine how prevalent they are, what they look like on average, and how their vitality compares with that of other groups.

Project on Congregations of Intentional Practice: Overview of Research Findings

The congregations studied have found new vitality (viability, spiritual depth, renewed identity and mission, and, often, numerical growth) through an intentional and reflexive engagement with Christian tradition as embodied in the practices of faith, with the goal of knowing God.

OVERALL PATTERN

- These congregations practice Christianity in ways that are dynamic and organic, reconstructing tradition in terms of experience and wisdom rather than program and absolutes.
- Much of the vitality has arisen from participants (many of whom are newcomers) who conceive of Christianity as a journey or subjective quest to "find home" or "authentic faith" that is deepened by forming relationships with others on similar quests and engaging the wisdom of those who have gone before (i.e., tradition and history).
- These congregations emphasize contemplation in action, faith in daily life, finding God in all things, the reign of God in the here and now, and creating better communities; by joining spirituality to social concerns, they are constructing a theological alternative to both conservative evangelicalism and classic Protestant liberalism.

A Romantic Impulse

- Most of the congregations express strong interest in ancient sources, tradition, and history, mining those sources for practices, models, and insights that bear on their personal lives and communities.
- Tradition is understood to be flexible and fluid, something that contemporary Christians participate in (rather than simply inherit).
- Worship, beauty, and music are participatory and tend toward one of two expressive and experiential modes—either muted Pentecostalism or contemplative/liturgical (or, a blend of the two).

Practices

- The practices that predominated discussion were: worship, hospitality, discernment, theological reflection, healing, forming diverse communities, testimony, and contemplative devotional disciplines.
- Practices observed but not necessarily discussed included creativity and the arts, especially innovative uses of music (not necessarily contemporary styles).
- Practices require commitment (they are "high demand"), but that commitment is typically internally and subjectively driven and not external or authoritarian.
- Engaging practices elevates the sense of intentionality throughout the congregation that leads to greater vitality and spiritual depth.

Public Presence

- The study congregations often defy "liberal" and "conservative" characterizations. People can find in these congregations a larger goal that allows them to transcend theological and political differences.
- Diversity appears as a fundamental virtue in all the congregations as a reflection of God's kingdom and is often tied to the practice of the Lord's Supper.
- Social justice and peacemaking are considered important practices in these congregations and are interwoven with the rest of the practices (especially worship and devotional practices).

- These congregations express anxiety about evangelism that they perceive as exclusive or fear-based; rather, they focus on personal connections and make modest claims regarding Christian conversion, choosing instead to link evangelism with hospitality, catechesis, and relationships.

LEADERSHIP

- The leaders reject managerial, programmatic, and technical models of leadership (although they are knowledgeable about and often trained in such models) in favor of leadership models drawn from Christian history, spiritual traditions, and biblical sources.
- Leaders willingly borrow across boundaries (mainline–evangelical; Protestant–Catholic; Western Christian–Eastern Christian; and racial divides) in order to further the mission of the church; they rarely avail themselves of denominationally produced materials in favor of creating their own resources from a variety of sources (including the congregation itself).
- The pastors and key lay leaders often possess spiritual charisma, but that charisma is not used to control the congregation; rather, charisma is shared or dispersed throughout congregational systems and creates grassroots commitment.
- Leaders initiate and motivate individual and congregational change through narrative; being able to articulate and link their own personal story, the congregation's story (and that of individuals in the congregation), and the larger Christian story appears to be a primary leadership capacity.

Specific Practices: Reading the Charts

The following charts summarize which practices were most frequently observed in the PCIP research. For the first chart, all passages in the data (transcripts, field notes, newsletters, etc.) were found that dealt with the topic of Christian practices.[136] Then we calculated the percentage of these passages dealing with each practice in the data from each of the core research congregations and for the entire set of data, including the validation set. For the second chart, the same calculation was performed for all passages dealing with worship.

Although the charts give percentage totals to help estimate the approximate significance of each practice within each congregation, these percentages are somewhat limited. For example, a long discussion about classical music would count the same as a short one in the calculation. Thus, to make comparisons among the congregations and practices, it is more helpful to look at how each practice ranked in the list. It is also worth noting that just because a practice did not appear in the data does not mean that it did not happen in a congregation; it simply was not a major topic for discussion or communal reflection.

The first chart, Key Christian Practices, summarizes ethnographic research—interviews, focus group conversations, and research observations—about Christian practices in the ten core PCIP congregations (supplemented by information provided by a larger validation group). Researchers gathered data as to which Christian practices had been most meaningful to the spiritual growth and vitality of these congregations. The percentage in the chart indicates how often the subject was observed in the data dealing with the overall topic of Christian practices. In each column, the three most frequent practices are highlighted. Practices specific to worship, preaching, or the arts are not included here.

Key Christian Practices

Practice	Santa María ECUSA Latino (VA, 250 (2004))	Epiphany ECUSA high diversity (DC, 325)	Redeemer ECUSA (OH, 375)	Holy Communion ECUSA (TN, 660)	Phinney Ridge ELCA (WA, 320)	Saint Mark ELCA (VA, 410)	Cornerstone UMC (FL, 200)	Calvin Pres. (PA, 220)	Goleta Pres. (CA, 210)	Redeemer UCC (CT, 130)	All (includes validation sample)
Discernment	—	8%	26%	4%	1%	15%	15%	18%	14%	5%	10%
Hospitality	27%	32%	16%	14%	32%	35%	20%	10%	18%	7%	18%
Testimony	—	8%	6%	—	6%	—	6%	—	3%	23%	5%
Reflection	33%	9%	29%	30%	30%	20%	16%	13%	13%	10%	20%
Forming Community	7%	—%	3%	15%	7%	5%	6%	8%	16%	8%	8%
Embracing Diversity	2%	24%	10%	11%	3%	7%	17%	8%	10%	19%	14%
Justice	15%	2%	—	—	12%	5%	6%	—	—	17%	5%
Healing	—	5%	1%	2%	—	3%	7%	7%	7%	—	3%
Stewardship	4%	8%	1%	2%	—	5%	3%	1%	—	5%	2%
Finding God in Everyday Life	4%	2%	4%	—	—	—	—	20%	—	1%	4%
Contemplation	7%	2%	4%	21%	9%	5%	3%	17%	17%	5%	9%

Location / Avg. att. during study period

The second chart, Key Worship Practices, summarizes ethnographic research—interviews, focus group conversations, and research observations—about Christian practices in the ten core PCIP congregations (supplemented by information provided by a larger validation group). Researchers gathered data as to which worship practices had been most meaningful to the spiritual growth and vitality of these congregations. The percentage in the chart indicates how often the subject was observed in the data dealing with the overall topic of worship. In each column, the three most frequent practices are highlighted. The frequent practice of the Lord's Supper, while very distinctive in Reformed settings, tended not to be a topic for discussion in Lutheran and Episcopal settings, where this practice is quite common. Asterisks represent congregations that have recently completed or are beginning a space renovation process.

Additional project findings are available in Diana Butler Bass and Joseph Stewart-Sicking, *From Nomads to Pilgrims: Stories from Practicing Congregations* (Herndon, VA: Alban, 2006).

KEY WORSHIP PRACTICES

	Santa María ECUSA Latino	Epiphany ECUSA high diversity	Redeemer ECUSA	Holy Communion ECUSA	Phinney Ridge ELCA	Saint Mark ELCA	Cornerstone UMC	Calvin Pres.	Goleta Pres.	Redeemer UCC	All (includes validation sample)
Location	VA	DC	OH	TN	WA	VA	FL	PA	CA	CT	
Avg. att. during study period	250 (2004)	325	375	660	320	410	200	220	210	130	
Musical style	Folk	Blended	Classical	Classical	Classical	Classical	Contemp.	Blended	Blended	Classical	
Using ritual in worship	75%	—	27%	43%	28%	38%	20%	6%	—	1%	28%
Quality in music	25%	29%	13%	7%	23%	10%	16%	35%	5%	32%	19%
Quality preaching that is practical	—	6%	40%	17%	4%	24%	10%	11%	24%	26%	18%
Balancing worship styles	—	11%	—	—	—	—	10%	—	50%	—	7%
Contemplative worship	—	17%	—	24%	2%	7%	—	11%	—	—	6%
Focus on baptism liturgies	—	—	—	—	22%	3%	—	—	—	—	5%
Ecstatic/Pentecostal influences	—	3%	—	—	—	—	20%	—	—	—	5%
(Re)design of liturgical space	*	*	*	—	—	*	—	11%	19%	—	4%
Worship and service complementary	—	17%	—	—	—	—	20%	24%	—	17%	2%
Frequent Lord's Supper	—	—	—	—	11%	3%	—	—	—	12%	1%
Focus on calendar, esp. Holy Week	—	3%	20%	—	—	7%	—	—	—	17%	2%
Using the visual arts in worship	—	—	—	5%	—	—	2%	—	14%	—	2%

NOTES

1. This line of argument was first advanced by Dean Kelley, *Why Conservative Churches Are Growing: A Study in Sociology of Religion* (New York: Harper & Row, 1972).
2. Dave Shiflett, *Exodus: Why Americans Are Fleeing Liberal Churches for Conservative Christianity* (New York: Sentinel, 2005).
3. The best description of emergent church is Eddie Gibbs and Ray K. Bolger, *Emerging Churches: Creating Community in Postmodern Cultures* (Grand Rapids, MI: Baker Academic, 2005). For this pattern in the mainline, see Marcus Borg, *The Heart of Christianity* (San Francisco: Harper San Francisco, 2003).
4. For a full listing of the churches and further information of the project's research design, see the Appendix. See also the project website, www.practicingcongregations.org. In addition, two previously published books discuss project findings: Diana Butler Bass, *The Practicing Congregation: Imagining a New Old Church* (Herndon, VA: Alban, 2004); and Diana Butler Bass and Joseph Stewart-Sicking, eds., *From Nomads to Pilgrims: Stories from Practicing Congregations* (Herndon, VA: Alban, 2006).
5. Peter Senge, C. Otto Scharmer, Joseph Jaworski, and Betty Sue Flowers, *Presence: Human Purpose and the Field of the Future* (Cambridge, MA: SOL, 2004).
6. This book treats postmodernism as a cultural ethos rather than a philosophical or literary category.

7. Zygmunt Bauman, "Morality in the Age of Contingency," in *Detraditionalization: Critical Reflections on Authority and Identity,* ed. Paul Heelas, Scott Lash, and Paul Morris (Oxford: Blackwell, 1998), 51.

8. I tell this story in detail in an earlier book, *Strength for the Journey: A Pilgrimage of Faith in Community* (San Francisco: Jossey-Bass, 2002).

9. Not long ago I heard the Reverend David Anderson, a fundamentalist Episcopalian, proudly say on NPR that he and his fellow conservatives were pushing to recreate "your parents' church."

10. This phrase is borrowed from Danièle Hervieu-Léger, *Religion as a Chain of Memory,* trans. Simon Lee (New Brunswick, NJ: Rutgers Univ. Press, 2000), 81.

11. Gary Dorrien, *The Making of American Liberal Theology: Imagining Progressive Religion* (Louisville, KY: Westminster John Knox, 2001), 117.

12. Notes, Case Statement, Redeemer UCC files.

13. James A. Monroe, *Hellfire Nation: The Politics of Sin in American History* (New Haven, Yale Univ. Press, 2003) 12.

14. E. Brooks Holifield, "Toward a History of American Congregations," in *American Congregations,* vol. 2: *New Perspectives in the Study of Congregations,* ed. James P. Wind and James W. Lewis (Chicago: Univ. of Chicago Press, 1998).

15. There are many agenda-driven accounts of why this is so; the most egregious examples are Thomas Reeves's *The Empty Church: The Suicide of Liberal Christianity* (New York: Free Press, 1996) and Dave Shiflett's *Exodus.* For the best scholarly analysis of the decline problem, see Roger Finke and Rodney Stark, *The Churching of American,* 1776–2005, 2d ed. (New Brunswick, NJ: Rutgers Univ. Press, 2005). Although Finke and Stark still insist, contrary to mounting evidence, that only "conservative" religions possess vitality, they nevertheless present a nuanced and helpful understanding of the trends.

16. For a more detailed account of Trinity's revitalization, see Butler Bass, *Strength for the Journey.* Nora Gallagher tells the same story from a more personal perspective in *Things Seen and Unseen: A Year Lived in Faith* (New York: Knopf, 1998) and *Practicing Resurrection* (New York: Knopf, 2003).

17. The classic book on the turn to the spiritual remains Robert N. Bellah et al., *Habits of the Heart: Individualism and Commitment in American Life* (Berkeley: Univ. of California Press, 1985).

18. On the extent and possible future of this development, see Paul Heelas and Linda Woodhead, *The Spiritual Revolution: Why Religion Is Giving Way to Spirituality* (London: Blackwell, 2005).

19. Jerry Adler et al., "In Search of the Spiritual," *Newsweek,* Sept. 5, 2005, 46–64.

20. Adler et al., "In Search of the Spiritual," 48–49.

21. Robert Wuthnow, *All in Sync: How Music and Art Are Revitalizing American Religion* (Berkeley and Los Angeles: Univ. of California Press, 2003), 15–16.

22. One of the most helpful and highly suggestive discussions of this is Princeton professor Robert Wuthnow's *All in Sync*.

23. Marcus Borg, *Reading the Bible Again for the First Time* (San Francisco: HarperSanFrancisco, 2001).

24. Huston Smith, *The Soul of Christianity: Restoring the Great Tradition* (San Francisco: HarperSanFrancisco, 2005).

25. For more on tradition, see Diana Butler Bass, "Tradition, Tradition!" in *The Practicing Congregation,* 35–55.

26. For more on Redeemer's story, see Lillian F. Daniel, *Tell It Like It Is* (Herndon, VA: Alban, 2006).

27. Robert Wuthnow, *After Heaven: Spirituality in America Since the 1950s* (Berkeley: Univ. of California Press, 1998).

28. Wade Clark Roof, *A Generation of Seekers: The Spiritual Journeys of the Baby Boom Generation* (San Francisco: HarperSanFrancisco, 1993).

29. The "return to tradition" is one of five patterns of emerging spirituality that Roof identified in his *Spiritual Marketplace: Baby Boomers and the Remaking of American Religion* (Princeton: Princeton Univ. Press, 1999). The quotations are from p. 29.

30. Roof, *Spiritual Marketplace,* 28.

31. Bishop Don Maier, "Journeying Toward Baptism," *The Lutheran,* Feb. 1999, www.thelutheran.org/9902/page32.html.

32. Michel de Certeau, *The Practice of Everyday Life* (Berkeley: Univ. of California Press, 1984), 97.

33. Henri Nouwen, *Reaching Out: The Three Movements of the Spiritual Life* (New York: Doubleday, 1975), 46.

34. Nouwen, *Reaching Out,* 47.

35. Nouwen, *Reaching Out,* 51.

36. Gregory of Nyssa, "As You Did It to One of These" (homily), in *And You Welcomed Me,* ed. Amy G. Oden (Nashville: Abingdon, 2001), 59.

37. Joan Chittister, *Wisdom Distilled from the Daily* (San Francisco: Harper-SanFrancisco, 1990), 130.

38. Father Daniel Homan, OSB, and Lonni Collins Pratt, *Radical Hospitality: Benedict's Way of Love* (Brewster, MA: Paraclete Press, 2002).

39. Oden, *And You Welcomed Me*, 36.

40. Epistle to Diognetus, in *And You Welcomed Me*, ed. Oden, 40.

41. John Chrysostom, Homily 16 on Second Corinthians, in *And You Welcomed Me*, ed. Oden, 42.

42. Nouwen, *Reaching Out*, 47.

43. Martin Marty, *When Faiths Collide* (Oxford: Blackwell, 2005), 128.

44. Richard Valantasis, *Centuries of Holiness: Ancient Spirituality Refracted for a Postmodern Age* (New York: Continuum, 2005), 43.

45. Frederick W. Schmidt, *What God Wants for Your Life: Finding Answers to the Deepest Questions* (San Francisco: HarperSanFrancisco, 2005), 7.

46. Schmidt, *What God Wants for Your Life*, 9.

47. Frank Rogers, Jr., "Discernment," in *Practicing Our Faith*, ed. Dorothy Bass (San Francisco: Jossey-Bass, 1997), 116, 118.

48. Wendy M. Wright, "Passing Angels: The Arts of Spiritual Discernment," *Weavings* 10(6), 1995, 11–12.

49. Mark McIntosh, *Discernment and Truth: The Spirituality and Theology of Knowledge* (New York: Herder & Herder, 2004), 19.

50. Benedicta Ward, trans., *The Sayings of the Desert Fathers: The Alphabetical Collection*, Antony 8 (Kalamazoo, MI: Cistercian, 1984), 3.

51. Valantasis, *Centuries of Holiness*, 45.

52. McIntosh, *Discernment and Truth*, 255.

53. Graham Standish, *Discovering the Narrow Path: A Guide to Spiritual Balance* (Louisville, KY: Westminster John Knox, 2002), 112.

54. Standish, *Discovering the Narrow Path*, 2.

55. Parker Palmer, *Let Your Life Speak* (San Francisco: Jossey-Bass, 1999), 88. See also Palmer's *A Hidden Wholeness* (San Francisco: Jossey-Bass, 2004).

56. Bruce G. Epperly and Lewis D. Solomon, *Walking in the Light: A Jewish-Christian Vision of Healing and Wholeness* (St. Louis, MO: Chalice Press, 2004), 17.

57. Epperly and Solomon, *Walking in the Light*, 17.

58. Walter Brueggemann, *Peace* (St. Louis, MO: Chalice Press, 2001), 20.

59. Zach Thomas, *Healing Touch: The Church's Forgotten Language* (Louisville, KY: Westminster John Knox, 1994), 44.

60. Quoted in J. Brent Bill, *Holy Silence: The Gift of Quaker Spirituality* (Brewster, MA: Paraclete, 2005), 16–17.

61. Quoted in Jane Vennard, *A Praying Congregation: The Art of Teaching Spiritual Practice* (Herndon, VA: Alban, 2005), vi.

62. Valantasis, *Centuries of Holiness*, 212.

63. David Schimke, "Turn Up the Quiet," *Utne Reader,* July–Aug. 2005, 54.

64. Schimke, "Turn Up the Quiet," 54.

65. Thomas Merton, *Thoughts in Solitude* (New York: Farrar, Strauss and Giroux, 1999), 40.

66. Jones, sermon, Feb. 29, 2004.

67. Church of the Holy Communion, "A Guide to Parish Life, 2004–2005."

68. Merton, *Thoughts in Solitude,* 49.

69. N. Graham Standish, *Becoming a Blessed Church* (Herndon, VA: Alban, 2004), 41.

70. Bill, *Holy Silence*, 91.

71. Vennard, *A Praying Congregation,* 1.

72. Bill, *Holy Silence,* 117.

73. For the full story of Redeemer's transformation, see Daniel's *Tell It Like It Is.*

74. Anthony Giddens, *Modernity and Self-Identity* (Stanford, CA: Stanford Univ. Press, 1991), 54; punctuation and italics as in the original.

75. Charles Taylor, *Sources of the Self* (Cambridge, MA: Harvard Univ. Press, 1989), 47.

76. Ernest Kurtz and Katherine Ketcham, *The Spirituality of Imperfection: Storytelling and the Search for Meaning* (New York: Bantam, 1993).

77. Kurtz and Ketcham, *Spirituality of Imperfection,* 13–14.

78. Steve Jacobsen, "Polycultures and Digital Culture in the Postmodern Age," in *From Nomads to Pilgrims,* ed. Butler Bass and Stewart-Sicking, 141–42.

79. Curtiss DeYoung et al., *United by Faith: The Multiracial Congregation as an Answer to the Problem of Race* (New York: Oxford Univ. Press, 2003), 28.

80. Desmond Tutu, *God Has a Dream: A Vision of Hope for Our Time* (New York: Image, 2004), 19–29.

81. Tutu, *God Has a Dream,* 20.

82. Quoted in DeYoung et al., *United by Faith,* 62–63.

83. Charles Marsh, *The Beloved Community: How Faith Shapes Social Justice, from the Civil Rights Movement to Today* (New York: Basic Books, 2005), 1–2.

84. Marsh, *Beloved Community*, 129.

85. Walter Wink, *The Powers That Be: Theology for a New Millennium* (New York: Doubleday, 1998), 4.

86. Stanley Hauerwas, "The Servant Community: Christian Social Ethics," in *The Hauerwas Reader*, ed. John Berkman and Michael Cartwright (Durham, NC: Duke Univ. Press, 2001), 377.

87. Roy Terry, Lisa Lefkow, and Brandon Wise, *Sojourners: An Adventure in Faith, A Guidebook* (Naples, FL: Cornerstone, 2004), 69.

88. This story is recounted by Lillian Daniel, "Minute Fifty Four," in *What Is Good Ministry?* ed. Jackson Carroll and Carol Lytch (Durham, NC: Pulpit and Pew, 2003), 6.

89. Marsh, *Beloved Community*, 211.

90. Eric Elnes, "From Message to Incarnation," in *From Nomads to Pilgrims*, ed. Butler Bass and Stewart-Sicking, 74.

91. "A Different Kind of Service," *Arizona Republic*, May 30, 2005; viewed online at http://nl.newsbank.com/nl-search/we/Archives?p_action= print&p_docid=10AE5F92EB0D9D51.

92. Anthony B. Robinson, *Transforming Congregational Culture* (Grand Rapids, MI: Eerdmans, 2003), 39–55.

93. R. Kevin Seasoltz, *A Sense of the Sacred: Theological Foundations of Christian Architecture and Art* (New York and London: Continuum, 2005), 343–344.

94. Borg, *Heart of Christianity*.

95. Gordon Lathrop, *Holy Things: A Liturgical Theology* (Minneapolis: Fortress, 1998, paperback), 5–6.

96. In an extensive study of the arts and religion, Princeton sociologist Robert Wuthnow found that "the influence of music and art on spirituality is becoming increasingly apparent." He discovered that "church members, recognizing the spiritual implications of the arts, are overwhelmingly interested in them" and that "innovative uses of music and art are also a source of new vitality" in some congregations. Wuthnow, *All in Sync*, 134.

97. For more on contemplative fire, see www.contemplativefire.org.

98. I have borrowed this phrase from Marcus Borg.

99. My friend, author Brian McLaren, describes this same quality as "generous orthodoxy." See Brian McLaren, *A Generous Orthodoxy* (Grand Rapids, MI: Zondervan, 2004). Judging from the response to his book, the longing for an open, nonjudgmental form of Christian practice is a more widespread cultural phenomenon than most scholars of American religion have guessed.

100. Don E. Saliers, "Singing Our Lives," in *Practicing Our Faith*, ed. Bass, 182.

101. Phyllis has told this story in a number of settings. She relates it in print in her *Prayer Is a Place: America's Religious Landscape Observed* (New York: Doubleday, 2005), 138–39.

102. See Todd Donetti, "Engaging Creativity," in *From Nomads to Pilgrims*, ed. Butler Bass and Stewart-Sicking.

103. Gallagher, *Things Seen and Unseen* and *Practicing Resurrection*.

104. Indeed, although my pilgrimage was among mainline Protestants, I met progressive evangelicals and liberal Roman Catholics with similar pilgrimage tales. Eventually, I met some Jewish pilgrims who testified to the same—and whose commitment to practice has much to teach Christians. I have no doubt that some Buddhists, Hindus, and Muslims might be able to identify with the difference between being spiritual tourists and pilgrims in faith.

105. This is the only story in this book in which everything—the people, church, denomination, and location—is disguised.

106. Bauman, "Morality in the Age of Contingency," in *Detraditionalization*, ed. Heelas, Lash, and Morris, 51.

107. Smith, *Soul of Christianity*, vii.

108. Heelas and Woodhead, *Spiritual Revolution*, 4.

109. By now, this is a thoroughly documented trend in American religion. Bellah et al., *Habits of the Heart*, remains the seminal book in understanding the growth of religious individualism. In addition, the impulse toward spiritual individualism may not be as "new" as some commentators appear to believe. Leigh Eric Schmidt traces this impulse in his *Restless Souls: The Making of American Spirituality* (San Francisco: HarperSanFrancisco, 2005). The poll is found in *Newsweek*, "In Search of the Spiritual," Sept. 5, 2005, 48–49. For a recent—and challenging—study on "spiritual but not religious," see Heelas and Woodhead, *Spiritual Revolution*.

110. Quoted in Heelas and Woodhead, *Spiritual Revolution*, 2.

111. See, e.g., Heelas and Woodhead, *Spiritual Revolution.*
112. In *Spiritual Marketplace,* Wade Clark Roof suggests that personal autonomy, something that many ministers decry, might actually be "spiritually rejuvenating" as a "means of positive self-assertion and inner discovery" (p. 149).
113. Diane's story is available in a privately printed pamphlet: Diane McClusky, *Christ-Guided Reiki* (Zelienople, PA: Calvin Church, 2005).
114. Steve Jacobson, "Polycultures and Digital Culture in the Postmodern Age," in *From Nomads to Pilgrims,* ed. Butler Bass and Stewart-Sicking.
115. Ken Carter reflects on consumerism and the church in "Saying Yes and Saying No: The Prayer of Jabez, The Passion of the Christ and a Tale of Two Congregations," in *From Nomads to Pilgrims,* ed. Butler Bass and Stewart-Sicking.
116. *Mission-Shaped Church: Church Planting and Fresh Expressions of Church in a Changing Context* (London: Church House Publishing, 2004), 9.
117. Vincent J. Miller, *Consuming Religion: Christian Faith and Practice in a Consumer Culture* (New York: Continuum, 2004), 179.
118. Thomas L. Friedman, *The World Is Flat: A Brief History of the Twenty-first Century* (New York: Farrar, Straus & Giroux, 2005). See also Manuel Castells, *The Rise of the Network Society,* 2d ed. (London: Blackwell, 2000).
119. Hervieu-Léger, *Religion as a Chain of Memory,* ix.
120. I'm not sure that she knows it, but Phyllis's typology of Christian history rather neatly reflects one developed by a medieval mystical friar by the name of Joachim of Fiore.
121. Roy Terry, "Becoming God's Church," *Congregations,* Fall 2005, 23–27.
122. Not only did they resist particular denominational labels, but in many cases they also resisted the broader term *Protestant.* For more on these trends, see Jackson Carroll and Wade Clark Roof, *Beyond Establishment: Protestant Identity in a Post-Protestant Age* (Louisville, KY: Westminster John Knox, 1993).
123. In the study congregations polled, between 85 and 95 percent of the members reported voting in the 2004 elections.
124. During the Civil Rights era, African Americans often spoke of "redeeming America" by saving the nation from the sin of racism. Their theological worldview—as well as their politics—was profoundly different from that of the white evangelicals who use the same language today.

125. In contrast to evangelical Protestants, Mormons, and Jews. Mainline Protestants split their votes evenly between Kerry and Bush; Roman Catholics voted for Bush by a slim majority (53%). John C. Green et al., "The American Religious Landscape and the 2004 Presidential Vote" at http://pewforum.org/publications/surveys/postelection.pdf.

126. The study congregations roughly matched the national statistics for mainline Protestants.

127. Marcus Borg, public lecture, Saint Columba's Episcopal Church, March 2005. See also Marcus J. Borg and John Dominic Crossan, *The Last Week: The Day by Day Account of Jesus's Final Week in Jerusalem* (San Francisco: HarperSanFrancisco, 2006), 119–23.

128. See Eric Elnes, *The Phoenix Affirmations* (San Francisco: Jossey-Bass, 2006) and www.crosswalk.com.

129. Green et al. claim that mainline support for Bush fell 10 percentage points from 2000 to 2004 (from 60 to 50 percent) while mainline turnout increased. This was reported on "PBS Perspectives," November 5, 2004.

130. Nora Gallagher, "Let's Not Talk About Our Faith," privately circulated essay.

131. Jim Harnish, "The Morning After," *Hyde Park Online*, pastoral letter, Nov. 4, 2004.

132. Jim Wallis, *The Call to Conversion: Why Faith Is Always Personal but Never Private* (San Francisco: HarperSanFrancisco, 1981), x. Emphasis mine.

133. John Avalon, *Independent Nation* (New York: Harmony Books, 2004), 12.

134. For more on appreciative inquiry as a research methodology, see Mark Lau Branson, *Memories, Hopes, and Conversations: Appreciative Inquiry and Congregational Change* (Herndon, VA: Alban, 2004).

135. The list and definition of the practices we considered derived from current writings on the subject, such as Dorothy Bass, ed., *Practicing Our Faith* (San Francisco: Jossey-Bass, 1997), and Dorothy Bass and Miroslav Volf, eds., *Practicing Theology* (Grand Rapids, MI: Eerdmans, 2001).

136. The book was: J. Deotis Roberts, *Bonhoeffer and King: Speaking Truth to Power* (Louisville, KY: Westminster John Knox Press, 2005).

137. They use a video and curriculum series entitled *Living the Questions*, see www.livingthequestions.com.

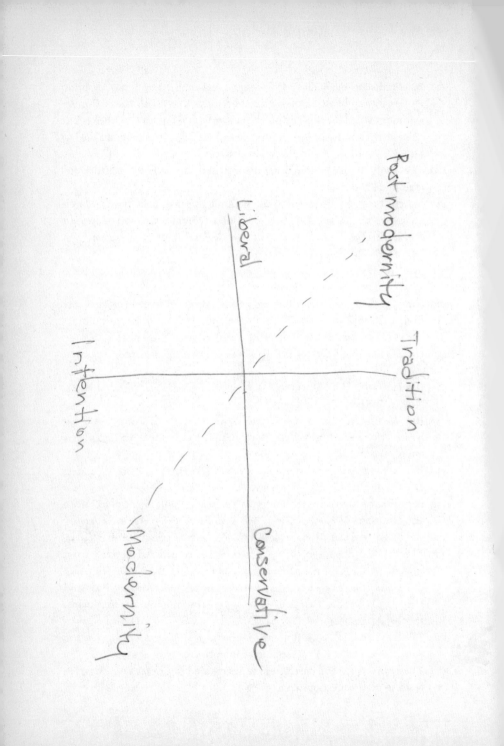

Post modernity

Liberal

Tradition

Intention

Conservative

Modernity

Characteristics

Practice
Discernment   Listening
        vestry
Hospitality
Testimony
Reflection
Forming community
Embracing diversity
Justice as key practice
Healing
Stewardship - broad
0 in daily life
Contemplation